Indian Social System

INDIAN SOCIAL SYSTEM

Amit Kumar

CENTRUM PRESS
NEW DELHI-110002 (INDIA)

CENTRUM PRESS

H.O.: 4360/4, Ansari Road, Daryaganj,
New Delhi-110002 (India)
Tel: 23278000, 23261597, 23255577, 23286875

B.O.: No. 1015, Ist Main Road, BSK IIIrd Stage,
IIIrd Phase, IIIrd Block, Bangalore-560085 (INDIA)
Tel: 080-41723429

Email: centrumpress@gmail.com
Visit us at: www.centrumpress.com

Indian Social System

First Edition, 2011

ISBN 978-93-80921-75-4

PRINTED IN INDIA

Printed at Tarun Offset Printers, Delhi-110053

Contents

Preface

The Indian society is millennia old and that much old is its system. A type of social system in India did stay alive. This system got refined from side to side the ages of history. Latest outlines were developed. A variety of cultures and civilizations prejudiced the Indian social system and it was refined supplementary. But, the spirit remained same.

The society learnt latest habits of sumptuousness and the average of living of the people in general was heaved. The best were better by all means, as forever. Then came the modern era and Western culture was commenced in India by strange monarchs in a big method. A new kind of politeness and complexity arrived on the sight with all its unenthusiastic aspects. No doubt, blessing of science and modern expansion came along, but, the Indian society, for the first time began to misplace its ground. Fortunately, Indian society could not at all be totally westernized, like numerous other societies. Again the basic Indian fundamentals were strapping as ever and that was the assurance of the innovation of Indian social system.

Now, the Indian social system has entered the latest century and the new millennium. New challenges have also come up. But, luckily, the classic Indian society is powerful sufficient. It has lived all odds and would survive in future. Although, the growing American and European influence is no good sign and the exposure of our new generation to powerful Western trends, is quite alarming, yet, one may be optimistic that, despite all waves, the essence of Indian society will remain intact, for the times to come. This book covers all the inclinations and sizes in an observed way. The undersigned is conflict of receiving a warm response from the related circles.

Author

1

India: An Introduction

India officially the Republic of India is a country in South Asia. It is the seventh-largest country by geographical area, the second-most populous country with over 1.2 billion people, and the most populous democracy in the world. Mainland India is bounded by the Indian Ocean on the south, the Arabian Sea on the west, and the Bay of Bengal on the east; and it is bordered by Pakistan to the west; Bhutan, the People's Republic of China and Nepal to the north; and Bangladesh and Burma to the east.

In the Indian Ocean, mainland India and the Lakshadweep Islands are in the vicinity of Sri Lanka and the Maldives, while India's Andaman and Nicobar Islands share maritime border with Thailand and the Indonesian island of Sumatra in the Andaman Sea. India has a coastline of 7,517 kilometres. Home to the ancient Indus Valley Civilization and a region of historic trade routes and vast empires, the Indian subcontinent was identified with its commercial and cultural wealth for much of its long history.

Four of the world's major religions—Hinduism, Buddhism, Jainism and Sikhism—originated here, while Zoroastrianism, Judaism, Christianity and Islam arrived in the first millennium CE and shaped the region's diverse culture.

Gradually annexed by the British East India Company from the early 18th century and colonised by the United Kingdom from the mid-19th century, India became an independent nation in 1947 after a struggle for independence which was marked by a non-violent resistance led by Mahatma Gandhi. India is a federal constitutional republic with a parliamentary democracy consisting of 28 states and seven union territories. A pluralistic, multilingual and multiethnic society where more than 300 languages are spoken, India is also home to a diversity of wildlife in a variety of protected habitats.

The Indian economy is the world's eleventh largest economy by nominal GDP and the fourth largest by purchasing power parity. Since the introduction of market-based economic reforms in 1991, India has become one of the fastest growing major economies in the world; however, the country continues to face several poverty, illiteracy, corruption and public health related challenges.

India is classified as a newly industrialised country and is one of the four BRIC nations. It is the world's sixth de facto nuclear weapons state and has the third-largest standing armed force in the world, while its military expenditure ranks tenth in the world. India is a regional power in South Asia. It is a founding member of the United Nations, the Non-Aligned Movement, the World Trade Organization, the South Asian Association for Regional Cooperation, the East Asia Summit, the G20 and the G8+5; a member of the Commonwealth of Nations; and an observer state in the Shanghai Cooperation Organisation.

ETYMOLOGY

The name India is derived from Indus, which is derived from the Old Persian word Hindu, from Sanskrit. The historic local appellation for the Indus River. The ancient Greeks referred to the Indians as Indoi the people of the Indus. The Constitution of India and common usage in various Indian languages also recognise Bharat as an official name of equal status. The name Bharat is derived from the name of the legendary king Bharata in Hindu scriptures. Hindustan, originally a Persian word for "Land of the Hindus" referring to northern India, is also occasionally used as a synonym for all of India.

HISTORY

Stone Age rock shelters with paintings at the Bhimbetka rock shelters in Madhya Pradesh are the earliest known traces of human life in India. The first known permanent settlements appeared about 8,500 years ago and gradually developed into the Indus Valley Civilization, dating back to 3400 BCE in western India. It was followed by the Vedic period, which laid the foundations of Hinduism and other cultural aspects of early Indian society, and ended in the 500s BCE.

From around 550 BCE, many independent kingdoms and republics known as the Mahajanapadas were established across the country. In the 3rd century BCE, most of South Asia was united into the Maurya Empire by Chandragupta Maurya and flourished under Ashoka the Great. From the 3rd century CE, the Gupta dynasty oversaw the period referred to as ancient "India's Golden Age".

Empires in southern India included those of the Chalukyas, the Cholas and the Vijayanagara Empire. Science, technology, engineering, art, logic, language, literature, mathematics, astronomy, religion and philosophy flourished under the patronage of these kings. Following Islamic invasions from Central Asia between the 10th and 12th centuries, much of northern India came under the rule of the Delhi Sultanate and later the Mughal Empire.

Under the rule of Akbar the Great, India enjoyed much cultural and economic progress as well as religious harmony. Mughal emperors gradually expanded their empires to cover large parts of the subcontinent. However, in northeastern India, the dominant power was the Ahom kingdom of Assam, among the few kingdoms to have resisted Mughal subjugation.

The first major threat to Mughal imperial power came from a Hindu Rajput king Maha Rana Pratap of Mewar in the 16th century. By early 1700s, the Sikh Empire and the Marathas had emerged as formidable foes of the Mughals. Following the death of Aurangzeb, the Mughal Empire entered a period of gradual decline and by mid-18th century, a large portion of the Mughal territory came under the control of the Hindu Maratha Empire.

From the 16th century, European powers such as Portugal, the Netherlands, France, and Great Britain established trading posts and later took advantage of internal conflicts to establish colonies in the country. By 1856, most of India was under the control of the British East India Company. A year later, a nationwide insurrection of rebelling military units and kingdoms, known as India's First War of Independence or the Sepoy Mutiny, seriously challenged the Company's control but eventually failed.

As a result of the instability, India was brought under the direct rule of the British Crown. In the 20th century, a nationwide struggle for independence was launched by the Indian National Congress and other political organisations. Several Indian radical revolutionaries, such as Subhash Chandra Bose and Bhagat Singh, led armed rebellions against the British Raj.

However, the defining aspect of the Indian independence movement was the nonviolent resistance led by Mahatma Gandhi and the INC. Under the leadership of Gandhi, millions of Indians participated in the Quit India civil disobedience movement against the British Raj. In September 1939, India declared war on Germany and at the height of the World War II, more than 2.5 million Indian soldiers were fighting against the Axis powers.

The Indian Army was one of the largest Allied forces contingents which took part in the North and East African, Western Desert and the Italian Campaign and played a crucial role in halting the progress of Imperial Japan in the South-East Asian theatre. However, certain Indian nationalists collaborated with the Axis powers to overthrow the British Raj. The Indian National Army, led by Bose, forged an alliance with the Axis powers and fought an unsuccessful military campaign against British India.

In 1943, a perceived shortage of food leading to large-scale hoarding and soaring food prices coupled with poor food distribution mechanism and inadequate response of the British officials resulted in a catastrophic famine in the Bengal region which killed about 1.5 to 3 million people. After World War II, a number of mutinies broke out in the Air Force and Navy and the INA trials caused considerable public unrest. On 15 August 1947, the British Indian Empire was dissolved following which the Muslim-majority areas were partitioned to form a separate state of Pakistan. The partition led to a population transfer of more than 10 million people between India and Pakistan and the death of about one million people. On 26 January 1950, India became a republic and a new constitution came into effect under which India was established as a secular and a democratic state. Since independence, India has faced challenges from religious violence, casteism, naxalism, terrorism and regional separatist insurgencies, especially in Jammu and Kashmir and northeastern India.

Since the 1990s, terrorist attacks have affected many Indian cities. India has unresolved territorial disputes with the People's Republic of China, which, in 1962, escalated into the Sino-Indian War, and with Pakistan, which resulted in wars in 1947, 1965, 1971 and 1999. India is a state armed with nuclear weapons; having conducted its first nuclear test in 1974, followed by another five tests in 1998. From the 1950s to the 1980s, India followed socialist-inspired policies.

The economy was shackled by extensive regulation, protectionism and public ownership, leading to pervasive corruption and slow economic growth. Beginning 1991, significant economic reforms have transformed India into one of the fastest-growing economies in the world, increasing its global clout.

GEOGRAPHY

India, the major portion of the Indian subcontinent, sits atop the Indian tectonic plate, a minor plate within the Indo-Australian Plate. India's defining geological processes commenced seventy-five million years ago, when the Indian subcontinent, then part of the southern supercontinent Gondwana, began a northeastwards drift—lasting fifty million years—across the then unformed Indian Ocean.

The subcontinent's subsequent collision with the Eurasian Plate and subduction under it, gave rise to the Himalayas, the planet's highest mountains, which now abut India in the north and the north-east. In the former seabed immediately south of the emerging Himalayas, plate movement created a vast trough, which, having gradually been filled with river-borne sediment, now forms the Indo-Gangetic Plain. To the west of this plain, and cut off from it by the Aravalli Range, lies the Thar Desert.

The original Indian plate now survives as peninsular India, the oldest and most geologically stable part of India, and extends as far north as the Satpura and Vindhya ranges in central India. These parallel ranges run from the Arabian Sea coast in Gujarat in the west to the coal-rich Chota Nagpur Plateau in Jharkhand in the east.

To their south, the remaining peninsular landmass, the Deccan Plateau, is flanked on the left and right by the coastal ranges, Western Ghats and Eastern Ghats respectively; the plateau contains the oldest rock formations in India, some over one billion years old. Constituted in such fashion, India lies to the north of the equator between 6°44' and 35°30' north latitude and 68°7' and 97°25' east longitude. India's coast is 7,517 kilometres long; of this distance, 5,423 kilometres belong to peninsular India, and 2,094 kilometres to the Andaman, Nicobar, and Lakshadweep Islands.

The Indian naval hydrographic charts, the mainland coast consists of the following: 43% sandy beaches, 11% rocky coast including cliffs, and 46% mudflats or marshy coast. Major Himalayan-origin rivers that substantially flow through India include the Ganges and the Brahmaputra, both of which drain into the Bay of Bengal.

Important tributaries of the Ganges include the Yamuna and the Kosi, whose extremely low gradient causes disastrous floods every year. Major peninsular rivers whose steeper gradients prevent their waters from flooding include the Godavari, the Mahanadi, the Kaveri, and the Krishna, which also drain into the Bay of Bengal; and the Narmada and the Tapti, which drain into the Arabian Sea.

Among notable coastal features of India are the marshy Rann of Kutch in western India, and the alluvial Sundarbans delta, which India shares with Bangladesh. India has two archipelagos: the Lakshadweep, coral atolls off India's south-western coast; and the Andaman and Nicobar Islands, a volcanic chain in the Andaman Sea.

CLIMATE

India's climate is strongly influenced by the Himalayas and the Thar Desert, both of which drive the monsoons. The Himalayas prevent cold Central Asian Katabatic wind from blowing in, keeping the bulk of the Indian subcontinent warmer than most locations at similar latitudes. The Thar Desert plays a crucial role in attracting the moisture-laden southwest summer monsoon winds that, between June and October, provide the majority of India's rainfall. Four major climatic groupings predominate in India: tropical wet, tropical dry, subtropical humid, and montane.

BIODIVERSITY

India, which lies within the Indomalaya ecozone, displays significant biodiversity. One of the seventeen megadiverse countries, it is home to 7.6% of all mammalian, 12.6% of all avian, 6.2% of all reptilian, 4.4% of all amphibian, 11.7% of all fish, and 6.0% of all flowering plant species. Many ecoregions, such as the shola forests, exhibit extremely high rates of endemism; overall, 33% of Indian plant species are endemic.

India's forest cover ranges from the tropical rainforest of the Andaman Islands, Western Ghats, and northeastern India to the coniferous forest of the Himalaya. Between these extremes lie the sal-dominated moist deciduous forest of eastern India; the teak-dominated dry deciduous forest of central and southern India; and the babul-dominated thorn forest of the central Deccan and western Gangetic plain. Important Indian trees include the medicinal neem, widely used in rural Indian herbal remedies.

The pipal tree, shown on the seals of Mohenjo-daro, shaded Gautama Buddha as he sought enlightenment. A latest report, less than 12% of India's landmass is covered by dense forests. Many Indian species are descendants of taxa originating in Gondwana, from which the Indian plate separated. Peninsular India's subsequent movement towards, and collision with, the Laurasian landmass set off a mass exchange of species. However, volcanism and climatic changes 20 million years ago caused the extinction of many endemic

Indian forms. Soon thereafter, mammals entered India from Asia through two zoogeographical passes on either side of the emerging Himalaya. Consequently, among Indian species, only 12.6% of mammals and 4.5% of birds are endemic, contrasting with 45.8% of reptiles and 55.8% of amphibians. Notable endemics are the Nilgiri leaf monkey and the brown and carmine Beddome's toad of the Western Ghats. India contains 172, or 2.9%, of IUCN-designated threatened species.

These include the Asiatic Lion, the Bengal Tiger, and the Indian white-rumped vulture, which suffered a near-extinction from ingesting the carrion of diclofenac-treated cattle. In recent decades, human encroachment has posed a threat to India's wildlife; in response, the system of national parks and protected areas, first established in 1935, was substantially expanded. In 1972, India enacted the Wildlife Protection Act and Project Tiger to safeguard crucial habitat; in addition, the Forest Conservation Act was enacted in 1980. Along with more than five hundred wildlife sanctuaries, India hosts thirteen biosphere reserves, four of which are part of the World Network of Biosphere Reserves; twenty-five wetlands are registered under the Ramsar Convention.

POLITICS

India is the most populous democracy in the world. It has operated under a multi-party system for most of its history. For most of the years since independence, the federal government has been led by the Indian National Congress. Politics in the states have been dominated by national parties like the INC, the Bharatiya Janata Party and various regional parties. From 1950 to 1990, barring two brief periods, the INC enjoyed a parliamentary majority. Within Indian political culture, the Indian National Congress is considered centre-left or "liberal" and the Bharatiya Janata Party is considered centre-right or "conservative". The INC was out of power between 1977 and 1980, when the Janata Party won the election owing to public discontent with the state of emergency declared by the then Prime Minister Indira Gandhi. In 1989, a Janata Dal-led National Front coalition in alliance with the Left Front coalition won the elections but managed to stay in power for only two years. As the 1991 elections gave no political party a majority, the INC formed a minority government under Prime Minister P.V. Narasimha Rao and was able to complete its five-year term.

The years 1996–1998 were a period of turmoil in the federal government with several short-lived alliances holding sway. The BJP formed a government briefly in 1996, followed by the United Front coalition that excluded both the BJP and the INC. In 1998, the BJP formed the National Democratic Alliance with several other parties and became the first non-Congress government to complete a full five-year term.

In the 2004 Indian elections, the INC won the largest number of Lok Sabha seats and formed a government with a coalition called the United Progressive Alliance, supported by various Left-leaning parties and members opposed to the BJP. The UPA again came into power in the 2009 general election; however, the representation of the Left leaning parties within the coalition has significantly reduced. Manmohan Singh became the first prime minister since Jawaharlal Nehru in 1962 to be re-elected after completing a full five-year term.

GOVERNMENT

India is a federation with a parliamentary form of government, governed under the Constitution of India. It is a constitutional republic and representative democracy, "in which majority rule is tempered by minority rights protected by law." Federalism in India defines the power distribution between the centre and the states. The government is regulated by a checks and balances defined by Indian Constitution, which serves as the country's supreme legal document.

The Constitution of India came into force on 26 January 1950. The preamble of the constitution defines India as a sovereign, socialist, secular, democratic republic. India has a bicameral parliament operating under a Westminster-style parliamentary system. Its form of government was traditionally described as being 'quasi-federal' with a strong centre and weaker states, but it has grown increasingly federal since the late 1990s as a result of political, economic and social changes. The President of India is the head of state elected indirectly by an electoral college for a five-year term. The Prime Minister is the head of government and exercises most executive power. Appointed by the President, the Prime Minister is by convention supported by the party or political alliance holding the majority of seats in the lower house of Parliament. The executive branch consists of the President, Vice-President, and the Council of Ministers headed by the Prime Minister. Any minister holding a portfolio must be a member of either house of parliament.

In the Indian parliamentary system, the executive is subordinate to the legislature, with the Prime Minister and his Council being directly responsible to the lower house of the Parliament. The Legislature of India is the bicameral Parliament, which consists of the upper house called the Rajya Sabha and the lower house called the Lok Sabha. The Rajya Sabha, a permanent body, has 245 members serving staggered six year terms.

Most are elected indirectly by the state and territorial legislatures in proportion to the state's population. 543 of the Lok Sabha's 545 members are directly elected by popular vote to represent individual constituencies for five year terms. The other two members are nominated by the President from the Anglo-Indian community if the President is of the opinion that the community is not adequately represented.

JUDICIARY

India has a unitary three tier judiciary, consisting of the Supreme Court, headed by the Chief Justice of India, 21 High Courts, and a large number of trial courts. The Supreme Court has original jurisdiction over cases involving fundamental rights and over disputes between states and the Centre, and appellate jurisdiction over the High Courts. It is judicially independent, and has the power to declare the law and to strike down Union or State laws which contravene the Constitution. The role as the ultimate interpreter of the Constitution is one of the most important functions of the Supreme Court.

ADMINISTRATIVE DIVISIONS

India consists of 28 states and seven Union Territories. All states, and the two union territories of Puducherry and the National Capital Territory of Delhi, have elected legislatures and governments patterned on the Westminster model. The other five union territories are directly ruled by the Centre through appointed administrators. In 1956, under the States Reorganisation Act, states were formed on a linguistic basis. Since then, this structure has remained largely unchanged. Each state or union territory is further divided into administrative districts. The districts in turn are further divided into tehsils and eventually into villages.

States:

- Andhra Pradesh
- Arunachal Pradesh
- Assam
- Bihar
- Chhattisgarh
- Goa
- Gujarat Haryana
- Himachal Pradesh
- Jammu and Kashmir
- Jharkhand
- Karnataka
- Kerala
- Madhya Pradesh
- Maharashtra
- Manipur
- Meghalaya
- Mizoram
- Nagaland
- Orissa
- Punjab Rajasthan
- Sikkim
- Tamil Nadu
- Tripura

- Uttar Pradesh
- Uttarakhand
- West Bengal

Union Territories:

- Andaman and Nicobar Islands
- Chandigarh
- Dadra and Nagar Haveli
- Daman and Diu
- Lakshadweep
- National Capital Territory of Delhi
- Puducherry

FOREIGN RELATIONS

Since its independence in 1947, India has maintained cordial relationships with most nations. In the 1950s, it strongly advocated for the independence of European colonies in Africa and Asia and played a pioneering role in the Non-Aligned Movement. India was involved in two brief military interventions in neighbouring countries--the Indian Peace Keeping Force in Sri Lanka and Operation Cactus in Maldives. India has a tense relationship with neighbouring Pakistan and the two countries went to war in 1947 and 1965 over the Kashmir dispute.

After the Sino-Indian War and the 1965 war, India's relationship with the Soviet Union warmed and continued to remain so until the end of the Cold War. In 1971, a third war broke out between India and Pakistan which resulted in the creation of Bangladesh. Additional skirmishes have taken place between the two nations over the disputed Siachen Glacier. In 1999, India and Pakistan fought an undeclared war over the Kargil district. In recent years, India has played an influential role in the SAARC and the WTO.

India has provided as many as 55,000 Indian military and police personnel to serve in thirty-five UN peacekeeping operations across four continents. India is also an active participant in various multilateral forums, particularly the East Asia Summit and the G8+5. Recent overtures by the Indian government have strengthened relations with the United States and the People's Republic of China. In the economic sphere,

India has close relationships with other developing nations in South America, Asia and Africa.

MILITARY

India maintains the third-largest military force in the world, which consists of the Indian Army, Navy, Air Force and auxiliary forces such as the Paramilitary Forces, the Coast Guard, and the Strategic Forces Command. The official Indian defence budget for 2010 stood at US$31.9 billion. In 2008 SIPRI report, India's annual military expenditure in terms of PPP stood at US$72.7 billion.

The President of India is the supreme commander of the Indian Armed Forces. India maintains close defence cooperation with Russia, Israel and France, who are the chief suppliers of arms. Defence contractors, such as the Defence Research and Development Organisation and Hindustan Aeronautics oversee indigenous development of sophisticated arms and military equipment, including ballistic missiles, fighter aircraft and main battle tanks, to reduce India's dependence on foreign imports.

China's repeated threats to intervene in the 1965 war in support of Pakistan convinced India to develop nuclear weapons to counter Chinese nuclear tests. India conducted its first nuclear weapons test in 1974 and carried out further underground testing in 1998. Despite criticism and military sanctions, India has consistently refused to sign the CTBT and the NPT which it considers to be flawed and discriminatory. India maintains a "no first use" nuclear policy and is developing nuclear triad capability as a part of its "minimum credible deterrence" doctrine.

On 10 October 2008, a civilian nuclear agreement between India and the United States was signed, prior to which India received waivers from the IAEA and the NSG which ended restrictions on nuclear technology commerce and recognised India as the world's sixth de facto nuclear weapons state. Following the NSG waiver, India has also signed civilian nuclear energy cooperation agreements with other nations including Russia, France, the United Kingdom, and Canada.

ECONOMY

The International Monetary Fund, India's nominal GDP stood at US$1.3 trillion, which makes it the eleventh-largest economy in the world, corresponding to a per capita income of US$1,000. If purchasing power parity is taken into account, India's economy is the fourth largest in the world at US$3.6 trillion. The country ranks 142th in nominal GDP per capita and 127th in GDP per capita at PPP.

With an average annual GDP growth rate of 5.8% for the past two decades, India is one of the fastest growing economies in the world. Before 1991, the Indian government followed protectionist and socialist-inspired policies because of which the Indian economy was largely closed to the outside world and suffered from extensive state intervention and regulation. After an acute balance of payments crisis, the nation liberalised its economy and has since moved towards a free-market economy. Since then, the emphasis has been to use foreign trade and investment as integral parts of India's economy. Currently, India's economic system is portrayed as a capitalist model with the influx of private enterprise. India has the world's second largest labour force, with 467 million people. In terms of output, the agricultural sector accounts for 28% of GDP; the service and industrial sectors make up 54% and 18% respectively.

Major agricultural products include rice, wheat, oilseed, cotton, jute, tea, sugarcane, potatoes. Major industries include textiles, telecommunications, chemicals, food processing, steel, transport equipment, cement, mining, petroleum, machinery and software. India's external trade has reached a relatively moderate share of 24% of GDP in 2006, up from 6% in 1985.

In 2008, India's share of world trade was about 1.68%; in 2009, it was the world's fifteenth largest importer and eighteenth largest exporter. Major exports include petroleum products, textile goods, gems and jewelry, software, engineering goods, chemicals, and leather manufactures. Major imports include crude oil, machinery, gems, fertilizer, chemicals. During the late 2000s, India's economic growth averaged 7.5% a year. Over the past decade, hourly wage rates in India have more than doubled. In 2007 McKinsey Global Institute report, since 1985, India's robust economic growth has shifted 431 million Indians out of poverty and by 2030, India's middle class population will rise to more than 580 million people. India ranks 51st in the Global Competitiveness Report and if diversified, it ranked 16th in financial market sophistication, 24th in banking sector, 27th in business sophistication and 30th in innovation; ahead of several advanced economies.

Seven of the world's top 15 technology outsourcing companies are based in India and the country is viewed as the second most favourable outsourcing destination after the United States. India's consumer market is currently the world's thirteenth largest and is expected to become the fifth largest by 2030. India has the world's fastest growing telecommunication industry, adding about 10 million subscribers during 2008–09 period.

The country has the world's second fastest growing automobile industry, with domestic sales increasing by 26% during the 2009–10 period and exports increasing by 36% during the 2008–09 period. Despite India's impressive economic growth over recent decades, it still contains the largest concentration of poor people in the world.

The percentage of people living below the World Bank's international poverty line of $1.25 a day decreased from 60% in 1981 to 42% in 2005. Since 1991, inter-state economic inequality in India has consistently grown; the per capita net state domestic product of India's richest states is about 3.2 times that of the poorest states.

Even though India has avoided famines in recent decades, half of children are underweight and about 46% of Indian children under the age of three suffer from malnutrition. In 2011 PwC report, in terms of PPP, India's GDP will overtake that of Japan in 2011 and by 2045, India's GDP will surpass that of the United States. Additionally, over the next four decades, India's average annual economic growth rate is expected to stand at about 8% and therefore, it has the potential to be the world's fastest growing major economy over the period to 2050. The report also highlighted some of the key factors behind India's high economic growth rate—young and rapidly growing working age population; growth of manufacturing sector due to strong engineering skills and rising levels of education; and sustained growth of consumer market due to rapidly growing middle class population. However, the World Bank suggests that for India to achieve its economic potential, it must continue to focus on public sector reform, infrastructure, agricultural and rural development, removal of labour regulations, education, energy security, and public health and nutrition.

DEMOGRAPHICS

With an estimated population of 1.2 billion, India is the world's second most populous country. The last 50 years have seen a rapid increase in population due to medical advances and massive increase in agricultural productivity due to the "green revolution". The percentage of Indian population living in urban areas has consistently grown; from 1991 to 2001, India's urban population increased by 31.2%. In 2001, about 285 million Indians lived in urban areas while more than 70% of India's population resided in rural areas. As per the 2001 census, there are twenty seven million-plus cities, with the largest cities being Mumbai, Delhi and Kolkata. India's literacy rate is 64.8%. The state of Kerala has the highest literacy rate at 91% while Bihar has the lowest at 47%.

The national human sex ratio is 944 females per 1,000 males. India's median age is 24.9, and the population growth rate of 1.38% per annum; there are 22.01 births per 1,000 people per year. Though India has one of the world's most diverse and modern healthcare systems, the country continues to face several public health-related challenges. The World Health Organization, 900,000 Indians die each year from drinking contaminated water and breathing in polluted air. There are about 60 physicians per 100,000 people in India.

LANGUAGES

India is home to two major linguistic families: Indo-Aryan and Dravidian. Other languages spoken in India come from the Austro-Asiatic and Tibeto-Burman linguistic families. Neither the Constitution of India, nor any Indian law defines any national language. Hindi, with the largest number of speakers, is the official language of the union. English is used extensively in business and administration and has the status of a 'subsidiary official language;' it is also important in education, especially as a medium of higher education. In addition, every state and union territory has its own official languages, and the constitution also recognises in particular 21 "scheduled languages".

RELIGION

As per the 2001 census, over 800 million Indians (80.5%) were Hindu. Other religious groups include Muslims (13.4%), Christians (2.3%), Sikhs (1.9%), Buddhists (0.8%), Jains (0.4%), Jews, Zoroastrians and Bahá'ís. Tribals constitute 8.1% of the population. India has the third-highest Muslim population in the world and has the highest population of Muslims for a non-Muslim majority country.

CULTURE

India's culture is marked by a high degree of syncretism and cultural pluralism. India's cultural tradition dates back to 8000 BCE and has a continuously recorded history for over 2,500 years. With its roots based in the Indus Valley Tradition, the Indian culture took a distinctive shape during the 11th century BCE Vedic age which laid the foundation of Hindu philosophy, mythology, literary tradition and beliefs and practices, such as dharma, karma, yoga and moksa.

It has managed to preserve established traditions while absorbing new customs, traditions, and ideas from invaders and immigrants and spreading its cultural influence to other parts of Asia, mainly South East and East Asia. Indian religions form one of the most defining aspects of Indian culture.

Major dharmic religions which were founded in India include Hinduism, Buddhism and Jainism. Considered to be a successor to the ancient Vedic religion, Hinduism has been shaped by the various schools of thoughts based on the

Upanishads, the Yoga Sutras and the Bhakti movement. Buddhism originated in India in 5th century BCE and prominent early Buddhist schools, such as Theravada and Mahayana, gained dominance during the Maurya Empire.

Though Buddhism entered a period of gradual decline in India 5th century CE onwards, it played an influential role in shaping Indian philosophy and thought. Indian architecture is one area that represents the diversity of Indian culture. Much of it, including notable monuments such as the Taj Mahal and other examples of Mughal architecture and South Indian architecture, comprises a blend of ancient and varied local traditions from several parts of the country and abroad. Vernacular architecture also displays notable regional variation.

SOCIETY AND TRADITIONS

Traditional Indian society is defined by relatively strict social hierarchy. The Indian caste system describes the social stratification and social restrictions in the Indian subcontinent, in which social classes are defined by thousands of endogamous hereditary groups, often termed as jatis or castes. Several influential social reform movements, such as the Bramho Shomaj, the Arya Samaja and the Ramakrishna Mission, have played a pivotal role in the emancipation of Dalits (or "untouchables") and other lower-caste communities in India.

However, the majority of Dalits continue to live in segregation and are often persecuted and discriminated against. Traditional Indian family values are highly respected, and multi-generational patriarchal joint families have been the norm, although nuclear families are becoming common in urban areas. An overwhelming majority of Indians have their marriages arranged by their parents and other respected family members, with the consent of the bride and groom.

Marriage is thought to be for life, and the divorce rate is extremely low. Child marriage is still a common practice, more so in rural India, with half of women in India marrying before the legal age of 18. Many Indian festivals are religious in origin, although several are celebrated irrespective of caste and creed. Some popular festivals are Diwali, Ganesh Chaturthi, Ugadi, Thai Pongal, Holi, Onam, Vijayadashami, Durga Puja, Eid ul-Fitr, Bakr-Id, Christmas, Buddha Jayanti, Moharram and Vaisakhi. India has three national holidays which are observed in all states and union territories—Republic Day, Independence Day and Gandhi Jayanthi.

Other sets of holidays, varying between nine and twelve, are officially observed in individual states. Religious practices are an integral part of everyday life and are a very public affair. Traditional Indian dress varies across the regions in its colours and styles and depends on various factors, including climate. Popular styles of dress include draped garments such as sari for women and dhoti or lungi for men; in addition, stitched clothes such as salwar kameez for women and kurta-pyjama and European-style trousers and shirts for men, are also popular.

THEATRE, MUSIC AND DANCE

Theatre in India often incorporates music, dance, and improvised or written dialogue. Often based on Hindu mythology, but also borrowing from medieval romances, and news of social and political events, Indian theatre includes the bhavai of state of Gujarat, the jatra of West Bengal, the nautanki and ramlila of North India, the tamasha of Maharashtra, the burrakatha of Andhra Pradesh, the terukkuttu of Tamil Nadu, and the yakshagana of Karnataka. Indian music covers a wide range of traditions and regional styles.

Classical music largely encompasses the two genres–North Indian Hindustani, South Indian Carnatic traditions and their various offshoots in the form of regional folk music. Regionalised forms of popular music include filmi and folk music; the syncretic tradition of the bauls is a well-known form of the latter. Indian dance too has diverse folk and classical forms.

Among the well-known folk dances are the bhangra of the Punjab, the bihu of Assam, the chhau of West Bengal, Jharkhand, sambalpuri of Orissa, the ghoomar of Rajasthan and the Lavani of Maharashtra. Eight dance forms, many with narrative forms and mythological elements, have been accorded classical dance status by India's National Academy of Music, Dance, and Drama. These are: bharatanatyam of the state of Tamil Nadu, kathak of Uttar Pradesh, kathakali and mohiniyattam of Kerala, kuchipudi of Andhra Pradesh, manipuri of Manipur, odissi of Orissa and the sattriya of Assam.

LITERATURE

The earliest works of Indian literature were transmitted orally and only later written down. These included works of Sanskrit literature—such as the early Vedas, the epics Mahabharata—and Ramayana, the drama Abhijnanaua-kuntalam, and poetry such as the Mahakavya – and the Tamil language Sangam literature. Among Indian writers of the modern era active in Indian languages or English, Rabindranath Tagore won the Nobel Prize in 1913.

CINEMA

The Indian film industry is the largest in the world. Bollywood, based in Mumbai, makes commercial Hindi films and is the most prolific film industry in the world. Established traditions also exist in Assamese, Bengali, Kannada, Malayalam, Marathi, Oriya, Tamil, and Telugu language cinemas.

CUISINE

Indian cuisine is characterised by a wide variety of regional styles and sophisticated use of herbs and spices. The staple foods in the region are rice and wheat. Spices, such as black pepper which are now consumed world wide, are originally native to the Indian subcontinent. Chili pepper, which was introduced by the Portuguese, is also widely used in Indian cuisine.

SPORT

India's official national sport is field hockey, administered by Hockey India. India's hockey team won the 1975 Hockey World Cup and 8 gold, 1 silver and 2 bronze medals at the Olympic games, making it one of the world's most successful national hockey teams ever. Cricket, however, is by far the most popular sport; the India cricket team won the 1983 Cricket

World Cup and the 2007 ICC World Twenty20, and shared the 2002 ICC Champions Trophy with Sri Lanka. Cricket in India is administered by the Board of Control for Cricket in India; and domestic competitions include the Ranji Trophy, the Duleep Trophy, the Deodhar Trophy, the Irani Trophy and the NKP Salve Challenger Trophy. In addition, BCCI conducts the Indian Premier League, a Twenty-20 competition.

India is home to several traditional sports which originated in the country and continue to remain fairly popular. These include kabaddi, kho kho, pehlwani and gilli-danda. Some of the earliest forms of Asian martial arts, such as Kalarippayattu, Yuddha, Silambam and Varma Kalai, originated in India.

The Rajiv Gandhi Khel Ratna and the Arjuna Award are India's highest awards for achievements in sports, while the Dronacharya Award is awarded for excellence in coaching. Chess, commonly held to have originated in India, is regaining widespread popularity with the rise in the number of Indian Grandmasters. Tennis has also become increasingly popular, owing to the victories of the India Davis Cup team and the success of Indian tennis players.

India has a strong presence in shooting sports, winning several medals at the Olympics, the World Shooting Championships and the Commonwealth Games. Other sports in which Indian sports-persons have won numerous awards or medals at international sporting events include badminton, boxing and wrestling.

Football is a popular sport in northeastern India, West Bengal, Goa, Tamil Nadu and Kerala. I-League is the premier Football competition in the country. India has hosted or co-hosted several international sporting events, such as the 1951 and the 1982 Asian Games, the 1987 and 1996 Cricket World Cup, the 2003 Afro-Asian Games, the 2010 Hockey World Cup and the 2010 Commonwealth Games. Major international sporting events annually held in India include the Chennai Open, Mumbai Marathon, Delhi Half Marathon and the Indian Masters. The country is scheduled to host the 2011 Cricket World Cup and the first Indian Grand Prix in 2011.

2

Astrology as a Key Part of Indian Society

INDIAN ASTROLOGY

Astrology is a branch of science that greatly influences the Indian society and culture. Dating back to Vedic India astrology is popular even today. Whether it is birth, marriage, death or a commencement of a new work; astrologers are in huge demand ion the Indian society. Like the other branches of science astrology is quite arresting. The details on the astrological elements and the movement of the stars are also incorporated in the Vedic texts as well.

GEMSTONES

Gemstones are defined as organic materials, mineral or rock that are used for several purposes. Like for instance, they are used in jewelleries, ornamentations and other art forms. Gemstones like pearl or opals are commonly styled into art or jewellery and they do not require any sort of polishing or cuts. They can be called as gemstones, but not gems. On the other hand, Diamond is a type of gem that needs proper cutting as well as polishing for making its true beauty visible. Gemstones are also known as crystalline rock. Gemstones appear like a piece of attractive mineral.

ORIGIN OF GEMSTONES

The origin of gemstones is from deep beneath the earth, while the others are formed from hot fluids and other chemical components. The gemstones that are formed deep beneath the earth ultimately brought to the surface by explosions of molten rocks. Some stones are also crystallised slowly from hot fluids and gases as they cooled and solidified eventually. These stones are formed far below the surface of the earth. Others stones are formed from liquids that are filtered into crack and pockets in the rock. Some stones are formed when rocks were heated and pressurised by the natural earth movements, and then again formed as a new, different mineral altogether.

CHARACTERISTICS OF GEMSTONES

The characteristics of gemstones can be explained by technical terminology. This is the specific subject for the gemologists. Gems are characterised by means of their refractive index, specific gravity, hardness, dispersion, luster, etc. They may exhibit pleochroism or double refraction. Gemstones may also have a distinctive absorption spectrum and luminescence. The gem may occur in certain locations; this is popularly known as 'occurrence'.

CLASSIFICATION OF GEMSTONES

There are around 30 popular varieties of gemstones and many rarer collector gemstones. Some varieties of gemstones have been treasured since pre-historic times while several others were discovered recently. Gemstones are classified on the basis of succeeding characteristics such as Crystal Structure, Optical Characteristics, Chemical Composition, Specific Gravity, and Durability.

GRADING OF GEMSTONES

Many years ago, there were only two types of gemstones. Some of them were precious while some were semi-precious. Some basic principles are involved in grading gemstones of both types. There are 4 C's regarding gemstones. These can be mentioned as colour, clarity, cut, and carat weight. One of the significant factors for determining the value of coloured gemstones is comprehensive colour grading. Unlike diamonds, where the cut is one of the most important factors, the 'colour' of coloured gemstones can influence as much as fifty per cent of a gemstone's value. Most of the gemstones are cut and polished for usage. Stones, which are opaque, are commonly cut as cabochons whereas the transparent gems are normally faceted.

COLOUR OF GEMSTONES

The actual colour of a gemstone is because of the reflective and absorptive properties of any elements or impurities within the precious stone. This colour does not include any optical effects caused by reflection or refraction. It is said that gemstones are the most deeply coloured natural material. In fact they have become a sort of synonymous with colour that nowadays mostly people recognise them with their colours. The colours of gemstones have a wide range of variations.

SYNTHETIC GEMSTONES

Some gemstones are manufactured to replicate other gemstones. But these artificial synthetic gemstones copy the look and colour of the real stone but possess neither their chemical nor physical characteristics as well. There are around 130 varieties of minerals that have been cut into gems with 50 species in common use.

POWER OF GEMSTONES

Gems are largely used as an astrological remedy to counteract unpleasant effects of different planets. The ancient prophets of India used to call them as 'ratnas'. They also used them to help an individual native. Among the many gemstones, the lunar astrology advocated the use of nine stones to counteract the adverse effect of the planets. But these gemstones should be carefully selected just as to the planetary positions and these can bring about prosperity, mental peace and success.

SEMI-PRECIOUS GEMSTONES

The use of semiprecious stones has been very popular in the country since time immemorial. There are around 84 different types of gemstones, out of which only 8 gems have been described as precious and the remaining are called semi-precious gems. Most of them are used for making cutlery, idols and ornamental items.

SIGNIFICANCE OF GEMSTONES

Gemstones often carry significant role in the wearer's life. People like to wear them but most of them do not have any idea how the gemstones are made and why they are so precious. Many gemstones have healing and medicinal power that protect against the bad effect of planets. They are also known to boost the spiritual power in a person's body. Research has proved that gemstones usually heal people suffering from dangerous and fatal illnesses by energizing them as well.

GEM THERAPY

The healing power of gems is not entirely an illogical belief. If it were, oral administration of gems as oxides and powder would never be so extensively practiced and so effective. Ayurvedic medicines and the Greek system, known as the Unani system in India, both utilize gems. Practitioners of these systems have studied gems and their typical effects on human organs, because gems are mineral in pure crystalline form and human body is composed of the same materials. Gems provide the lacking colour in any human body for which the person may suffer from various diseases.

NAVRATNA GEMSTONES

Navratna gemstones are the set of nine precious stones that are related to nine ruling planets. A person should wear either the ring of a single gemstone or a set of nine precious stones. This navratna gemstone is worn to increase the power of planets and for removing their malevolent effects.

GEMSTONES FOR PLANETS

There are many gemstones, which are effective for planets. These can be mentioned as Blue Sapphire that is gemstone for

Saturn planet, Cat's eye that is gemstone of Ketu planet, Coral, which is the gemstone for Mars planet, Emerald that is the gemstone for Mercury planet, Gomed that is gem stone of Rahu planet, Ruby that is the gemstone for Sun, Pearl that is the gemstone for Moon, and Yellow Sapphire that is the Gemstone of Jupiter planet.

TYPES OF GEMSTONES

There are various types of gemstones present. All the gemstones are basically differentiated in two distinct groups of precious and semi-precious stones. Diamonds have also been considered as the most valuable of such stones. Other precious gemstones are rubies, emeralds, topaz, zircon and sapphires used in a wide range of purposes. Amethyst, opal, aquamarine, jade, turquoise, garnet, agate, onyx, apis lazuli, and malachite are some of the popular semi-precious stones. Gemstones are highly prized and are known for their beauty, durability, and rarity.

ZODIACS

The zodiac belt is the band of stars that surrounds the earth like a ring. There are 12 main constellations that form this great ring around us. Amongst the millions of stars in the sky, the 7 planets and two invisible planets (in Vedic Astrology) are in constant motion. Each Zodiac is named after patterns, or configuration of animals and features that can be visualised by looking at them in the starry nights. The figures got linked with the symbolic trait endowed by that zodiac to the earth's inhabitants. Astrology is guided entirely by zodiac signs. Twelve Zodiacs in Horoscope are categorized by the very element that represents them namely Water, Earth, Fire and Air.

FIRE SIGNS

Fire signs are Aries, Leo and Sagittarius. The expression 'Fiery in nature' applies perfectly to these signs. Resembling their symbolic element, the people born under these signs posses a fiery drive and liveliness in their behavior. The constant urge to accomplish things is very evident in those lustrous sign holders. Fire also gives a great deal of pride and warmth to the people. The people under element of fire are highly independent. Fire is considered very pure in Hindu texts. It can also be destructive. Similarly, every passionate action taken by the people born under these signs can break and make their karma with ease.

WATER SIGNS

Water signs are Cancer, Scorpio and Pisces. Many water qualities can be seen in the emotional beings born under these signs. Their own emotions run deep, and they have absolutely no problem in sensing and soaking other's emotions as well. The signs ruled by water are very intuitive. Water can take the shape of the vessel in which it is held. This shows the adaptability of the element and people born in it. This zodiac borne have to take care that they do not hold on to their emotions for too long, as water standing can become stagnated. They have to let the emotions flow gently like a moving water.

AIR SIGNS

Air signs are Gemini, Libra and Aquarius. People born in these zodiacs have a fast and at times multidirectional quick thinking. They take all information with the swift movement of their own. This sign also give good power of speech and communication capabilities. The movement of air is uncontrollable and changeable and so is the basic thought process of these people. Air hates confinement and needs the freedom to move and the same is true for the people influenced by the element. People in these signs need to give a direction and shape to their movements and life.

EARTH SIGNS

Earth signs are Taurus, Virgo and Capricorn. Once formed across the period of time, earth takes the definite shape, and refuses to let it go. The same is true for the characteristics of these signs. People born under it seem grounded and down to earth. They do not like to budge from their opinions and basic character. Their slow, conventional approach to life is the anchoring force for many. They form a good foundation and support system for all the things to accomplish. The people born under it need to be in harmony with all the elements around them, as well as with themselves, to save the world from rare but possible disruptions.

Their compatibility can also be judged on the basis of the relationship of these elements. Interestingly, The mutual compatibly of the people born under a particular sign depends upon the compatibility of the elements governing them. All the signs are compatible with the other signs born under the same element. And there are some elements that are not compatible with the other elements.

These are as follows:

- Fire signs and water signs are not so compatible. The emotional nature of water sign can be too demanding for the fiercely independent sign of fire. The enthusiasm of leading a life of desires can actually neglect the deep seeded need of emotional security.
- Water signs gel well with Earth signs, thus these two signs are compatible, as emotional needs of water signs go well with firm and warm security of earth. The reverse is true for the other sign.
- Earth signs do not gel well with air signs, since Rigid thinking and slow movements of the earth signs can be quite confining to the freedom loving airy people. And earth cannot adapt to the quick and changeable thoughts and actions of air.
- Air and Fire signs are mutually compatible. Both elements facilitate each other`s existence with beautiful easygoing nature.
- Fire is neutral to earth, as both elements have no effect on each other. Thus a basic emotional detachment exists when these two signs are operating together. They are neither too compatible, nor incompatible. In such cases, the level of compatibility is dependent on individual`s nature.
- Water and air signs are again neutral to each other.

The effects, when theses two come together are not specific or predictable. But still they can have profound effect on each other. The signs can also be categorized just as to the manner it behaves or acts in situations, and the kind of energy that governs them. There are three such categories:

1. *Cardinal Signs*: These are Aries, Cancer, Libra and Capricorn. These are highly action-oriented signs with changeability and forthrightness in their actions to accomplish things. People born in these signs are usually the leader or the charge takers. They usually lead the teams or group of people to a specific goal.
2. *Fixed Signs*: These are Taurus, Leo, Scorpio and Aquarius. These are the ones, which remain glued to their habits and thinking. They resist changes. They can be quite determined in getting what they want once they make up their mind. And they can go through enormous patience and odds on the way. Stubbornness is another characteristics associated with theses signs.
3. *Mutable Signs*: These are Gemini, Virgo, Sagittarius and Pisces. These do not have any fixed pattern of doing things. They explore each and every facet of affairs, and can adapt to any situations. They explore different sides and directions. Sometimes that is how they get things done brilliantly. They can be good organizers and followers.

NAKSHATRAS

Nakshatras in Astrology have exclusive system of prediction which is based on the position of the moon in a given constellation in Vedic astrology. In the Vedic system of Astrology, the 27 constellations are the key to understanding celestial influences on the planet. These 27 constellations are actually the 27 Nakshatras. Vedic or Hindu astrology offers a most powerful analytical technique which is based on the

Nakshatra of a person at the time of birth. The zodiac is divided into 12 signs and 27 constellations. Each covers 13 degrees and 20 minutes of the zodiac. Each Nakshatra is defined as the head of a specific group of stars. The term 'Nakshatra', can be broken down into its component parts such as 'naks', which means 'sky' and 'shetra', which means 'region', which when translated stands for 'Sky Map'. Another translation is derived by using a different analysis; it says 'naksha' is 'map' and 'tara' is 'star' and so 'Nakshatra' means 'Star Map'. Both these meanings clearly bring out the significance of the 27 Nakshatras or constellations.

Since ancient times the Moon was looked for calculating time and connecting to the stars. 'Nakshatras' is the name that is given to the constellations or mansions of the Moon, as the Moon resides in each of these constellations for one day.

The system of constellations is very ancient and dated back about more than 5,000 years. Its reference is found in the ancient Vedic scriptures. The concept of Nakshatra is known to give more accurate results. Nakshatras are also considered the backbone of astrology and interestingly they are considered throughout the astrological analysis. Several interesting legends are associated with Nakshatras in Astrology.

As per the Hindu mythology, Moon had married all 27 daughters of king Dakshan, who are the star constellations (or the 27 Nakshatras) in the sky. He used to spend more time with his beloved queen Rohini and because of this reason his other wives complained to their father. In spite of the repeated interference of king Dakshan Moon did not change his habit.

Finally the king lost his cool and cursed the Moon. As a result, the size of Moon started diminishing. All the gods intervened and requested the king to withdraw the curse. King Dakshan then assured that if Moon visits all his wives, he would recover his lost strength for half a month. Thus, this is stated as the reason why Moon visits all the 27 constellations during a month.

Moon travels across the sky and around the earth through this pathway. They define characteristics and influence of the planets placed in them. Janma Nakshatra is the Nakshatra in which the moon is placed at the time of birth. It plays a major role in shaping a person's thinking patterns, inherent capabilities and destiny. Because of being the pathway of Moon, Nakshatras are also known as lunar mansions.

Moon travels through one Nakshatra in a day. Each Nakshatra is divided in four parts called Padas or charan. Consideration of Pada is also very important during chart analysis as each Pada of Nakshatra gives a different result. Each zodiac covers nine Padas in total. The calculation begins by Ashwini Nakshatra which covers from zero degrees of Aries, and ends in 30 degrees of Pisces covered by last Nakshatra of Revati.

Nakshatras are classified in several ways and the classification is made just as to basic attribute. The primary motivation is Kama -sensual desires; Artha material desires; Dharma living life based on spiritual principles; Moksha liberation from birth and death, sex, caste, species and so on. They are primarily revealed by their presiding deities, ruling planets and their symbolic form.

The Nakshatra and the signs of the zodiac both begin from the same point. The first Nakshatra or constellation of is Ashwini Nakshatra, the first Nakshatra, is the same as that of the first sign of Aries. Each sign contains the shared influence of the Nakshatras falling with it. The Nakshatras have a deeper effect. In Vedic astrology, Nakshatras are considered to be essential. The character traits of an individual are read more through the birth star than by the Sun sign. The saints, Nakshatras in Astrology represent the abodes into which the fruits of labour or Karma is transferred and stored. Thus, Nakshatras distribute the outgrowth of Karma just as to Hindu scriptures.

NUMEROLOGY

Numerology studies the different characteristics of all the numbers. Numerology in India is gaining popularity with every passing day. Numerology each number acquires the sensations of a particular planet and accordingly each alphabet has the vibration of a particular number. These numbers reveals some of the behaviour traits, emotional reactions, talents, strengths, obstacles of a person. It has also been mentioned that numerology discloses the traits of human beings that exist in the human sub-conscious mind. Numerology is basically the study of relation between human beings and numbers.

HISTORY OF NUMEROLOGY

It is believed that around some 10,000 years back Numerology originated in Egypt and Babylonia. With the passage of time, numerology in India has been improved and the studies and researches have been taken further. The branch of numerology encompasses diverse studies in a variety of sectors. The numerology report is made by using some simple devices namely the core and the core element that includes Soul Urge, Birthday, Life Path and Expression. Numerology gives much importance in the birth name and it is believed that birth names can reveal some of the important character traits of human beings.

CONCEPT OF NUMEROLOGY

Numerology is based on the concept that each number represents the vibrations of a particular planet and each alphabet corresponds to the vibration of a particular number. Right from the numbers influencing the core basis of the personality (birth date), or a changeable but important influence in a person's life (name), numbers act as compelling forces in human destinies. Numerology helps in understanding these influences and relationship of numbers and linguistic to gain more insight in a person's life. In ancient India, ancient sages also established relationship between numbers and names. However, in contemporary scenario, the concept is much more westernised and simplified.

PROCESS TO DETERMINE NUMEROLOGY

The process of numerology is simple and effective. To prepare a numerological report some basic points should be taken for consideration. To get the basics of numerology, the birth numbers are considered. Like for instance, if a person was born on 23rd July, 1978. The core birth date will be 23. Thus, it can be written as- 2 +3 = 5. Five is the basic number with the vibrations of Mercury. This person's personality will be coloured by the qualities bestowed by this number. Anyone born on 5th, 14th and 23rd of any month will have the basic number 5. For further conclusions, the entire birth date will be added.

Number 1 possesses the strong vibrations of Sun. Thus, the person is also coloured to an extent by the characteristics of number 1. Moreover, calculating the numbers of a name is equally simple. Each alphabet matches with a particular number. The numbers are mentioned below- A=1 B=2 C=3 D=4 E=5 F=8 G=3 H=5 I=1 J=1 K=2 L=3 M=4 N=5 O=7 P=8 Q=1 R=2 S=3 T=4 U=6 V=6 W=6 X=5 Y=1 Z=7

The numbers corresponding to the alphabets in the name has to be added up. For example, in case of the name Mani Ratnam.

The vibration of the given name corresponds to the all-powerful vibes of number 1. Thus the name imparts the colours of number 1 to the already present personality traits of that particular person. The basic numbers vibrate in accordance with a planet each. Thus, that planet also defines the characteristics imparted by it. Each number has some inherent qualities. The vibration of the given name corresponds to the all-powerful vibes of number 1.

Thus the name imparts the colours of number 1 to the already present personality traits of that particular person. Power of numbers influences the entire life of human being. Many significant inferences are made out from the birth date people are born on, numerological value of names, the number of the house people reside in, numbers of the kiths and kins the human beings are related to, the important years in human life and many other contexts. People who are born in the single, or core numbered date such as 1 to 9 of any months, are distinctly imprinted with that number's traits.

There are compound numbers from 10 to 31st of every date. 10 will correspond to number 1, (1 + 0). 23 will have the basic number 5, (2 + 3) etc. These compound numbers not only relate to the basic single numbers, but also to the karmic consequences hidden in them. Each compound number will give different effects on life patterns of the person. For example, a person with number 19 or 21 influence will automatically have a relatively rewarding life. On the contrary, a person born on dates 8 or 29 might have to face more challenges in life than average.

One might also say that the pre-decided destiny human beings have to follow in life manifests in form of the birth date people are born in. Numbers follow the rules of Karma. Still many effects of numbers are in the control of human beings. Most common trend to bring greater reward in our life is to change the spelling of the names of individuals to get favourable vibrations. Numbers influence administers even the professional life of the person.

For example, 5 is the number related with communication. Number 14 and 23 are considered as the karmic reward number. Many people born in these numbers are naturally gifted with flairs in writing and oratory skills. Any media related project would receive better vibes when related to these numbers. As a result, spellings of titles of serials and movies are checked and adjusted to suit the vibes of these numbers to give added effect. Also, spellings of people's names are usually changed to suitably bring them more favour in their respective fields.

No wonder, today, with the vast influence of numerology in India more and more people are opting for the change in their name's spelling. The numerologist should do a thorough checking of the horoscope to understand the already present karmic influences in the native's life, and then he should suggest the correct numbers to generate the appropriate influence in their life for overall success.

There are number of branches associated with the science of numerology that are developed across the centuries. More popular of them are Kabala, Chinese, Chaldean and Vedic numerology. All follow different patterns and believes. Today's numerologists follow the combined influence of these branches to gain more accuracy and detailed coverage for each and every aspect of human life.

NADI SHASTRA

Nadi Shastra is a distinctive type of astrology in which a person can read his destiny inscribed on Palm leaves thousands of years ago. Nadi Shastra is an ancient Astrology method for learning about a person's past, present and also the future. It is believed that Indian sages around thousands of years ago had the power to look into the matters of past as well as future of the universe. They recorded the life of a person and at some point of time those results were documented on palm leaves. Those documented findings are being referred by the Nadi astrologers over the years.

It is one of the most amazing confirmation of the intuitive powers and developed knowledge of the ancient sages, who possessed the capability of seeing the future of the entire universe. An expert Nadi reader reads one's past, present and future with incredulous details. The most astonishing fact about Nadi Shastra remains that a person reads his or her Nadi leaf only at a preordained time of his or her life; which have been predestined thousands of years ago.

Thus, a person learns about his life patterns by going through palm leaves that provide actual facts of his life on the exact time it was meant to be told. A great deal of Nadi Shastra is based purely on astrological foundations. There are various 'Samhitas or Nadi literature named after various ancient sages.

In Nadi Shastra, the thousands of life patterns are written based on the possible astrological combinations. It is presumed that the Rishis like Agastya, Vashishta, Kausika, etc. had outlined the lives of each person on palm leaves through their yogic and intuitive powers. Precise date of origin of Nadi Shastra is not known.

But, it is said that sages and yogis of about 2000 years ago are the authentic writers of the Nadi leaves. They wrote the destiny of each and every human being to be born on this earth. They even did the prediction of the time when the individual will read his leaf. It is believed that the records were originally written on animal skin and later were transferred to palm leaves. However, this knowledge is kept sacred and is handed down from generations to generations excluding any public disclosure. They have been preserved by applying oil extracted from Peacocks' blood on auspicious 'muhurtas'.

Although Nadi readers and leaves are scattered all over India, most of them are centered in Tamil Nadu. These calculations are written in Sanskrit language, but they were later translated in Tamil language under the Chola ruler ship. Because of this reason Nadi Shastra is often referred as the most prominent branch in Tamil Astrology. Maratha and Chola rulers were the great patrons of this art who endeavoured to preserve these sacred records.

Their major record collection was kept in Saraswati Mahal library in Tanjore. After the British invasion, the palm leaves were sold to various enthusiastic buyers. The Valluvar community of south India, who were the keen followers of astrology, bought maximum leaves. This is where the main hub of Nadi Shastra resides till date. But, Nadi reading is not prejudiced to any caste, region, or nationality. All human beings have their destiny recorded and preserved.

There are more than 24 Granthas in Nadi Shastra. Most of them are named after the sages who developed them. Many of the Granthas are stored in libraries or temple vaults. Many Nadi leaves are also stacked away for the use of future generations. Some important Nadi Granthas are Guru Nadi; Sutra Nadi; Markandeya Nadi; Nandi Nadi; Suka Nadi; Sudha Nadi; Saraswati Nadi; Dhruva Nadi; Satya Nadi; and Chandra Nadi.

Amongst these, Sukra and Dhruva Nadis are significant ones; they give quite accurate life history. There are two types of original Granthas on Dhruva Nadis, namely Satyacharya and Jai muni, based on Sayan system unlike other Nadis that are based on Nirayan system. Satya Nadi deals with the prominent people in every field, along with details about their life and accomplishments. In various Nadis like Bhrigu Samhita, horoscope is related with the Nadi Shastra, the outcome of which is derived by different permutations and combinations. This is unlike many Nadis who use Nadi Amsha (part of any sign) and go on detailing about person's event and happening in life.

READING IN NADI SHASTRA

A Nadi seeker's thumbprint is firstly taken for selecting the suitable possibilities of leaves stack. After a rudimentary classification, search of the right leaf begins. The search is usually time taking, and may range from few minutes to few hours, few days and perhaps even years. In step two, certain questions are asked connected to the present situations in life. After these steps, a leaf is reached, where all the answers are correctly predicted. This is defined as general reading in Nadi Shastra, where a person's past and future is read broadly. Nadi readings are classified as 'kandams' or chapters.

Nadi Shastra is getting more and more popular in the present times. Nadi Shastra makes stronger a person's belief in destiny being the guiding force of one's existence.

SADE SATI

Sade Sati refers to a time period of seven and half years dominated by the influence of Saturn in our life. In India, Sade Sati or Saturn spells dread and apprehensions. In Vedic astrology, moon is the major force that governs our life. This is unlike western astrology, where 'Sun sign' is considered far more important than 'Moon sign'. Moon sign or Janmarashi in our horoscope is the zodiac in which the moon is placed at the time of our birth.

Saturn is the cold, stern planet, famously known as a tough taskmaster. It causes delays, gloom and frustration wherever it goes. Sade sati is the time when our Janmarashi comes under the influence of Saturn. Saturn transits through each zodiac or Rashi, in two and a half years. Sade sati is the time when Saturn is transiting through the sign previous to the Janmarashi (two and half years), in the Janmarashi itself (again two and a half years) and the sign next to Janmarashi (again two and half years making it a course of 7 and half years in total). Saturn's transit in each Rashi is known as Dhaiyya.

For example, if a person was born in 'kark' (cancer) rashi then, Sade sati will begin for that individual the day Saturn will enter the previous sign, that is Mithuna rashi or Gemini. While the Saturn is going through Mithuna Rashi, the period will be known as 'Pratham Dhaiyya' (first phase). That native's second Dhaiyya will start when Shani will enter Kark rashi itself. This will be major Dhaiyya with the profound outcome in full blow. The individual's Third Dhaiyya will begin when Saturn will enter the next zodiac, *i.e.* Leo (sihm). The person's Sade Sati will finish the day Saturn will exit from Leo. Meanwhile, that individual will be having various forms of setbacks and losses depending on the Dhaiyya and his own horoscope. People having horoscopes where Saturn is well placed, tend to progress in Sade Sati instead of suffering from reverse effects. Similarly, a strong well-placed moon also makes the horoscope holder highly immune from the effects of Sade Sati.

Hence, the phases of Sade sati are not same for everyone. For rare few people the period can turn out to be fatal, for most it is most trying one, while it proves to be highly prosperous time period for few others. For an individual, different Dhaiyya give different effects on health, wealth, career, marriage and relations. Saturn is the ruling planet for Capricorn and Aquarius. It is also the yoga karaka (that planet which has the power and energy to bring growth, progress, prosperity, good luck and good fortune) for Taurus and Libra rising signs. When Sade-sati occurs for Taurus, Libra, Capricorn and Aquarius moon signs, the Sade-Sati tends to be less negative. Since, Saturn takes 29 and half years approx. to complete the entire circle of zodiac belt, a Sade sati can occur upto three times in a human lifespan. It is said that the third Sade sati takes adverse effects on a person's health and can even result in his death.

1ST DHAIYYA

In the first cycle, when Saturn transits 12th house from moon for 2 and a half years, the evil results are felt by the parents and near relations of the native. The health of grandmother can be affected and may result in her death. The eyesight of the native can be affected necessitating the use of spectacles. Saturn here creates extra expenditure. The position of Saturn may affect the financial position. As Saturn aspects second house, it may retard environmental activities. If in a birth chart, Saturn is passing through the last phase of life, it may force native to get sanyas. In addition to the during this period, the father of native may have set back or reversal, loss etc. in his profession and will lead to an extra, unwanted and uncalled for expenditure which may become unbearable for the native.

2ND DHAIYYA

During this cycle, Saturn transits the moon sign for 2 Â½ years. During this period, it affects the native himself in domestic and professional fields. It also denotes ill health and death of some relations, fear from enemies, journey to distant places and separation from relations like brothers, sisters, wife or family etc. May cause imprisonment, miseries, loss of wealth, fatigue and general debility, loss of friends, Obstructions and delay in undertakings, failure in attempts and increased expenditure.

3RD DHAIYYA

Saturn when transits in 2nd house from Moon, third cycle of Sade Sati starts. It affects one's health, children and it may even cause death if it comes late in life. During this transit, loss of health, happiness, loss of position, increased expenditure, financial stress and physical weakness might be felt. If there is any gain of wealth from others, then the same will be lost, and one can also have get deception through wicked men.

May cause death of children too if other combinations to confirm the same are present. Many believe that Sade Sati is the debt of karma, which each individual has to pay in his life. Still, astrologers suggest certain remedies to lessen the ill effects of Sade sati. Visiting Hanuman temple, to offer tribute to deity who won over Shanidev is one such popular one. Charity of black udad and oil is also a widespread action to pacify Saturn. Sade sati is the astrological phenomenon during which the effects are felt by the individual and his/ her relatives. It is not a phase to be scared of. The biggest advantage of Sade sati is that it teaches us important sessions in life which if learnt properly makes up the basic foundation of every success and achievement, we make henceforth. Laziness and wrong attitude has to be discarded as the repeated failures teach us. The unwanted and unnecessary things are discarded. It is also the time to take a detachment from materialistic success and failures, instead of fretting over them. Sade sati gives perfect opportunity to be in touch with our spiritual self. In the long run, any person who value higher learning in life and accomplishments obtained after a series of trials will think that the existence of Sade Sati has made his life more meaningful.

PALMISTRY

Palmistry or Hasta Rekha Vigyan is the most popular branch of Samudrik Shastra. Although, palmistry is being studied in a more scientific fashion in west or Europe, the original Samudrik Hasta Rekha embodies Vedic philosophy within itself in coalition with all the cosmic forces available. Up to 153 lines are recognized and studied well in the palm. A more spiritual insight in the readings is done by defining. Palmistry has also been derived from Greek 'chiromancy' connoting 'foretelling through palm reading'. The word 'chiromancy' is formation of two words, Greek 'cheir' and 'manteia'. In recent times, Pamistry is being practiced all over the world. The art of analyzing the palm as a blue print of person's past, present, future, karmas, personality and life issues originated in the ancient mystique land of India. The hands of every individual are the constant recipients of the continuous flow of electrical impulses from the brain. In fact the coordination between the conscious and subconscious mind with that of the hands is almost miraculous.

The nerve endings and energy flow in the palm is responsible for etching out the presence of lines and mounts on them. Studying these lines and other signs to know the details about a person comes under the practice of palmistry. Every sign in the palm foretells something about the characteristic, talents, strengths etc of a person. Since the free will of the person is the most important cosmic force of all, palm lines and signs are changeable through the changing circumstances in human life. Palmistry commences with the obvious things and goes forward with countless elaborate affairs followed by proper judgment and elucidation that lead to the ultimate foretelling of an individual. The hands of individuals are reckoned as active and passive hands. In Palmistry, the passive hands are of great importance as it has been considered that the passive hands transmit innate human characteristics and the active hand entails the 'karma' of the individuals. Even as per Vedic Palmistry, the passive hands convey the karmic imprint of a person or the past life of a person. The study of Palmistry is dependant on reading the mounts of the palm, the lines in the palms, and the structure of fingers.

The process of palm reading is done maintaining some basic notions. The study of Palmistry divides the hands of an individual into three major parts namely the fingers, the middle of the palm and the lower half of the hand. Each part foretells important traits of the individual viz. the fingers of the hands are the representations of the higher self and the mind of the individual whereas the middle half of the palm depicts the conscious mind of the person and the mundane life. On the other hand, the lower portion of the palm defines health, basic drives of the subconscious and the original instincts of an individual.

The palm reader considers a number of Palmistry lines for giving perfect result of palm reading. The Palmistry lines are Head Line, Heart Line, Fate Line, Life Line, Simian Line. Significant changes between the two palms stand for the radical changes or degradations that the individual had gone through in life. In addition to that, even the colour and quality of the fingernails and skin; the prominence of the knuckles, different qualities of the hand, considering the lines and shapes of the palm and fingers; the sizes of the fingers and palms and several other things are scrutinized by the palm reader to make a perfect palmistry report. In almost all schools of Palmistry, the shapes of hands are considered of major importance as they define some important traits of individuals. As per Palmistry, the shapes of the hands are ramified into four or ten major categories though the modern palmists use only four common types of hands namely the Air, Earth, Fire and Water.

3

Importance of Costumes in Indian Society

The diversity of the Indian states has give rise to a wide range of costumes. While the traditional costumes never go out of fashion, the latest trends in the textile industries never go unnoticed. The best part of the India costumes is the fusion. It is an intelligent combination of traditional and modern that is mostly popular in India today. Certain costumes like the sarees and dhoti-punjabi are exclusive to Indian sub-continent.

INDIAN COSTUMES

Indian Costumes are as varied and diverse as the culture of the country. The many beautiful, bright and unique attires of the country vary even from state to state due the great geographical diversity of the country. The costumes in India largely depend on the climate, local inhabitants and the religion that is followed by the people of that region. Apart from these, the costumes in India are also worn depending on the natural fibres that are popularly grown in that particular area. For these reasons, the costumes of tropical regions, dry regions, coastal areas and the extremely cold regions differ from one another. Despite the current prevalence of western style of dressing, when festivities and other occasions are in vogue Indian traditional costumes are the preferred forms of attire. An outstanding feature of Indian costume is the bright hues and fine textures of the clothes. A rather arresting sight is portrayed by the Indian people in their wonderfully coloured attire. Indian attire is as diverse as its subcultures.

Every region is distinct in its language, lifestyle and food and this diversity is reflected in its traditional dressing as well. For example, a half sari worn to college in the southern states is completely different from the dressing norms followed in northern India. Intermingling due to social changes and improvement in communication has managed to give India a pan-Indian look. However, people from all subcultures are slowly adapting to a more homogeneous way of dressing.

TRADITIONAL COSTUMES

Traditional clothes are still worn during traditional ceremonies or in the interior pockets of the country. Traditional costumes in India primarily depend on the climate and natural fibres grown in a region. For instance, in the cold northern state of Jammu and Kashmir, people wear a thick loose shirt called a 'phiran' to keep them warm; whereas in the tropical warmth of south India, men wear a sarong like garment called the 'mundu', while women drape 5 metres of cloth around their bodies in the graceful folds of the saree, the national dress of Indian women.

In the state of Rajasthan and Gujarat which are rather dry, the men wear a dhoti around their lower limbs and a kurta, which is a shirt-like garment on the upper part of the body. The Rajasthani men are also known for the colourful turbans that they wear. Their heads are covered by a cloth made of fine cotton known as the Odhna or the dupatta.

The state of Punjab is famous for the renowned Phulkari work which is seen woven on the shawls, worn over a blouse known as the choli and a long skirt called the ghaghra. In urban India, women, commonly wear the 'salwar kameez' or the 'churidar', and the 'saree' is worn on formal occasions. Men wear 'kurtas' and pajamas, or a 'sherwani' for formal wear. Men these days usually wear a trouser along with a shirt.

The most common costume worn by Indian women, in fact the national dress of Indian women, is the Saree. It is a six yard cloth which is draped in different styles in different regions. This is shaped by the lifestyle and the religious inclination. The urban Indian style is by far the most common.

Stiff tangails, flowing silks, elegant chiffons and heavy brocades, all of them can be easily maneuvered into this style.

The ladies generally use the 'pallav' (edge) of the saree to cover their heads. For the men, the common traditional outfits are the Kurta Pajamas. Lungis and dhotis are also worn by Indian men. Usually the lungi is worn in many parts of India like south India, but depending on the social practices of the region it may be restricted to indoor-wear. A sherwani is generally worn for special occasions. The men also use turbans and caps of various types. The Muslims use a different cap (topi) from those in the northeast and the Sikh turban forms an essential part of his identity and is very different from the ones worn by others on festive occasions.

WESTERN COSTUMES

It is a point to note that while the traditional Indian costumes are still largely worn by a vast majority of people in the country, the spread of globalization and cross-culturalism has also led to the popularity of traditional costumes in the country. A majority of the Indian population today follow the western mores when it comes to dressing.

Thus the men can be seen dressed in pants, t-shirts, shirts and jeans, the women may be variously outfitted in jeans, tops, shirts, skirts and dresses. However, this style of dressing is mostly restricted to the urban areas and the rural areas still display a pre-dominantly traditional style of dressing. Also during weddings, festivals and other occasions and celebrations, traditional costumes are the way to go all over the country.

TRIBAL COSTUMES

The Indian tribes use a particular dressing pattern just as to their native style. The women of Santhal tribe usually drape a white saree with red borders. The Meghval women wear puthia, while the Kumhar women dress much like the women of Gujjar tribe and wear a black and red-checkered 'saadi' of thick woven fabric draped around the waist. The Jogi women wear a 'chola' as the upper garment, which is usually made of red printed fabric, the lower garment is a skirt made of 'katari chhint'. Among the tribal communities of the north-east, such as the Mizos, the Manipuris, the Khasi tribe, the Naga tribe and the Arunachilis, the people are seen wearing beautifully coloured woven clothing much like a sarong, and and woven shawls which represent the identity of each tribal group. Similarly, there are many more Indian tribes who dress just as to their deep rooted tradition.

ACCESSORIES

Accessorising a particular garment is a rather integral part of Indian dressing. Costume accessories and costume jewellery are items that are widely used in India to complement fashion. Thus in India most women can be seen adorned in earrings, nose ornaments, rings, anklets and brightly coloured bangles. Some paint a dot of colour or apply a readymade Bindi, on their foreheads. The bindi is also a fashion statement and may be matching to the colour of the dress.

Thus the great diversity of the country is seen reflected in the dressing style of the different people. The variety of Indian costumes is immense, and the style of dressing and costume of a person goes a long way in indicating his ethnicity, region, religion and sub-culture in India.

COSTUMES BY STATES IN INDIA

RAJASTHAN

Costumes of Rajasthan are extremely bright, colourful and elegant. The beautifully designed and vibrantly coloured clothes lend cheerfulness to the dull-coloured monotone of the sands and hills. Interesting costumes and jewellery of these desert people are not mere ornaments for them. Everything from head-to-toe including the turbans, clothes, jewellery and even the footwear establish the identity, religion, and the economic and social status of the population of Rajasthan. The clothes worn by the people of Rajasthani people have been designed keeping in mind the climate and conditions in which they live.

Costume Worn by Rajasthani Men

The pagari (turban), angarkha, dhoti, pyjamas, Cummerbund or patka (waistband) form an integral part of a Rajasthani male's attire.

PAGARI

There is a proverb in Rajasthan which goes so, 'a raga in music, taste in food and knots in a pagari are rare accomplishments.' The turban is significant of many important things. The style of the turban, its colour and the way in which it is wound is of special significance to the people of Rajasthan as it is symbolic of the caste and region to which a person belongs. Turbans of Rajasthan, also known as pagaris, come in many different shapes, sizes and colours. Moreover, there are specific turbans for specific occasions as well.

The people of Udaipur are accustomed to wearing a flat pagari, while pagaris of the people of Jaipur are angular. The safa from worn by the men of Jodhpur has the distinction of having slightly curved bands. In Rajasthan about 1000 different types of pagaris can be found. A common pagari is usually 82 feet long and 8 inches wide. A 'safa' is shorter and broader. Whereas the common man in Rajasthan wears a turban of one colour only, the men from rich families wear designs and colours which are suited to the occasion.

Angarkha

Angarkha, which can be loosely translated as body protector, is a garment which is mostly made of cotton. When there occasions of celebration and festivities in the region, people can be seen wearing printed angarkhas or those which have been subject to the popular tie and dye method. The two principal kinds of angarkhas which are common to Rajasthan are kamari angarkha and the long angarkha. The former type styled like a frock and reaches till the waist. The latter is longer and goes beyond the knees.

Dhotis or Pyjamas

Dhotis or pyjamas are used to cover the lower part of the body. The dhoti is a piece of cloth which measures 4m by 1m and requires quite a bit of practice to be worn properly. Ateh commonly worn dhotis are white in colour. However on special occasions people also wear silk dhotis with a border of zari.

Patka

Patka was a garment worn by people of upper classes and royal families. It is a cotton cloth which measures about 1.5 metres by 1 metre. It was traditionally kept on the shoulders or worn around the waist to tuck in the weapons during medieaval times. However it is no longer in use and has become out of date, though one can still see Brahmins who wear traditional dupattas on their shoulders.

With changing times, the traditional style of dressing has also undergone a change. The Rajasthani man is often seen to dress in the urban garb of trousers and a shirt, or, sometimes, in an attractive combination of both urban and traditional garments teamed together. They provide comfort and utility, while preserving the cultural identity as well. Synthetic fabrics that are easily available, durable and require little maintenance, have been slowly replacing cotton as the favoured choice of the consumer. Also mechanisation in the manufacture of textiles, jewellery, dyes and sewing techniques have enhanced this transformation of Rajasthani costumes.

Costume Worn by Rajasthani Women

The Rajasthani female's attire includes Ghaghra (long skirt), kurti or choli (tops and blouses respectively) and odhna. Most of the Rajasthani women wear the ghagra which is a long skirt that reaches up to the ankle. It has a narrow waist which increases in width and flares towards the base. The skirt is usually not folded at the lower end like normal skirts but a broad, coloured fabric known as 'sinjaf' is sewn below to make it stronger. The width and the number of pleats in the 'Ghaghra', are said to symbolise the wealth of a person. The ghagra comes in many colours and styles. The ghagras which are most popular among Rajasthani women are those which are cotton ones which are coloured or printed with mothra, chunari and laharia prints. Much like the pagaris of the men folk.

The Odhni is a specialty of Rajasthani costume. It is a piece of cloth which is about10 feet long and 5 feet wide. One corner of the Odhni is tucked in the skirt while the other end is taken over the head and right shoulder. The colours and motifs which are found on the Odhnis are particular to caste, type of costume and occasion. Both Hindu and Muslims women wear 'odhnis'. An 'odhni' with a yellow background and a central lotus motif in red called a 'pila' is a traditional gift of parent to their daughter on the birth of a son.

Today, the traditional costume of the Rajasthani women is almost in a state of transition. The women are opting for new fabrics, designs and accessories. This transition of Rajasthani costumes now becomes more apparent among the affluent, the educated and those who, through their work or otherwise, have gained exposure to a range of other external influences.

Costumes of Royalty in Rajasthan

Royal costumes in Rajasthan reflect the regal taste of the state. The rich and luxurious dresses that were created for the royalty were made under the careful attention of special departments that were in charge of royal costume. The 'Ranghkhana' and the 'Chhapakhana' were departments that took care of dyeing and printing the fabrics respectively. The 'siwankhana' ensured faultless and clear tailoring. There were two special parts, namely the 'toshakhanand' and the 'kapaddwadra', that took care of the daily wear and formal costumes of the king.

The Rajput kings were quite close to the Mughal court. Cosequently they dressed up in their most colourful and formal best. Richly brocaded material from Banaras and Gujarat, embroidered and woven Kashmiri shawls and delicate cottons from Chanderi and Dhaka were procured at great cost to make the various outfits of the Kings and nobility of Rajasthan.

The changes ushered in by modernisation were felt even in the changing costumes of the Rajasthani people. The popular culture that prevails in Rajasthan, the influence of television, cinema, magazines, newspapers and most importantly migration and urbanization have contributed to the modifications in traditional costume. However, traditional garments are still extensively worn in Rajasthan even today and the change has merged harmoniously with tradition, maintaining the spirit of Rajasthani dress.

PUNJAB

Costumes of Punjab are indicative of the bright and vibrant culture and lifestyle of the people. The costumes are a mix of colour, comfort and beauty. It may be noted here that the state of Punjab is well known for the use of phulkari in its costumes. It is a kind of flower work embroidery done most often on shawls. These shawls are worn over a tight-fitting choli and ghagra. Phulkari forms the traditional costume of rural women of this region.

In earlier days, Phulkaris were made for everyday wear. Usually the border and field of the shawl were not so densely embroidered, with much of the ground cloth exposed. For ceremonial purposes, a special kind of phulkari known as "bagh" (garden) was made in which the whole of the ground was covered with embroidery, so that the base cloth was not visible at all.

Costume Worn by Punjabi Women

Popular, comfortable and convenient dress worn by the women of Punjab is the churidar kurta. This was traditionally the dress worn in Punjab, but is now worn almost everywhere, particularly among the younger generations. Punjabi girls and women also wear salwar kameez's with bright coloured duppattas. A salwar kameez has two pieces of clothes- the kameez, or shirt or top piece; and the salwar, (pants) or bottom piece. A duppatta is a piece of colourful cloth that women wear around their necks.

Salwar kameez's and duppattas come in a variety of colours and designs. Punjabi girls and women wear salwar kameez's with bright coloured duppattas. The women can also be seen wearing shawls adorned with the beautiful phulkari shawls. The shawl is completely covered in thick silk embroidery and folk motifs done in jewel-tones on an ochre background.

Accessories Worn by Punjabi Women

Punjabi women can be seen bedecked in gold. They adorn themselves with necklaces, bangles, rings, nose-pins, earrings, toe-rings, anklets and ornaments to pin up the hair with. Sikh women and men are seen wearing the kada, a steel bangle, at all times. After adolescence, and almost certainly after marriage, women are expected to wear traditional Indian clothing. However it may be mentioned here that this trend is rapidly changing and women can be seen wearing a variety of western wear. Jeans, Jackets, Trousers, Skirts and other form of western outfits are worn by the women of Punjab today.

Costume Worn by Punjabi Men

The traditional costume of the men of Punjab comprises a kurta pyjama. The kurta is a kind of loose shirt which is long and straight-cut. The pyjamas are loose, baggy pants which are tied at the waist. Some men also wear the kurta with the loongi or tehmat, which is a kind of sarong. During winters they can be seen wearing bright colourful sweaters. Some of the boys and even the brown up men can be seen wearing loose pants or slacks with a collared shirt or t-shirt. The Sikhs among the Punjabis can be distinctly identified by their attire as they are obliged by religion to wear turbans known as 'puggs'. Traditional Punjabi shoes, called juttis are extremely popular with men in both the rural and urban areas. They are extremely comfortable and also look very elegant.

The modern urban Punjabi men have also adopted the western style of dressing and are equally at ease in a pair of jeans and t-shirt as they are in the loongi and kurta. For the purposes of formal wear, Punjabi men can be seen wearing shirts and trousers. Thus the costumes of Punjab can be best seen in all their beauty and resplendent colours in the state of Punjab, especially in the rural areas.

KERALA

Costumes of Kerala evidence the innate simplicity of the

lifestyle of the Malayali people. The people from 'God's own country', both men and women, are mostly seen dressed in off-white and white attires. The principal dress which the people of Kerala wear is largely traditional in nature. The traditional form of dress worn by the Keralites is Mundu and Neriyathu (a piece of white cloth having borders of golden zari symbolising royalty) for both men and women. The women also wear 'sari' (a five to six metre long cloth which is embroidered with golden border) and jacket.

Costume Worn by Women of Kerala

The traditional garment worn by the women of Kerala is the 'mundum neriyathum.' The conventional piece is the 'mundu' which is the lower garment and it consists of two cloth pieces. The 'mundu' is worn around the hips and beneath the navel. This hand-woven cloth made of cotton, is very comfortable to wear in the summer season.

The cloth is creamy or white in colour and possesses a coloured strip called border or 'kara'. The women of Kerala wear mundu in this way except for the women of Christian origin. For them, the 'mundu' is folded up in multiple folds and this part is hung at the back. Over the 'mundu', women take on a special type of blouse, covering the navel.

The 'neriyathu' is the name of the upper garment which is put over the blouse having one of its ends inserted in the mundu and the other long end worn over the front torso. This is worn in a diagonal way, from the right hips to the left shoulder looking like a sari. Both the 'neriyathu' and 'mundu' is stiffened and then worn with a blouse matching the border or Kara's colour. This costume is worn every day and in the festive seasons people wear the same but with an ornamental 'kara' or a border which is either copper coated, golden or artificial coloured with temple or peacock design.

The colour of the blouse is decided by the marital status and age of the women. Unmarried young Keralite girls take on green blouse whereas the married ones wear red blouse. At the time of the celebration of the famous festival of Onam, women belonging to different age groups wear it and participate in the folk dance known as 'Kaikotti Kali Dance'. The women belonging to the Muslim community in Kerala, more particularly in the northern and central regions of Kerala, take on a long dark black or blue garment along with purdah and also cover up their abundant and long hair with beautiful kerchief.

The 'mundum neriyathum' was the traditional costume of the people of Kerala. But today, it has become an old fashion and is mostly worn by the old women of the state. Nowadays, it is being taken over by the 'set-sari' which has become the dress of the Keralite women as a quasi 'mundum neriyathum' and today as the 'Kerala sari'. Nowadays, they are mostly seen attired in sari and blouse.

Costume Worn by Men of Kerala

The men are more conservative than the women. In keeping with the old tradition of Kerala they wear white, which was once universal for both sexes. Their main garment is the long cloth called mundu, which is tucked at the waist and reaches to the ankle, giving its wearer a peculiar mincing walk, unless, to stride more freely, he kilts it to the knees.

Many men wear no garment the waist, but those who belong to the higher castes at least drape a towel-like cloth over the shoulders, and if they consider themselves modern they wear shirts which, like the mundu, are always washed to a dazzling whiteness. This garb is worn by men of all religions and all classes, except for the small westernized minority who have gone over to bush shirt and cotton slacks. The poor people of Kerala live simply from necessity, but their wealthier compatriots make simplicity a cult, so that among Malayalis one rarely sees the ostentation which in northern India is almost regarded as a duty of the rich. The local traditions set a value on eating sparingly and doing without elaborate furniture; one may wear fine rather than coarse cotton, but one does not wear silk. The traditional wear of the Hindu men residing in the state of Kerala is Kasavu Mundu. This dress is very much popular in the rural or remote areas. This attire is a piece of cloth made of cotton, three to four metre long having a silk border. Lungy or Kaily acts as an informal dress for Keralite men. But while moving out of their house, these men take on a shirt and mundu as well as a neriyathu over their shoulder and apply a paste of sandal on their chest and brows which provides them a much dignified appearance and a royal look.

The Keralite Muslims wear the same but they just wear an additional cap over their head. The Muslim style of wearing mundu is somewhat dissimilar to that of the Christian and Hindu Keralites.

Daily Wear of the People of Kerala

The daily use garments for the people of Kerala are saris and churidar or salwar-kameez for women and for men, trousers and shirts. The western type of dressing is also well-known among the generation of the young.

With continuous change in designing and fashion, the dress codes of the Keralites have changed considerably. The traditional form of dressing is reserved for special occassions and the women and men of today's Kerala are seen wearing a range of dresses. The people of this state have accepted the northern mode of dressing with men wearing trousers and tea-shirts which is a comfortable item for travel and their female counterparts have accepted the churidhar of north Indian style

ANDHRA PRADESH

Costumes of Andhra Pradesh are Saree and Blouse for women, and Dhoti and Kurta for men. The women of all communities together with Muslims wear Sarees and blouses. The skill of draping the saree is in itself an expression of a woman's creativity. Some Muslim women also put on Salwar Kameez Dupatta. Among the Hindus and Christians men usually wear a Dhoti and Kurta. The Muslims in general wear pyjamas instead of dhotis and kurta and the Fez cap, which though is not so common now. Andhra Pradesh is the insignia of the cultural convergence of South India. This fourth largest state of India, displays the wide spectrum of varied population, residing in this land, with their diverse cultural heritage.

Costume of a place reflects upon the cultural traditions, the lifestyle, the tastes and preferences and finally the impact of present modernity on the mindsets of its inhabitants. The myriad costumes of Andhra Pradesh, attest the place to be a potpourri of the ancient and the modern. The folk, rural element is a component of Andhra Pradesh's society.

The half-nomadic tribes, hailing from Lambadi or Banjara or Sugalis, are an agricultural sector of the social fabric of Andhra Pradesh. They earn their livelihood through harvesting, sowing, reaping and so on. It is evident that the costumes they would cater to would represent their life-pattern, class, and likings, in addition to their use of dresses that suit their climatic and geographical conditions, and social context Sarees of the original handlooms of Andhra Pradesh are complete with ethnicity and richness of texture. Dharmavaram in Andhra Pradesh has world wide repute for the production and distribution of gorgeous silk sarees. These Dharmavaram sarees make for ornate costumes, appropriate for bridal wear, ceremonies, like wedding party, or festivals.

The hallmark of these splendid sarees is that their borders are generally brocaded with gold plating. The Gadwal sarees, manufactured in Gadwal of Andhra Pradesh, are one of the most exclusive linen, available in the world. What is unique is the saree's cotton body, with pure silk borders and pallu (the tail-end of the saree). The Ikkat saree was first woven in the Nalgonda district of Andhra Pradesh. Now its chief production-sites are Puttapaka, Pochampalli and Chautuppal villages of Andhra Pradesh.

A proper know-how is indispensable in their creation. It requires a weaving -pattern, wherein the yarn is arbitrarily dyed in zigzag or geometric structures. The last category of sarees and not the least is the Mangalgiri saree, prepared from fine cotton, in Mangalgiri. All these sarees are the most happening costumes of Andhra Pradesh, not only, but in India and other parts of the globe also.The Kalamkari fabric contains the paintings of mythological figures and events with vegetable colours. Kalamkari sarees, kurti (tops), salwar-kameez, have become the order of the day and have become the popular costumes of Andhra Pradesh. This particular art form is prevalent in Machilipatnam of Andhra Pradesh. Urbanity in its refined form rules in the epicenter of sophistication, Hyderabad.

Here it is normal to come across burqha-clad, veiled Muslim woman, working at the same company with today's cosmopolitan girls, attired in salwar-kameez and jeans-shirts. The crowning glory of the costumes of Andhra Pradesh is the awesome Hyderabad's pearls. The enthusiastic Nizams of Hyderabad inaugurated pearl trade. The pearl small-industries, craftsmen and jewelers are situated near the well-known Charminar. The cost of pearls varies just as to radiance, shape and size.

Lambadies are a familiar tribal group in Andhra Pradesh and are well-known for their colourful costumes. The Lambada men have taken on the regional dress but the women folk have to this day preserved their gorgeous colourful and heavy garments, with lot of mirrors and beads studded on them. They dress in wide skirts in many gay and loud shades of red, orange and blue. The magnificent finesse of the costumes of Andhra Pradesh definitely highlights the deft craftsmanship of the different handlooms and textile-industries.

Furthermore, pearls have always been a woman's pride. Therefore, the costumes of Andhra Pradesh cast such an enigmatic spell, that not only the denizens of the state, are spellbound with their aura, but also the tourists who flock there, to appease their appetite for exotic garments and pearl-jewellery.

KARNATAKA

Costumes of Karnataka consist of regal silk sarees, which happen to be the traditional costumes of this place. Karnataka is the silk hub of the country. Karnataka silk has a wide spectrum. It has abundant variety, namely, smooth silks, sleek chiffons, and gorgeous brocades. These saris not only decorate women in the state, but also establish its sway in other parts of the country and in foreign nations. Indeed, Bengaluru and Mysore are the epicenters of silk-industries in South India. The marvelous shine, the super quality thread and the interweaving of gold threads in exclusive creations, attribute to the profound popularity of the sari as the favorite costume.

The Kanjeevaram or Kanchipurram silks, of Kanchipuram in Karnataka, dazzle the eye with the rich texture, mind-blowing colours, and fabulous designs. The Kanchipuram Silk Saree is a hand-woven creation. The silk yarn is dyed to bring the desired colour and afterwards Jari is interleaved into the yarn. Pure Jari is a silk thread, intertwined with a thin silver wire and then gilded with pure gold.

The Jari adds the element of shimmer in the yarn. The technique of Kanchipuram-making calls for Sarees the conjunction of three threads to concertedly make the silk thread used for weaving. This gives the sari a durable quality. Hence, the outstanding Kanchipuram sarees usually turn out to be the bridal costume of Karnataka.

Among the other popular items, Mysore silk, deserve mention. The magnificent mantle, the lustrous zari and the rich silk, make the saree assume an enchanting look. These sarees are less expensive than the queen of silks, Kanchipuram silks. Therefore, its reasonable costs make it more affordable for the ordinary people and, still give them the elegance, they are searching for. Arani Silks, Valkalams, Kora Silks, Patola Sarees, exclusive Designer Mysore Silk Sarees, Crepe Silk Sarees, Chiffon Sarees, and Raw Silk saris can satisfy the aesthetically aware population of Karnataka.

Sarees with this impressive variety is thus the traditional costume of Karnataka. The Kornadu sarees are fascinating in their fusion-display of cotton and silk. The saris are woven in a blue cotton yarn together with a silk yarn in other multiple shades. The motifs in the sarees are varied and the body of the sari either bestowed with checks or stripes. These sarees are used as daily comfort wears.

The Mysore crepe silk, is apt as costume for office or workplace, more because of its light-weight, and easier maintenance. It is supple opaque crepe silk complemented with Jari margins. These saris are dyed in spectacular colours after the completion of the weaving. The Ilkal and the

Mokalmuru sarees stand as the ethnic motif of Karnataka. It is used for regular wear and tear and also as traditional costume, by a fashion-conscious Karnataka lady. Karnataka presents before the world its harmonisation of modernity and tradition.

When Bangalore reigns as the Silicon Valley of India, it is evident that women and men will also adhere to the formal office wear, suitable for working environs. Today's girls might wear Mysore crepe salwars, or Karnataka handloom's cotton salwar or saree, or even Western jeans and trousers, while going to office.

When it comes to considering the office costume of Karnataka men, they wear formal shirts, or T-shirts or trousers, without having the privilege of many options. However, on special occasions, men might dress themselves in ornate versions of their traditional costume, the Panche, which is Dhoti-like apparel. In recent times, only the rustic men of Karnataka stick to Panche, as their everyday costume. Mysore Peta is the traditional headdress for Karnataka.

The magic wand of technology has cast its spell on Karnataka. But surprisingly enough, the demand for the traditional costume of Karnataka, especially those of women, has not declined, but is on the rise with the passage of time. Recent technological improvement rather has set the textile industry of Karnataka on a boom. This state has established an ideal example of blending present priorities with tradition, to achieve the best of costumes.

MEGHALAYA

Costumes in the state of Meghalaya show the ethnicity of the tribes namely the Garos, Khasi and the Jaintias. Nestled in the peaceful hills of the north-eastern part of India, the beautiful state of Meghalaya houses these three famous hill tribes of India. It is interesting to note that the Garos are the most skilled weavers of the region. Probably, every family earns their livelihood through weaving. Indeed, the traditional costume for women, called Jainsen, is an unstitched garment wrapped around to cover the body. It is woven from mulberry silk cultivated in the local region. The crowning glory of the costume of Meghalaya is the Endi silk shawl.

Sonidan is the hub of Fndi or Errandi silk-production in Meghalaya. The hill communities rear Philosamia ricini, the silkworm, feeding on castor leaves. These nature's artists, the silkworms, produce rich protein fibre and accordingly spin round the open-ended cocoon. It is from this fibre that the coveted silk is generated.

Endi silk is the product of the domesticated silkworm, Philosamia ricini that feeds mainly on castor leaves. Sericulture is a popular small-scale industry of Meghalaya. The silk-weavers use the Endi silk threads to weave splendid shawls, that are not only warmth-retentive or supple, but assets to boast of. These shawls are invested with natural soothing shades of crÅ me, white, brown, beige and gold. They are favorites of not only the local tribal, but also of any fashion-addict of India.

The weaver-ace Garos cater to different forms of costume, in keeping with the air of the ambience they are residing in. In the remote areas of Garo hill villages, the women drape eking, a short cloth round the waist, while the men put in a loincloth. But the Garo women go for a longer version of cotton attire in the crowded zones. A Garo woman dons a blouse, and wears a Lungi like mantle of unstitched cloth called Dakmanda, by fastening it round the waist.

The Dakmanda is an example of hand-woven cotton fabric. Its specialty is the six to ten inch broad borders embellished with attractive motifs or floral patterns. The Khasi sect comprising fifty per cent of the total population in India, emit a discrete aura, owing to the costume they wear. The traditional costume of the Khasi man in Meghalaya is unstitched lower apparel, akin to Dhoti, completed by a jacket and headgear or turban. However, in the recent times, men display themselves in traditional garments only on social festivals and ceremonies, to keep the flame of tradition, glowing. Western concept of dressing has entered the realms of costume-design in Meghalaya. However, the element of tradition is much alive in the costume of the Khasi women. It entails a Jainsen, concealing till the ankles, which is topped off by a blouse. These garments, she ties the edges of tap-moh khlieh, a cotton shawl, round her neck or pins at the shoulders, to serve somewhat like an apron.

During occasions, Ka Jainsem Dhara, a long piece of Assam Muga silk, is added to this attire, so as to assume a radiant appearance. But the base-material for these costumes is mill-manufactured, as the Kashis are not so much attached with weaving today. Another strip of woolen cloth called Jainkup, is used by the senior women. Jainkup is not so much in vogue among the younger generation. Khasi women, have the affordability to deck themselves in ornaments of pure gold and silver, made by local jewelry-smiths. The costume of the male members of the Jaintia tribe bears similarities with that of the Khasi men. However, the costume of the Jaintia women in Meghalaya is a little different from the other groups.

A Jaintia woman envelops her head with a cloth-piece with checks called "Kyrshah", at the times of harvest-work in the field. She covers herself from the shoulders to the ankles, with a velvet blouse, along with a sarong called Thoh Khyrwang wrapped round her waist. She also ties round her shoulders an Assam Muga silk cloth, flowing down to the ankles. There exists a practice among Jaintia men and women, to present themselves in gaudy, resplendent costumes, on festive and happy occasions.

Dressing without the embellishments of ornaments, is lusterless for Jaintia women. They adorn themselves with earrings and other ornaments of gold and silver. It is a custom to dress in head ornaments, like, a silver circlet worn round the head as a forehead decoration. Both the Khasis and the Jayantis, flaunt themselves in a pure gold pendant kown as Kynjri Ksiar. The elegance and grace inherent to the ethnic costumes of Meghalaya complements the scenic beauty of the picturesque landscape of Meghalaya.

SIKKIM

Costumes of Sikkim reflect the social and cultural lifestyle of the major communities namely Lepchas, Bhutias and Nepalis. However, in the cities and urbanised sectors of the state,

Marwaris, Biharis, Bengalis, South Indians and Punjabis, have settled to conduct business and serve in government services.

The original inhabitants of Sikkim, the Lepchas, flaunt themselves in costumes, furnished with resplendent colours. The traditional costume of the Lepcha male is Thokro-Dum which involves a white pajama, stretching only to the calves, Yenthatse, a Lepcha shirt and Shambo, the cap. The texture of the male dress is rough, and long-lasting, suitable for the hardy toil in the field and forest.

The hereditary costume of Lepcha women is Dumvum or Dumdyam, a kind of smooth and cosy ankle-long dress, draped like a saree, Tago a loose-fitting comfortable blouse, Nyamrek, a belt and Taro, a cap. The magnificent ornaments exhibited by the Lepcha women, entail, earrings, called Namchok, Lyak a necklace, Gyar, a bracelet, and so on. The Bhutia community, hailing from the adjacent country of Tibet, has over years become rooted in the culture and social norms of Sikkim.

The traditional costume of Bhutia males comprises Kho, also known as Bakhu. It is a loose mantle which is tied at the neck on one side, and at the waist region with a silk or cotton belt. Added to this basic garment, a Bhutia man dons Jya Jya, a waist coat, the shirt, called, Yenthatse, shirt, Kera, a cloth-belt and Shambo, the cap.

A Bhutia woman's general costume consists of Kho or Bakhu, Hanju, a silky full-sleeve loose blouse, Kushen, a jacket, a different pattern of the cap, Shambo and Shabchu, the shoe. Pangden, the stripy apron, the signifier of marital status is a symbol of married Bhutia females. The ornaments enhancing the appearance of the Bhutia women are Yencho, the earring, Khao, the necklace, Phiru, the pearl ornament, Diu, the Gold bangle, and Joko, the ring. Bhutia people are obsessed with the pure form of gold, *i.e.*, 24 carats, and have most of their ornaments crafted from pure gold.

Nepali, another predominant group of Sikkim, has sustained the ethnicity of their own culture in their costume. The Nepalese men dress themselves in Shurval, a Churidar Pajama, topped off by a shirt, known as Daura. It is associated with Aaskot, wrist coat and their belt, called Patuki. The traditional costume of the Nepali women of Sikkim is endowed with fabulous hues. Pharia, the saree, gorgeous in vibrant shades, definitely augments the grace of the Nepali women.

The dressing gets the right finish with a long loose blouse, is fastened from four sides and hence is called Chaubandi Cholo. Another variety in blouse is the Tharo Cholo. The upper portion of the body is daintily enveloped with a piece of cloth with wonderful prints. It is called Hembari.

The dance costume of the Nepali women is amazing. Pachauri, a colourful piece of cloth, suspended from the head to the waist, is utilised as adornment during dance performances. The ornaments that give a gaudy appearance to the Nepalese women are Sir-Bandi or tiara, *i.e.*, a jeweled head-ornament, Kantha, a necklace, Naugeri, a pearl-necklace, Charanihari, again a necklace, Tilhari, a green bead with an elongated gold pendant, attired mainly by married women, Bulaki, a nose-ring, Dungri, a nose-pin, Tik-mala, Chandrahar, Chepti son, an ear ring, Gadwari, an earring, a silver Chura, a bracelet, and Kalli, a thick, substantial, silver anklet.

The other Marwari, Bihari, Bengali or Punjabi communities cater to their traditional costumes of salwar-kameez dupatta, saree, woolen textiles, and even to Western outfit, like jeans, T-shirts, trousers, anything which suits their taste and preferences. Costumes of Sikkim, reflects in the resplendence of the dress and ornaments of the people, their love for beauty and inventive finesse.

DADRA AND NAGAR HAVELI

Dadra and Nagar Haveli, situated on the west of the western Ghats,is replete with the ethnic culture of tribes. The main tribes include Dodhia, Kokna and Varli. Above 62%of the population in Dadra and Nagar Haveli is tribal.

The costume of the men of Varlis origin, the largest tribal community, comprises of a loin-cloth, a waist-long coat, and a headgear *i.e.*, a turban. The Varli women, wrap themselves round the waist in Lugden (a one yard sari), reaching down till the knee and another piece of cloth called Padar. Women love to deck themselves in silver and white ornaments. Dhodia men, cover themselves in a white knee-length Dhoti, topped off by a shirt or a waistcoat. They, like the Varli to act as the headdress, a cap of white or coloured shades. The Dhodia men are inclined towards wearing ornaments, such as earrings and silver chains, encircling the waist.

The traditional costume of the Dodhia women, on the other hand, is a dark blue saree, stretching upto the knees, and with the aanchal, enveloping the front portion of the body. Beads necklaces of resplendent hues, metal bangles on wrists and dainty metal Kadas (a kind of anklet) round the ankles, augment the natural beauty of the woman folk. The costume of the Koknas, is much akin to that of the other tribes. The sturdy Kokna men, don themselves in Dhoti, coming down till the knees, a waist coat or shirt. A turban furnishes a Kokna man with dignity.

Kokna women flaunt themselves in sarees of myriad colours, either knee-long or toe-long. An additional adornment catered by the Kokna men and women is a tattoo-painting, on the forehead and on other parts of the body. It is wonderful to watch that the costumes of Dadar and Nagar Haveli, has a simple as well as aesthetic complexion.

KUTCH

Exquisitely stylized and intricately embroidered, the kutchi attire is simply eye-catching. Dazzling with vibrant colours, flooded with striking mirror work and stunning jewellery it's one of the most alluring customs in India. The mirror work and embroidery work forms an integral part of Kutchi Handicrafts irrespective of the community or ethnic group to which they belong, however the workmanship differs. In fact the various communities can be identified by the pattern of handicrafts and dress or costumes they were. For instance, the Garacia Jat women wear only red or black chunis while Rabari women wear black open blouses or cholis with odhnis to cover head. In the rural areas women wear Chaniya choli during the whole year, Chaniya choli's are of many designs and fashion. Typical Kutchi costume is incomplete without 'Abha' or 'Kanjari'. 'Abha' is the name of the typical choli worn by women folk and 'Kanjari' is a long blouse beautifully embroidered and with mirror work. Most men in Kutch wear loose trousers, a long-sleeved under-jacket, and a short coat, a plain or silk-bordered cloth. Normally men prefer white clothes except the Muslims who prefer coloured clothes.

Abhas, the traditional costume of the region of Kutch, has entered the world of high fashion. Successfully adapted to modern styles by Anjali Mangaldas, this beautiful garment has become a rage with the fashion conscious women. In the village of Kutch, the women looked beautiful in their fabulous Abhas as they swayed to the music. The twinkling lights played mischievously over the gold and thread embroidery while the sequins and badla work sparkled continuously.

A woman in an abha, the traditional costume of the Khatri, Memon and Korja Muslim communities of Kutch is a sight to behold. This garment from Kutch, a district in Gujarat, has a history that is as colourful and exciting as the garment. In ancient times the women wore the abha embellished with beautiful tie-dye designs, zari thread embroidery that was very minute and intricate embroidery in coloured silk or cotton thread in a combination of a variety of stitches, integrating minuscule mirror discs into its elaborate and distinct pattern.

The word abha-has been derived from aba a word commonly used in the Middle Eastern countries which means a top garment or a mantle. The abha based on an age-old traditional classical cut and style, is basically a kalidar kurta without a slit on the sides, with a lose flair and it hangs lower than a normal kurta. The abha has been a collectors item since the last four generations. The abha has been a collectors item since the last four generations. The best have even been part of collections auctioned in the west by Christys and Sothebys Research scholars have not yet been able to pinpoint the historical period or influence on these costumes. Unfortunately modernity has compelled these lovely costumes into museums or wooden boxes in far off villages. The genuine abhas could be date back nearly a century.

ASSAM

Muga or the golden silk fibre of Assam constitutes the lion's share of the costumes of Assam. The characteristic of the durable Muga silk is that it lasts for years and adds radiance to itself, after every wash. It is interesting watching the silk-cultivation in Assam. One can watch the silkworm in its cocoon stage, till the unfolding into worm's generated silk-thread, and finally the conversion of the threads into the gorgeous saris at the handloom. Almost twenty eight thousand families are engaged in silk-rearing in Assam. The delicate designs, finely woven, on the saris cater to patterns in nature, for example the flora and the fauna. Embroideries also incorporate, acquainted and culture-related things, such as architecture and stone-sculptures on the Madan Kamdev Temple in Assam.

Now-a-days, Muga artisans, indulge in experimentation. They offer contrast creations of pinkish red or greenish blue and other innovative as well as traditional colours of red, blue, yellow, green, against the inherent golden colour of the fabric. Assam silk saris Bridal wears are decked with gold and silver threads, to make the bride catch a marvelous get-up on her special occasion. The Assam silk saris are perfectly suitable for parties, wedding ceremonies and mirthful festivals. It endows on any woman, who wears it, an aura of elegance. This high quality textile of Assam, Muga silk, serves as the material-base, even for the traditional costume of Assam, called Mekhla Chadar. The Mekhla is an awesome ensemble, which resembles a sari, and is yet not a sari.

The distinction lies in the fact that a Mekhla is composed of two or three pieces of cloth, whereas a sari is a single piece of cloth. One half of the Mekhla is worn as the skirt or petticoat or Lungi, while the other half, Chaddar, is akin to the sari's Anchal, used as the upper-garment for the skirt. Added to the Chaddar, blouses are worn, below Chadar, to complete the dress. The Mekhla skirt bears a broad border and is thicker in texture, but the Anchal is light-weight for easier handling. A Mekhla is hence a mix and match of Aanchal and Lungi. However, the Chadar, is adorned with spell-bound weavings, integral to the weaving-ace Assamese. The Chadar is worn in a special criss-cross pleated-form, down the front side. Assamese women look marvelous in these fascinating costumes of Assam.

Bodo tribe of Assam resides amidst the lush greenery of Assam. The Bodo tribal womenfolk acknowledge Mekhla as their prevalent costume. Along with the Chaddar, an upper-wrap called Riha. In fact, this happens to be the usual costume of the rustic people of Assam. The men of the Bodo tribe, dresses themselves in Dhoti (an Indian loin cloth) and Chaddar, made from Endi (a material made from conglomeration of silk and cotton). Very similar to the costume of the Bodo tribe, is the dressing style of another, tribal community, the Mech tribe, and silk-weavers in profession. The Dimasa tribes are renowned for their expertise in silk-culture and weaving-prowess. They are indeed the producers of Endi.

A Dimasa woman covers herself in a skirt-like attire, known as the as Rigu, topped by an embellished vest-like cloth, called Rijamphai. Ceremonies and merry occasions see the women, decorating themselves in more ornate Rijamphai, locally named as Rikhaosa. Again, like the Bodo men, Dimasa men, wears, a Risha, this is a loin cloth of deep green colour. He puts in a vest, called Rimsao. He also attaches on his head, a turban woven from pure cotton or Endi. The costume of the Thai Phake tribe stands illuminated with respect to its attractive charm. A Thai Phake woman uses a striped girdle, called Chin which stretches from the waist down to the ankles. There exists a cloth belt encircling her waist. It is called Chairchin. It has a width of about 6 cm and a length of 1.5 m. Young girls resort same upper-cloth structure, with the only difference being in size. It is called Fafek.

The Thai Phake women are inclined towards beautification of themselves. They enhance their prettiness, by wearing multicoloured blouse, called Chekhamchum. While attending invitation or paying visit to far-flung places, they flaunt themselves in dignified white shawl-like cloth called Chaddar. At times of wedding, this Chaddar acts as the customary veil to the bride. The costume of the Thai Phake man is to some extent same. He wears a chequered green loin cloth, invested with black stripes and red, yellow or white lining, called Fatong. Upwards, he matches his Fatong, with a shirt called Sho. He also bears a white turban called Fa ho ho. While venturing out, the Thai Phake men, adorns himself in a white shirt with long sleeves, enriched with a plain bordered white shawl called Fa fek mai, to make himself presentable at the place of his visit. Jewellery is a fundamental aspect of costume of any place.

The remarkable feature of Assamese jewellery is Khopo Phool, an earring which appears like an orchid. The outlook is like two small shoes paired together and crowned by a floral construct, which is again connected to a chain. Gaam Kharu is a large-sized silver bangle with shimmering gold polish. Another fashionable earring is Lokaporo, wherein two gold or ruby or mina or enamel-plated, bird figures are conjoined together, back to back. Assamese costume has cast an enchanting spell on not only India, but on foreign nations also, because of their mind-blowing perfection.

HIMACHAL PRADESH

Costumes of Himachal Pradesh comprise an awesome diversity owing to the plethora of culture and religion. Again the costumes of each community are different, be it the Hindu Brahmins, the Rajputs, and the tribal people like Gaddis, Kinnars, Gujjars, Pangawals and Lahaulis.

By heritage, the Dhoti-clad Brahmin priests roam around in Kurta, coat, waistcoat, turban, *i.e.*, Pagri, and with a hand towel, placed upon the shoulders and with a valuable copy of Panchang, an astrological yearbook, carried under the arm, for important consultation. His attire is thus in keeping with the cold atmosphere, and curiously enough with his priestly profession that involves astrological predictions too.

The Rajputs wear body-hugging churidar pyjamas, a long coat, a starch-stiffened turban with a unique mould, and shoes with pointed edges. The boasted thick moustaches and a dignified frown in the forehead-region, is symbolic of manliness in Rajput society. Now a days, though not so much in vogue, but previously the Rajputs adhered to the Purdah or veil system for their women. Their wives and daughters used to venture out within the enclosed confines of curtained palanquins.

The costume of the women hailing from the Brahmin and the Rajput clans are quite traditional. These women normally dress themselves in kurtas (shirt-like oriental blouse), salwars, ghaghri(Indian long skirts), choli (blouses or tops with intricate embroidery) and rahide (nice crimson headscarves decked with golden fringes).The farmers and worker classes required to toil, go for kurta, a loincloth and a cap. They cater to long pyjamas, for attending ceremonies, like marriage ceremonies or special occasions, such as festival.

Nevertheless, Western influence is visible on the costumes of the younger generation of Himachal Pradesh these days. Hand-woven excellence is the hallmark of the costumes of Himachal Pradesh. The native women are famous in weaving headscarves. The utility shoes made from grass, are perfect for keeping the feet warm. The difference in style and the quality of Kurtas, saris and gowns woven by indigenous weavers, serve as the insignia of Himachal handlooms. Peculiarities in kinds of feminine ornaments are well demonstrated by the bangles and rings produced from horsehair. These weave-ace people are the dexterous creators of exclusive shawls.

These shawls are famous for their elegance and smooth textures, as well as fascinating patterns, are assets for any costume-lover. The soothing suppleness of the renowned Pashmina shawl is the specialty of the handlooms of Himachal Pradesh. Manufactured from the hair of Pashmina goat, these shawls find their demand worldwide. Among the favorite types of shawls, 'Dhobroo' and 'Pattu', are the leading. The fancy needlework available on these shawls has its source in the Kangra and Chamba schools of paintings.

Thapada is also a broad shawl, embroidered with marvelous embroidery. Embroidered blouses and caps gives a glimpse of the commendable taste of the Himachal inhabitants. The embroidered caps of the Kulu, Sirmair, Kinnaur and Lahaul are all brands of skilled craft by themselves. The striking shawls originating from Kulu, Lahaul, celebrate the ages-old Pahadi designs. Exquisite patchwork, quilts, doll and elephant figures constructed of rags are all native productions, which serve as vital constituents of the gorgeous attire for the bride. The wool products are knitted from Byangi wool. Wool weaving acts as a major vocation in Himachal. The dwellers of Lahaul-Spiti and Kinnaur are deft in this task who weaves ornate draperies for special occasions.

Dyeing and printing of fabrics makes for a traditional craft in the region. The Farahada and the Chhiba group people are the experts in this business. And the resultant is that we come across, abundance of resplendent dyed and printed fabrics and costumes in Himachal Pradesh. To be very precise, the splendid costumes of Himachal Pradesh owe a lot to the impressive craftsmanship of the prolific weaving-talents and the outstanding handlooms of the state.

MADHYA PRADESH

Costumes of Madhya Pradesh Description: Costumes of Madhya Pradesh show multiplicity in various aspects. Handicrafts and different textile techniques have given rise to a rich diversity of costumes of Madhya Pradesh. Costumes of Madhya Pradesh comprise handicrafts and diverse textile techniques which have given rise to a rich array of costumes of Madhya Pradesh. The majority of the people of Madhya Pradesh attest Dhoti as their traditional costume. Safa, a kind of turban, is the headgear, which is the common feature of Madhya Pradesh's costume.

Furthermore, a white or black jacket called Bandi or Mirzai, is a part of the men's attire, specifically in Bundelkhand and Malwa. The myriad colours of this traditional costume of the men of Madhya Pradesh, gives the men a radiant and dignified appearance. The womenfolk of Madhya Pradesh dress themselves in Lehenga (long Indian skirt) and Choli (Indian blouse).Another additional strip of cloth called Orni or Lugra is draped around the head and shoulders, to retain a decent and sobre look. Red and black, are the favourite shades for this feminine costume. Bandhani (locally called Bandhej) cloth is produced on a huge scale in Maundsar, Indore and Ujjain. The fabric is painted with molten wax and is dyed with cold dyes to create a cloth variety called Batik. Contrast patterns on Batik cloth are quite well-known. The delicate Chanderi sarees and Maheshwari sarees produced in Madhya Pradesh are hand-woven, and they are quite renowned all over India.

It is interesting to watch that the air of Western dress-pattern has already started blowing in the towns and Kasbas of Madhya Pradesh. Mill-manufactured clothes are in vogue in urban areas. In fact, modern dresses form an integral part of the daily costume in Madhya Pradesh. Ready-made dresses, with a medium coarse quality, rampant in weekly markets are the daily costume. Special occasions and delightful festivals witness people roaming around in utmost revelry. Their costumes in such wonderful moments are resplendent, colourful costumes, enriched with fascinating prints. Immaculate white garments are celebrated as the foremost priority.

Tribal people, for presenting themselves in public wear short-sized Dhotis, but in the remote ambience of the forests they feel cozy in minimal garment, called langot. The children, or the school-going group of Madhya Pradesh, have uniforms, very similar to the student's costume of other states. Boys visit school in short-pants and shirts; whereas, girls, cover themselves in ghaghri, a kind of Indian skirt, or in Western frock. It is definite that a costume is incomplete without shoes, which are a necessity and no more a luxury. The villagers of Madhya Pradesh wear raw-leather shoes, made by the village-cobbler. These shoes are tough and lasting in order to endure the immense toil of he primarily agricultural rustic people of Madhya Pradesh.

Ornaments are a natural accompaniment to Indian costumes, and that of Madhya Pradesh, is no exception to this rule. The tribal women of this state augment their beauty in silver or Kathir ornaments. Their treasure-chest incorporates

Kadas (bracelets) and Kangni (bangles) on hand and Hansli and Haar (necklace). Aluminium or silver bracelets decorate the wrist and armbands, the upper-arm. Bali or little ear-studs, Zele on the forehead, silver Kandora on the waist-line, payal (anklet) and Bichhudi on the toes, gives the tribal woman a gorgeous look.

The accessories of the refined and educated elite women have a different charm. They go for similar types of ornaments, but they have the affordability to indulge in the delight of gold. Young girls, hanker for silver or aluminum-made Pyjeb to embellish their feet. Their necks are adorned with sleek silver or golden chain, bearing often, attractive pendant or locket. Semi-precious or today's imitation jewelry are quite popular among the young generation of girls.

Tattoo painting is an important constituent of the costume-pattern of Madhya Pradesh. In tribal-crowded zones like Bhil, Bhilala, Banjara, Meghwal, Charan, Kahar and Kumhar, the tribes, who are by profession potter, engage in a lot of captivating tattooing. Particularly, the women of these tribal sects prefer drawing on their arms tattoos of flower, self-name or picture of a god, an ox, *i.e.* subjects from the wide range of the flora and the fauna encircling them. To conclude, one must praise the intermingling of tribal as well as non-tribal cultures in Madhya Pradesh, which has given the costumes of this region, an element of ethnicity and discreteness, fundamental to the social system of Madhya Pradesh.

MIZORAM

The beautiful and serene Mizoram, situated on the Northeastern corner of India, is the home of the Mongoloid relatives, living for years in the Equality-championed hill societies. The costumes of Mizoram bear conspicuous resemblance with that of the other hill-states of the Northeast. The fundamental patterns speak volumes for the prevalence of the ethnic heritage, typical of the costumes of the North East. The hot favorite costume of a Mizoram woman is Puan. The vibrant colour and the outstanding designs are the reasons behind this marvelous costume. Puanchei, the gorgeous attire of Mizo girls is a must during weddings and festivals such as 'Chapchar Kut' and 'Pawl Kut'. Ngotekherh is a cotton and hand-woven festive-attire apt for kuts, *i.e.* festivals, namely 'Chapchar Kut', 'Mim Kut' and 'Pawl Kut'. The shades in the cloth are black and white. The black portion of the textile is constructed from some kind of synthetic fur.

Kawrchei is akin to Ngotekherh, as it is the costume for revelry and merry-making. It is a fabulous blouse for Mizo girls. They too are hand-woven and cotton material. This are usually worn along with 'Puanchei' and while performing the various dances of the Mizos In earlier times, these were all hand woven but nowadays these are mostly machine made. They are made from cotton and the colours are made by a thing called 'Ting'. Along with this, a blouse, which is of the same pattern, is usually worn.

The Lusei men believe in simplicity, when it comes to deciding their traditional costume. They drape themselves in an almost. 7 feet long and 5 wide cloth-piece. It reaches the left shoulder to the back and then passes under the right arm, to cover the chest, with the remaining end concealing the left shoulder. In cold season, some additional attires are worn, one on top of the other, along with a white coat, comes down from the throat enveloping till the thighs. White and red bands, invested with designs adorn the sleeves of these coats.

During the hot months, people tie these clothes around the waist to feel comfortable. Moreover, at times to avoid the blazing sun, a Lusei man contrives a piece of cloth as a turban or Pagri. The entire costume of the Lusei men is made of cotton, cultivated in the region itself. Usually, the costumes come in white colour, but sometimes men want to wear other shades, for example, blue colour bestowed with stripes. There is hardly any difference existing in the costumes of the ordinary Lusei and the head of the community. Only during festive occasions, the costume is different.

The traditional costume of the Lusei women is the dark blue cotton petticoat, worn round the waist and tightly held by a girdle or belt of brass wire. This is uniform, worn by all women, stretches itself upto the knees. This petticoat is topped off by short white jacket and a cloth, wrapped in the same way as the men's. However, the resplendent item in the Lusei girl's costume is the headgear, worn during dances. This headdress is composed of a coronal, built from brass and coloured cane, endowed with porcupine quills, and upper edges of these quills are added green wing-feathers of the common parrot, carrying at their tips tussocks of wing covers of green beetles.

In the Lusei society, where men and women are considered equal, women indulge in smoking like men, through a hookah-type pipe,which is 9 inches in height.

The warrior's costume in Lusei society entail a cloth passed round the waist, a knapsack, fortified with a bear or tiger hide over one shoulder, a gun in one hand an weapon called dao on the other. A valorous Lusei, who had been conferred upon the honorable title of the Thanhchhuah, wears a particular cloth to signify his status, while the one who has wiped off people in war have special headdress, known as "chhawndawl" and "arke-ziak".

The Hmars tribes are weaving-experts, deft in creating multiple patterns. Among them, one must mention the Thangsuo Puon, meaning famous cloth in Hmars vocabulary. This the prized possession of the victorious and the destroyer of optimum number of foes in war. Those valiant Hmar warriors wear them, and even their wives, sometimes relish in the pride of their husband's might, by wearing them.

Puon Laisen is a red cloth with two black stripes at the middle. The cloth is gifted with several designs like Sakat Zang Zie, Disul, etc.

The handwoven Hmaram, also called Kawkpui zikzial are very much in vogue among the children and girls. They are put in on the occasions such as 'Chawn Day', 'Chhawnghnawh Day' and 'Chapchar Kut'. Zakuolaisen this is a blouse piece with crimson stripes used mainly by the unmarried girls.

The little but praiseworthy costumes of Paiteis are captivating. Thangou Puon, ranks as the most significant costume of Paiteis community. Only, a brave warrior who has slaughtered rivals in inter-tribal tussle or in war is allowed to claim ownership of this costume. Again, the producer of maximum quantity of crop can wear the Thangou Puon. Paite is project themselves in the Puon Dum, their national cloth to attend commiseration, formal meetings and observance of National Dayand so on. It matches with the gravity of the situation etc. It appears with black lines along with white, yellow, red or green stripes.

Puon Pie, a quilt woven cloth, is a must for every girl, while coming down to settle in her husband's abode, post marriage. The costume of the Riang group of Mizoram is similar to that of the other tribes. The use of colours, designs, cuttings and finally the style of dressing, associated with costumes, casts light on the artistic prowess of the people of Mizoram.

TRIPURA

Tripura, the frontier hilly state of the North-East, is the land of skilled weavers, gifted with proper know-how.The women of the local tribes, such as the Khakloo, the Halam, the Lushei and the Kuki-Chin tribe, excel in the art of weaving, as is attested in the diligent traditional costumes, which they diligently preserve.

There is a striking resemblance in the traditional costume of the Khakloo and the other fellow tribes. The plain dressing style is apt for the hilly climate, and for regular work. The infants are hardly given clothes except when it becomes essential in the winter and rainy season. The children put on a loincloth. The daily work-costume of a full-grown male is a towel-like sheet of loin cloth, called Rikutu Gamcha, topped off by a self-woven shirt, called Kubai. To combat the blazing heat of the sun and to continue working in the open heat, the men resort to a pagri, *i.e.*, a turban. Western influence is prominently visible on the young boys of today's Manipur, because they prefer wearing shirts and pants.

The infants are normally kept undressed, although in winter and monsoon season, garments suitably shield them. Children, covers themselves in a loin-garment.

The Khakloo, and at large the Tripuri women, envelop themselves in a greater size of cloth-piece, known as Rinai.

This long as well as broad cloth is draped around the waist and reaches the knee. She dons herself in a shorter piece of cloth called Risa. This upper-attire passes under the arms, and conceals the entire chest-region of the body. Risas are often invested with beautiful embroideries. Now-a-days, the younger generation of girls prioritize blouses over Risa, as being more management-friendly. However, still among few clans, the wearing of Risa during wedding is mandatory. Women folk also are found to use some kind of headdresses while at work outside.

The neck areas of women are adorned with plethora of beads and coin strands. The element of finery is dim in the costume of the women of the Lushei tribe. Every woman wear a dark blue cotton fabric, to serve as a skirt or petticoat. This cloth, wrapped around the waist, is held firmly by a corset of brass wire or string. The Rinai-like cloth, which falls down to the knees, is associated with an upper-attire; a short white jacket and a cloth to invest in their appearance the sobriety.

In the mirthful times of revelry, the female costume, gets an extra item, a dignified headgear, specifically during dance-performance. This headdress is a coronal, made of brass and coloured cane, further embellished with porcupine quills. Moreover, the upper edges of these quills are studded with the green feathers of the parrot's wings, decorated at their tips, with tussocks of contrasting red wool.

The earlier costumes of the Kuki-Chin women had deigns, imitated from the patterns, seen on the hide of snakes. They bore several names, such as Thangang, Saipi-khup, Ponmongvom, and Khamtang. However, these clothes were previously the prerogative of the women of the aristocrat background, like those from the chief's family and other noble-blood. Indeed, the simplicity yet attractiveness of the traditional costume of Tripura, is attributed to the artistic fervor and weaving-talent of the natives.

LAKSHADWEEP

The blue sea lashing against the beaches of Lakshadweep, shimmering in the golden radiance of sunlight makes

Lakshadweep a dream-destination. The abundance of colours enriches the traditional costumes of Lakshadweep. The scenic landscape is hence in tune with the resplendent costumes, all of which are marvels to watch at.

The plain, but colourful costumes of Lakshadweep, and the Amini cluster of islands, deserve praise, for their inherent sense of artistry. The tribal men, of this coastal land, other than Minicoy, don themselves in white or coloured lungi, coming as a rectangular piece of cloth, with its edges, stitched together. Not only men, but also women tie a silver thread round the waist. This acts as a girdle for a senior person, who pulls the lungi through the string to hold it firmly round his waist. Normally, for daily wear and tear, men do not covers themselves upwards the waist. However, in ceremonial participation, they flaunt themselves in cotton or silk drapery, invested with impressive embroidery. This cloth is passed around the shoulders. The younger generation, exhibit themselves in shirts.

The traditional costume of women comprises of Kachi, a rectangular piece of cloth, but unstitched unlike that of men. Kachis are, often made of silk fabric. This Kachi, enveloping a woman from the waist, is tucked into the waistband of silver thread. The shades of Kachis are generally black or white with black borders. However, the silk Kachis, commonly come up in red body with contrasting black borders.

The jacket, on the front side, contains fine -embroidery, done with glass or gilt bits. It is topped off by a full-sleeves close-fitting jacket around the waist. The colour-smeared scarf, known as Thattam, serves as a wonderful headdress. There is a discrete charm about the costume of the Minicoy population. The various stratas of this community namely, the Manikfans, the Thakrufans, the Thakrus and the Raveri project their own traditional dress. The Manikfan class has an air of elegance about them, reflected in their customes too. Manikfan men dress themselves in the customary lungis and shirts costume.

However, the men of the remaining classes have embraced trousers, similar to the pattern of jeans, as their daily costume.. The trousers are available in black, white, blue, pink or green hues. The trousers are worn from the waist and are supported with a cord. A coloured embroidered tapelines along the sides as and around the ankles. The custom is a little different for the Thakrus and Thakrufans. None is entitled to wear such trousers, except those courageous males, who have undertaken sea-expeditions. The scenario is again different for the Raveri class. Raveri men achieve ownership of wearing these clothes, after becoming mature adults.

Waistband associates the trousers. The waistband is a strip of white cloth. The upper part of the women's body is left without clothes. The headgear emerges is a stripy red or black cloth. The number of protrusions, be it four or two, is maintained in accordance to the class-status of the various classes.

The younger generation has exhibited a liking for trousers and shirts to their costumes. The costume of the Minicoy women is an under-garment, with blue or green colours, along with a long cloak, called libus, stretching from shoulder to ankle. The libus is usually seen as a brick-crimson cloth, marked with black stripes. This cloth has an opening only at the neck, with embroidery decorating that part. The costume for the ceremonial occasions, are decked with floral patterns. The practice of wearing a headdress prevails among these women. It is a strip of black cloth. At times, women use a veil-like covering, white in colour and expanding from the face down to the chin.

Ornaments are in vogue among the islander women, apart from the Minicoy women. A waist-ornament called aranchan, bangles called vala or kodakam, for the wrists, ear-rings, koodu and alikkath, and a necklace, urukku, are the popular jewelry items. The waist-belt could be of gold or of silver. The two types, classified, are the kannadi aracha, with an width of one inch, possessing a lock; and the adippu, worn around the chain.

The vala is an ordinary bangle has a glamorous kodakam, functioning as a bracelet. The design of koodu, an eardrop is special. It has a pyramidal structure. Alikkath are small rings embellishing the ear. The Urukku is however, the necklace, is a remarkable item, is a string of black beads, interspersed with gold. The plenty of ornaments, beautifying a bride for the most special important occasion of her life, are bestowed with greater detail. The Minicoy women are economical about their ornaments choices.

There exist some prohibitions regarding the use of jewelry. It is the privilege of the Manikka women, the female belonging to Manikfan class, that they can demonstrate themselves in the lustrous gold ornaments, because, women of other classes, can lay their hands on silver ornaments only.

In general, all women wear a modram, a finger-ring. The intricacy of design, and the good choice of colours and quality of fabric of the costumes of Lakshadweep, call for recognition and praises of their taste and preferences.

DELHI

Costumes of Delhi have a unique pattern. The traditional costumes of Delhi are churidar or salwar kameez dupatta for women, and kurtas and pyjamas for men. Delhi, the microcosmic India, and the national capital of the country, treasures a rich cultural heritage of splendid diversity and secular democracy that the country stands for.

The air of Delhi is abuzz with the mantra of variety and ethnicity, founded on the truth of intermingling of cultures, tastes and preferences. People from diverse states have come and settled in Delhi for education, business, career, etc. and along with them; they have also brought their culture, languages, dressing style, etc. Delhi is a fashionable city and it is showcased in Delhi's costumes; here youth and adolescents are very fashion conscious.

The cosmopolitan Delhi denizens have reflected this tradition of an all-accommodative mindset, in the choice and setting of the costume-trends. A living example is the admired female costume of Delhi, Salwar—Kameez, which refers to a dress of baggy trousers, narrowed down towards the bottom, topped off by a long shirt or tunic like dress, and a cloth -piece called dupatta, covering the front upper portion. This costume of Salwar-Kameez, hugely popular among girls, is not inherent to India. The pattern of this Turko-Persian, or Turko-Mongol costume, was imported into the Indian horizon, with the advent of the Turko-Iranian dynasty of the Delhi Sultanate. Salwar-suits with sequined embroidery or semi-precious stones' embroidery, mirror-work, ari work, cut-work, or simple but elegant cut, prints, hand paints, all alluring on excellent fabric is the characteristic of salwar-kameez in Delhi these days. A very noteworthy attribute of today's costumes of Delhi is that, modern innovations have started impressing their signatures on the traditional element of the costumes of Delhi. For instance, sari is the traditional Indian costume for women. But a modern-day Delhi sari, can very much be invested with design, shades and get-up. The same applies for Ghagra-choli and salwar-kameez. Ghagra is an oriental ankle-length skirt, and choli is the upper blouse. The distinct charm of today's Ghagra Lehenga Choli of Delhi is the modern designs, colours, and cut of a traditional attire.

In fact this conjunction of the old and the new is the mark of excellence of the costumes of Delhi. The dress-designers namely Ritu Kumar, Neeta Lulla and Sabyasachi Mukherjee are weaving magic with their embroidery splendour, including Zardozi, a Persian form of embroidery, done with gold or silver thread, and introduced by the Muslim rule in India. Exclusive silk materials, tissue cloth, crepe, georgette, chiffon and other types of fabric possessing a rich texture, work as the perfect base for shimmering Zardozi. Zardozi can be on sari, or salwar-kameez, ghagra lehenga choli, or Kurta-pajamas, and sherwanis, worn by men, and even on skirts and blouses, to obtain a gorgeous appearance.

Women of Delhi are well-aware of fashion-updates. Along with the ethnic costume of sari, or salwar-kameez or churidar-kameez (churidar is a body-hugging trouser), Western jeans tops, shirts, T-shirts, skirts, varying in sizes and shapes, blouses, and so on, crowd a fashionable and modern-day woman's wardrobe. These costumes are not only wear-friendly in the course of daily busy schedule of modern-life, but also enrich a woman's aura of style and smartness. Resplendent semi-precious jewelry, crafted by the deft craftsmen of the neighbouring Jaipur and Rajasthan, including fascinating Kundan work, at present compete with the original gold, silver, diamond or authentic gem-studded ornaments. They are increasingly becoming a woman's passion in Delhi.

When it comes to making themselves presentable in proper costume, the men of Delhi are not lagging behind. The senior and the venerated generation cater to the ethnic costume of India, namely, Dhoti, Kurta, Sherwani-salwar, Kurta-Salwar, kurta-pajama. They are not only keen to preserve the culture they belong to, but also assert the Indianness of their identity, as well as their values, which get well-communicated through this costume-type. Jawaharlal Nehru, the first Prime Minister of India, exhibited himself in Sherwani with Nehru collars (collar-style, popularised by him) and Nehru cap.

His costume was helpful in emphasising his role as the national leader to the country. The young generation, however, usually dress themselves in formal shirts, trousers, jeans, T-shirts and the other modern-day chic male garment, happening to be the daily costume, even workplace dress for men. However, on ceremonial occasions, men try out ornate Sherwani-churidars, Dhoti-Kurtas, or Kurta-Pajamas, frequently turning out to be a designers or a boutique's collection. Men sometimes adorn themselves in ornaments like bangles, wristbands, to augment their manliness, along with stylish wrist-watches. Traditional shoes, like, Nagra shoes, is usually worn with Sherwanis, to effect a royal outlook, on special occasions. The expanding range and plethora of patterns, related to the costumes of Delhi, have made Delhi a dream-destination of the costume-lovers, allured by the availability of the recent in-things as well dignified traditional dress there. Costumes of Delhi make the style statement and are a yardstick for the clothing industry nationwide. Over all, the costumes of Delhi have manifold facets of cultural and ethnic identities despite its primarily global look.

TAMIL NADU

Costumes of Tamil Nadu for the most part comprise the traditional wears. The women of this state are decked with these traditional sarees that mark them from rest of the communities. The ageless charm of these sarees is the identity of the people of Tamil Nadu. Being the abode of South Indian silk sarees with rich zari work, the costumes reflect the traditions of India and Tamil Nadu itself. India has always been looked at as a land of enigmatic resources and many have staked their lives just to acquire it and call those their own.

The distinctness amongst the four corners within the country makes this very factor even more interesting when admired. The South Indian costumes possess a certain aura within their dress materials, with zari work predominating amongst women and white dhoti amongst men. Costumes of Tamil Nadu absolutely falls within this genre, with women dressing up intricately for any festive occasion and men also are looking towards the similar direction. Costumes of Tamil Nadu dominate with traditionalism speaking out every time for both the sexes. In Tamil Nadu women don the ubiquitous Indian saree and blouse, whereas, men wear 'lungi' together with a shirt and 'Angavastra.' Saree, the sheer six yards of pure excellence is one such costume that ladies of all ages prefer to don for each special festivity.

The traditional Tamil woman chooses to drape her heavy Kanchipuram saree around herself, the lower part of the calf exposed, the extra piece of pallu established thereby wrapped around her waist. What is remarkable about this draping fashion is that a woman wears the most dazzling of Kanchipuram saree in the most informal manner.

Sarees have a special place in the costumes of Tamil Nadu, and are an indispensable part of the state's heritage. Saree is the traditional dress of Indian women and Tamil Nadu women as well. In Tamil Nadu, sarees are available in a variety of materials like cotton, chiffon, crepe silk, organza, silk, georgette, Pattola silk, micro silk, etc. Till a few years ago, the half-saree or Pavada besides serving as the traditional dress was also the most admired costume of young girls in Tamil Nadu. Full-length skirt, short blouses and a davani (shawl) successfully completed this dressing style. This traditional pleated dress however has been replaced by salwar kurtas, jeans and trousers. The style, colour and texture of a saree cloth vary and it might be manufactured from cotton, silk or one of the various man-made materials. A Saree from Tamil Nadu possesses an everlasting charm due to it not being cut or tailored for a particular size. Sarees are available in the state in a wide variety of fabrics, ranging from silks, cottons, chiffons to georgettes and crepes.

Costumes of Tamil Nadu are although not just restricted to the fairer sex only; men also occupy a considerable position. Men are generally encountered dressed in lungi, together with a shirt and Angavastra. The traditional and tremendously popular lungi originated in the South and it is purely a short length of material worn around the thighs, resembling a sarong. A dhoti is a rather longer lungi, but with an additional length of material hauled up within the legs. The lungi is a rectangular cloth, normally manufactured from cotton, draped around the waist and pleated in front at the groin. The Angavastra is an elongated piece of cloth wrapped around the shoulders. In earlier times it was donned instead of an upper garment, but nowadays men wear an angavastra over a shirt.

JAMMU AND KASHMIR

Costumes of Jammu and Kashmir reflect the richness of the culture and landscape of the region. It has been historically seen that the early Aryan descendants who lived in this region, interacted with various prosperous civilizations like the famous Greeks, the Romans and the Persians. Such influences of its cultural ethos and tradition coupled with the climatic factors find a reflection in the attires of its people. Most of the garments are made of wool, silk with intricate embroideries and cotton. In these mountainous regions, the traditional 'pheran' is the most popular form of dressing among both men and women. The pheran has a lot of beautiful embroidery work done on it and is decorated with floral motifs and designs.

Costumes Worn by Kashmiri Men

The pheran is the most commonly worn garment among men. Hindu men usually wear churidars while the Muslim men are dressed in salwars beneath the formidable pherans. The pheran is a loosely fitted woollen garment which makes use of the 'kangri'. The kangri is an earthen vessel which is filled with flaming coal. It is then placed within a container made of natural fibre. The kangri is usually placed in the front, skillfully shrouded by the pheran. It functions as an internal heating system in order to keep the wearer warm during the extreme cold winters.

The 'pathani' suit, also referred to as 'Khan-dress', is a popular garb among the men, especially in Srinagar. Turbans are common among Muslim men. Skull caps are extremely prevalent, especially among the peasants and the 'karakuli' or fur skull caps along with the Pashmina shawls worn by men often symbolize royal lineage. The Pashmina shawls are made from traditional woollen textiles which are obtained from mountain goat. Intricate work is done on both sides of these shawls. The special Kashmiri embroidery work, Kasida, is done in such a manner that the patterns appear in a uniform manner on both sides of the fabric. The Pashmina belts and 'kamarbands" are common too. The Muslim men wear lace-free shoes known as Gurgabis. Brocade, camel hair and cashmere are the main elements that are used in the making of coats and fleece for men.

Costumes Worn by Kashmiri Women

The pheran is the prominent attire for Kashmiri women as well. Traditionally, there are the 'poots' and the pheran, comprising two robes placed atop the other. The pheran worn by women usually has zari embroidery on the hem line, around pockets and mostly on the collar area. The pherans worn by the Muslim women are traditionally characterized by their broad sleeves and reach up to the knees. However, the Hindus of Jammu and Kashmir wear their pherans long, stretching up to their feet with narrowed down sleeves. Often, the pherans are wrapped tightly by a piece of creased cloth called 'lhungi'. The Hindu women wear a headdress called the 'taranga', stitched to a suspended cap and it narrows down at the back, towards the heels. The taranga is an integral part of the wedding attire among

Hindus. Elaborate zari embroideries or floral patterns around the neck and the pockets are a prominent feature of a Muslim woman's pheran. Brocade patterns adorn their long sleeves.

The pheran is accompanied by red headgears known as the 'kasaba'. The kasaba is stitched in the form of a turban and is pinned together by ornaments and silver brooches. A pin-scarf suspended from the kasaba descends towards the shoulder. It is worn by the Muslim women as a part of their regular attire.

The 'abaya' is also commonly worn by them. For unmarried Muslim women, the costumes vary to some extent. The elaborate headgears are replaced by exquisitely ornate skull caps embellished with threads of gold, talismans and gems.

Accessories Worn by Kashmiri Women

The intricate patterns of a woman's costumes in Jammu and Kashmir are further enhanced by the use of various accessories. Earrings, anklets and bangles are widely used apart from the use of ornamentation in clothing. Silver jewellery is popular among the Muslim women and they adorn themselves with neckpieces, bracelets and heavily bejeweled chains. 'Dejharoos' or golden pendants are worn by the Hindu women. These dejharoos comprise two decorative gold pendants which are suspended through gold chains or silk threads. It is symbolic of a woman's married status among the Kashmiri Pandits.

Costumes Worn by Ethnic Groups of Kashmir

The Jammu and Kashmir landscape is dotted with various ethnic groups. The Dogras are tribes residing amidst the hilly topography of Jammu. The Dogra womenfolk are found attired in fitted pajamas and tunics accessorized with a suitable headdress. Similar fitted pajamas and kurtas of considerable length constitute the costume of the Dogra men. The use of kamarbands and turban are prominent among the Dogra elders. The Gujjars, also residents of Jammu, are the second-largest group of ethnic tribes inhabiting in Kashmir. The members of this tribe are mostly shepherds. The Gujjar women are dressed in loose sleeved tunics coupled with baggy salwars. They cover their head by an elaborate headgear, akin to the ones worn by the women in Turkish villages. The costumes of the inhabitants of the Ladakh region of Jammu and Kashmir deserve special mention because of their extraordinary variety. 'Kuntops' are woolen gowns worn by women. It is accompanied by a 'bok', a brightly decorated shawl that can aid in carrying packages and even children. The men wear 'Goucha', a woollen robe made of sheep skin fixed at the neck. It is wound at the waist by a bright sash called 'Skerag'. It extends to about 2 metres in length and 20 cm in breadth. The Skerag serves as an enclosure for the Ladakhi men to carry their bare essentials. Men in Ladakh wear velvet multihued caps while the women adorn turquoise coloured hats named 'Perak'. In tradition, upon a woman's demise, the perak is handed down to her eldest child. In Ladakh, footwear made of Yak skin and wool is known as 'Papu'.

It has been seen that over the years, the people of Jammu and Kashmir have adopted the dressing style and habits of the west as well as those of other regional Indian cultures. This is noticed primarily among the men have appropriated the western attire to a great extent. The sari is more popular among the Hindu women after the 1930s Reform Movement. However, despite these influences, the traditional pheran continues to remain the symbol of the culture and couture of Jammu and Kashmir.

BIHAR

Bihar, the land that has inculcated traditional old values to the core, is noted for its hand woven textiles in the field of costume. Particularly, the rustic crowd of Bihar adheres to the traditional pattern of dresses and jewellery. Though most of the population of the state still remains in rural areas the costumes worn by them are still traditional. The clothes for the people of different religions are a bit divergent.

The senior male citizens of Bihar, irrespective of Hindu or Muslim, favour tradition, when it comes to costumes. If a Hindu elderly person prefers Dhoti (an Indian loin cloth), a Muslim person might dress himself in Lungi (a type of petticoat for men) or Pyjama (loose trousers). As an upper garment, men usually go for Kurta (loose, normally cotton, Indian, T-shirts), and shirts. However, the men resort to attractive apparels for ceremonies, festivals and social gatherings. Kurtas, Churidar, Pyjamas and Sherwani are the ideal costumes, chosen for such special occasions, where accurate attitude owes a lot to an impressive dressing style.

The Muslims, Sikhs, and Christian males are habituated in luxuriating in the fragrance of perfumes and "attar" on an every day basis. It is interesting to note that men of Bihar inhabit a penchant for ornaments. They decorate themselves with bala or bali (bangles) in Shahabads, Kanausi in Patna and Gaya. Again Gowalas (the milkmen) flaunt themselves in Kundals (earrings). However, malas or bead necklaces are on the rise these days, than, the other ornaments.

The costume of the women folk of Bihar is chosen carefully in keeping with tradition. As per tradition, married women, smear the hair- parting zone with powder of Sindoor or vermillion. Tikli, a forehead-adorning little ornament is added to the hair-partitioning area. On the forehead, a Bihari married woman, be she an urban or a rural one, usually applies bindi.

A lot of Bihari women, love applying Kajal *i.e.* eye-pencil, or antimony eye-make-up called Surma, to improve the appeal of their eyes. They also indulge in flattering their senses with soothing aromatic oils that leave them perfumed, and refreshed, in the mind and body. Tattoo-paintings are broadly prevalent among Bihari women. They give detailed attention to their hands, and beautify them with Mehendi-designs (a kind of tattooing, done with colours fetched from herbal product like, amla or shikakai).

Ornaments with elaborate designs and extravagant look, such as Chandrahar, Tilri, Panchlari, Satlari, and Sikri are the common accessories, accompanying a woman in Bihar. Indeed, the plethora of accessories, replicate upon the craze for jewellery and ornaments. Women's passions for jewellery are not restricted to necklaces only. They buy and wear myriad ornaments for arms, wrists and fingers.

The most popular are bangles, rings, for hands and the anklets (worn around ankles). Beauty-consciousness is an inherent characteristic of feminine nature. And in this respect, even the tribal women of Bihar, are not lagging behind. Even the men participate in these regular grooming-sessions. Tribal people, inclusive of both men and women, wrap a thin strip of cloth round the waist. By rule, they maintain two pieces, of cloth, one for home-use and the other for going out. Their men are accustomed to wearing Dhotis, whereas women attire themselves in sarees. Drawing tattoo on the forehead, arms and legs is very much in vogue among tribal population. This is especially in harmony with their belief in magic. To sum up, simplicity is the mantra which provides an aura of elegance to the costume of this tribal elegance of Bihar. The costumes of Bihar, thus exhibit the richness, refinement and immeasurable worth of a heritage that remains ever-glorious, even in the face of changing times.

JHARKHAND

The nascent state of Jharkhand, which got its political dimension as a state, only in November 2000, has been previously the southern portion of Bihar. This state, bearing the popular sobriquet, Vananchal, meaning land of woods, happens to be the habitat of ages-old tribal population. The major tribes of Santhal Pargana, for instance the Paharis and the Santhals follow a dress-code, unique in appearance. Tribal females traditional attire is the Panchi and Parhan. Parhan, the lower garment is topped off by the upper Parhan.

Men however maintain their decency with only one piece of cloth, called Bhagwan. Side by side with the tribals, live the non-tribal people. These people envelop themselves in the traditional costume of Jharkhand, and almost the whole of India, dhoti, pajama, kurta and shirts. Men while featuring in ceremonies, adorn themselves in better quality and attractive-looking kurta, pajama and sherwani. Women cover themselves in sarees and blouses. Women, belonging to well-off families, or costume-crazy women, can hardly ignore the dazzle of the ethnic as well as awesome Tussar silk sarees, manufactured in Jharkhand. Tussar silk is cultivated in the Kharsawa district of Kuchai area of Jharkhand. The silk is produced by the mature silkworm, as natural protein fibres round its cocoon. The rearing of the source, silk-worms is the task of the deft tribal labourers, indispensable in the weaving of silk threads into wonderful Tussar silk sarees. Indeed, the increasing demand for Tussar silk can be met, only due to the prowess of these silk-weavers and silk-farmers.

The silk sarees, are endowed with a lustrous texture, and often with traditional paintings or print, demonstrating tribal dances, and tribal festivals, *i.e.* various nuances of tribal life. Recently, the newly launched Anjana and Swarnarekha silks of Jharkhand are ruling the market. Fashion-conscious women are flaunting themselves in this new innovation, respecting ethnicity.

The tribe-centric culture of Jharkhand, has exhibited its preference for plain but elegant accessories. Gold, silver and beads ornaments are indeed aesthetic and hence, eye-captivating. The local women, beautify themselves with the help of this ethnic and artistic costumes of Jharkhand.

People of Jharkhand harbour a love for perfumes and their aromas. So they have the habit of applying perfumes, in general. People of higher status of the society use the modern European dresses. The people also use perfumes oil. It is a veritable truth, that if someone wants to view the sophistication and the magnificence of native-talents in India, then that individual must make a visit to the tribal heaven of India, Jharkhand and enjoy the lovely costumes, they can present forth.

MAHARASHTRA

Costume of Maharashtra comprises a nine yard sari as the traditional costume for the women, and dhoti and shirt as the traditional costume of the men folk. Maharashtra, one of the largest and most populous states of India, demonstrates an array of costumes, suiting the purpose of any occasion, as well as weather conditions. The traditional costume of women in Maharashtra is a nine-yard long saree, called Nauvari. This saree bears a resemblance to male trousers. This specific style of draping does not require a petticoat or a slip beneath it.

The Nauvari saree has a historical background. During the Maratha rule, women were entrusted with the grave responsibility of helping their male partners, at emergency period of wars. To facilitate easy movement, the Maharashtrian women then introduced the Nauvari Saree.

The fabric of Nauvari Saree is usually cotton, and for special occasions, silk tops the priority list. Paithani sarees happen to be the treasured creation of Maharashtra's textile-industry. The Paithani saree, invested with an 18 inch to 25 inch pallu, owes its origin to adept textile-designing. The Brahmin ladies of Maharashtra wear sarees in a particular pattern where the pleats are located at or near the back and these are tucked in waist and the decked part of the saree is left open on the shoulder part. They use choli with the sarees and often polkas and blouses.

The Maharashtrian women prefer to deck themselves in beautiful jewelleries. Most of the designs of the jewelleries are of Peshwa and Maratha style. Among the most favoured jewelleries are the haar, nath or nose ring decorated with pearl or vibrant coloured stones. Some of the necklaces they wear include bangdya, Kolhapuri Saaj, tode and patlya.

Silk is woven to constitute the body of the royal Paithani silks. And into this rich silk texture, pure Jari-made of gold and silver threads, are interwoven, to give the Saree the ornamented get-up. The bright Paithani sarees are very popular as the bridal costume in Maharashtra.

The Paithani sarees are thus essentially linked to the culture and society of Maharashtra. The sarees have received their name after the place of its origin, Paithan in Maharashtra. The other weaving-sites of this exclusive item are Yeola, Pune, Nasik and Malegaon in Maharashtra. The men of Maharashtra uphold Dhoti as their cultural heritage. It may be worn along with a shirt or kurta, and Dhoti is often substituted with trousers. They also wear 'bandi' over the shirt and turban called 'pheta' and 'pagadi'. The festive occasions of the Maharashtrians allow themselves to indulge in the festive mood and during this time most of the men wear Churidar, Pyjama, Ackan or Survar.

In the urban areas of Maharashtra, and especially in its cosmopolitan capital, Mumbai, costumes display themselves in their variety best. Women put in Kurta-Pajamas, salwar-kameez, skirt-blouse, and jeans-trousers, exotic Sarees and so on. The urban Mumbai men on the other hand, flaunt themselves with the halo of grooming. They shift from wearing jeans, trousers, branded shirts, baggy trousers, T-shirts, all possible types of casual wears. On occasions, sherwanis, kurta-pajamas, ornate Dhotis, and other kinds of resplendent men's attire, rank among their favorites. Indeed, Mumbai the glam-epicenter of India, and the abode of Bollywood, is the trendsetter for costumes, for the whole of India. Fashion experiences its high, in the posh cities of Maharashtra, with fashion-designing institutes and business units, establishing their sway.

The state of Maharashtra, hence has achieved a splendid synthesis of the old and the new patterns in costume. Time and the effect of globalisation have brought a drastic change in the costumes of each and every state and Maharashtra as well. Though the modernisation has a great impact in the society, the tradition has not faded its glitter, thus the traditional dresses have not lost the glory of their past. It has also focused on the traditional and regional textile-accomplishments like Paithani as the 'in-thing' now.

NAGALAND

Costumes of Nagaland mainly comprise shawls which are an extensively used item of the state. For instance, the ornate warrior-celebrating shawl, called Tsungkotepsu is a characteristic of the Aos clan. Against the dark base colour of this particular shawl, there is a central white band with two horizontal black, red and white bands, brightening the outlook. On the median band are painted black with a pattern in black mithun figures, signifying affluence of the owner, and the depictions of elephant and tiger speaks of the courage of the concerned man, while the human head attests accomplishment in head-hunting and other tasks like wielding spear and dao. Aomelep su made from dog's hair, dyed red in colour, is the shawl flaunted by the rich men or the sons and daughters of affluent fathers. This shawl contains alternate red, yellow and black stripes to bring the striking effect of contrast. Rongsu shawl is wearable only by those who have a glorious heritage of Mithun sacrifice, committed by the forefathers and also by the individual himself.

The costume of the Ao women is a skirt, which is one and a quarter metre long and about two thirds of the metre, is draped round the waist and the surface outer edge is implanted for the grip. The skirts come up in an inexplicable variety. They differ from village to village and also from clan to clan. The popular types of the Ao skirts involve Azu jangnup su, endowed with red and yellow-black stripes, the Ngami su or fish tail skirt, and finally the Yongzujangau or cucumber seed skirt, woven in red on a black base.

The Angamis, a major Naga tribe, demonstrate themselves in clothes with white, red and black bands called Loramhoushu and black background with red and yellow bands, and at present with green, called lohe. The western Angami villages have their unique style of costume-design. Shawls of Lothas are graded by the number of gennas or festivals arranged by the wearer. Thus a man who has given the first genna wears the phangrhup. With the performance of the second genna, the strip broadens accordingly.

The third genna allows a man to put in the Ethasu. With the fulfillment of the mission, the successful man resorts to stone-dragging which permits him to wear Lungpensu. This latter one is a dark blue cloth with five stripes of light blue and with thin marginal stripes on either side. There is only one cloth in the wardrobe of the Angamis, which is indicative of social prestige. The phichu-pfe is the priest's costume.

A daily costume, meant for wear and tear, is the black shawl called ratapfe. Men wear black kilt, decorated with embroidered cowries in three or four lines. The cowries are bestowed with distinct importance. Women in general are clad in plain blue cloth and a white cloth with black marginal bands of changing breadth. Women often wear men's garment. The casual costume of a dress of Angami women includes a petticoat called neikhro, a sleeveless top called vatchi, a white skirt called pfemhou. The Ze-liangs-rong, a mixed group of Zemis, Liangmais and Rongmei exhibit themselves in costumes, considerably same with that of the Angamis. The commonest costume is a white cloth, contrasted with six black bands of varying measurements at both ends. The costume of the Zemei women is restricted to white-coloured clothes and skirts with very narrow black and red border.

The women of the remaining groups go for diversity. The cotton cultivated by them is the source for the material of the white or beige shawls and the skirts that they use. Black bands of different sizes on the border, alienated by red and pink borders also decorate the body of the shawl. This is a daily-purpose shawl. Multifarious patterns, lines and hues, of skirts and belts, and men's girdles, required during dances characterise the occasion-costume of the Rongmei.

The favourite dancing skirt is black with a broad, intricately embroidered red border and three white central bands, beautified with a narrow red line in the middle. There is a wide spectrum of shawls woven by the Yimchunger Nagas. Rongkhim is a fantastic shawl, wearable by a venerated warrior only. Kechinger Rongkhim is too a warrior-respecting shawl, though Rongkhim ranks first, with respect to mettle. The soldier who annexes the right hand of the killed enemy is acknowledged to win the right to wear this particular shawl. It is a black cloth, possessing narrow grey bands at two margins.

The exotic shawl tsungrem khim is an asset for the Yimchunger Naga women. The hallmark of the Konyaks is nye-myon the shawl worn by the senior villagers in important conferences and meetings. Nikola is a white shawl which functions as a woman's attire. Resplendently coloured shawl, known as Shatni is a luxury item, affordable by the wealthy Konyak woman. It is the custom, that an affluent man's daughter, during wedding is gifted with a Shatni shawl by her parents.

This particular shawl is maintained with care, as there is the peculiar law among the Konyaks, that at the time of her death, her corpse would be enveloped in this specific shawl. A shawl, dedicated to the blue-blooded Konyak chiefs or Ang and the elderly women of the village is called meyni. It is an awesome fusion of wide black and red bands, woven alternately. Well-off Konyaks decorate themselves in a splendid cloth called nyauni. It appears as red bands and red lines. The plethora of designs, motifs, patterns and vibrant shades make the world of Naga costumes a rainbow world.

UTTARAKHAND

Costumes of Uttarakhand reflect the culture and lifestyle of the ethnic communities, the Garhwalis and the Kumaoni. The graceful Uttarakhand is adjacent to the neighbouring states of Uttar Pradesh and Himachal Pradesh. Side by side, many Punjabis, Bengalis, and even Nepalis, from neighbouring Tibet, have settled in the state. The Garhwals residing in the Garhwal hills of Uttaranchal follow a costume-pattern suitable to the climatic conditions of the place they belong to. Wool fetched from goat or sheep is used to manufacture warm costumes, so as to ward off the biting cold in winter season.

Ghagri, an oriental long skirt, topped off by a Choli, an Indian blouse and an Orni, a cloth covering the head and the front portion, usually fastened to the waist, happen to be the traditional costume of the ethnic groups, namely, the Garhwalis and the Kumaonis. The traditional bridal costume of the Kumaoni is Ghaghra-Pichora, akin to Ghaghra Lehenga-Choli. Pichora is a Kumaoni veil or Rangwali, endowed with gold and silver tatting. But women also go for sarees. The hallmarks of Kumaoni woman are sindoor smeared on the forehead, and an enormous gold ring, called Nath. Further, Chareu, a black beaded necklace is worn by the married woman, is a holy accessory for Garhwali married woman. A luxury ornament item is Hansuli, a kind of necklace, preferred in gold by the rich, and in silver, by the less affluent, or poor. Some of the ethnic groups, drape themselves in mantle-like clothing, called Sarong, girdled by a waistband and completed with a top-blouse. Muslin textiles, specially muslin veils or Rangwalis are assets of Uttaranchal costume designing. They come in auspicious hues of yellow, signifying warmth and cordiality and red, symbolic of the holy bond of marriage.

The traditional male costume of Uttaranchal is the loin-cloth Dhoti, or the Lungi, used as the lower-garment. The Uttaranchal man dons himself in Kurta, to serve as the upper-attire. The men love to present themselves with headgear, or turban, a part of their traditional costume. Kurta -Pajamas are another good alternative for men of Uttarakhand. Both women and men wear sweaters or woolen jackets in winter, mainly sleeveless in form.

Ethnicity and tradition has very well been maneuvered to be at par with convenience, when it comes to considering the costumes of Uttarakhand.

CHANDIGARH

Chandihgarh, the capital city of both Punjab and Haryana, has ranked as one of the highest income-generating state-economy of India. This superb city, forging ahead on the advancing wave of improvement is bound to flourish in all possible aspects of life. The city populated with Hindus, including the Punjab is, Sikhs, Muslims and Christianity, certainly projects forth a potpourri culture respecting traditional norms but welcoming innovations as well. This amalgamation of tradition with modern newness is reflected in the costume-types of Chandigarh in India.

The urban ambience of Chandigarh, requires men to go for formal-office costumes. The long-sleeved shirt, with tie, coat and formal trousers make up a total office-suit for men, is very much in vogue. At times formal trousers are topped off by sobre T-shirts, that contributes to the dignified appearance of Multi-national executives, servicemen, businessmen, during office-work, conferences, meetings and important deals. In the winter months, men assume a stylish look with handsome jackets, or woolen garments, which wards off the biting cold of North India as well.

As casuals, jeans and other branded or quality cotton fabric, rule the list of men's favourite costumes. The traditional bridergroom's costume of Chandigarh, is the resplendent and sophisticated Sherwani, an attire suiting the inherent attribute of manliness. Sherwanis, invested with Western-eastern fusion, has the best outlook, and is in keeping with the contemporary air and traditional choices.

A Sherwani is a body-fitting, long coat-like garment, with ornate buttons, installed in the front side, which are buttoned up, while wearing. A Sherwani has a Nehru collar (collars worn by the first Indian Prime Minister, Jahawarlal Nehru, the trendsetter). This coat-like knee-length upper garment is perfectly matched with a body-hugging Churidar-trousers. The tall and sturdy Chandigarh grooms look regal in Sherwanis. Sherwanis usually, come in light shades like, off-white, or beige.

The grooms' Sherwanis are decorated with mind-blowing Zardozi (a kind of gorgeous Persian embroidery, decked with stones, gold and silver thread, and present with copper wire,with gold sheen, or gold coloured thread) and embroidery designs. They can be fashioned in different forms, for example the Peshawri or the Baloochi. Indian embellished shoes, for instance, Nagra, Khussa, Mojri in general, gives a finishing touch to this elegant groom costume, Sherwani.

The urbanized women of Chandigarh have laid their hands on both Indian and Western outfit. Their costume ranges from salwar-kameez, sari, kurtis, jeans, shirts, T-shirts, formal trousers, chic capris, to be very precise all the popular variety. The casual versions of these entire can serve as workplace costume, and costume for daily wear and tear. Salwar-kameez, which glorifies the innate beauty of the Indian woman, is the forever priority for the Chandigarh women.

The plethora of diversity in salwar-kameez involves, suit with mirror and Kundan embroidery, Persian embroidery, Aari and Resham work, Cut-work salwar-kameez, golden filigree salwars-suits, vegetable dye kurta churidar, Phirozi salwars, handloom jacquard salwar suit, camric cotton salwar suit, chikan suit (cotton fabric with self-design). Added to these, Zardozi salwar-kameez, Phulkari -work kameez and other ornamented salwar-suits. Sleeves of kameez can be of short, bell and umbrella shaped. The textile-manufacturers of salwar-Kameez play with different hues, starting from the bright shades like red, maroon, mustard, yellow, green, navy blue, black to the pastel and light colours, like baby pink, pink, sky-blue, saffron, peach, crème, beige, white and so on. The traditional bridal costume for the beautiful maidens of Chandigarh is the marvelous Lehenga-choli-dupatta.

Traditional wedding Lehenga-choli or Ghagra-choli and designer wedding Lehenga-cholis created out of a splendid synthesis of traditional costume-pattern and modern designs, cut, mix and shot colour shades, etc., happen to be the bridal love. A today's Lehenga can be a mantle of vibrant marron, finely toned with beige contrast, and golden Zardozi, harmonised with butawork.

The colours may vary from maroon, red, to the sunet yellow, to the pink, blues and pesta. The beautiful, long - flowing get-up of Lehengas, with a flare towards the bottom, make the bride appear like a pretty princess.The bride endowed with lustrous make-up and luminous Lehenga, also dons an equally adorned blouse, called Choli.

The dazzling Dupatta, the decorated and matching piece of cloth, either covers the upper front portion of the bride, as it passes round her neck, to the back of the head or is suspended from the back of her head, being pinned into her braided hair.

The brilliance of accessories is a must for bridal costume. Kundan and gold jewelry wonder, studded with ruby, emeralds, turquoise, coral, entails elaborate necklaces, chokers, malas (necklaces as garlands), haars or kanthas (a kind of necklace); bajubandhs (armbands) for brides, payals (anklets) and mangtikas (headdress-ornament) and finally the Zaridar, thread-embroidered sandals furnish the bride with an awedsome splendor.

Nowadays, the semi-precious jewelry, of breathtaking beauty, are simultaneously present with gold ornaments, in the bridal costume, of some brides. They augment the shimmer on the whole. It is evident, that the costumes of Chandigarh, bear the signature of tradition and modern designs at the same time, to arrive at the best.

ARUNACHAL PRADESH

Costumes of Andhra Pradesh reflect the cultural and ethnic way of life of the tribal people residing there. Indian ethnicity and tribal life finds its fullest expression in the serene hills and the sylvan surroundings of the picturesque Arunachal Pradesh. This eastern-most state on India's northeast frontier is crowded with twenty six native tribes and several sub-tribes, residing in 3649 dispersed villages. In general, the Arunachal people have a Mongoloid descent, though one tribe is diverse from the other in terms of distinct vernacular, dress and costumes.

Costumes of the different tribes of Arunachal Pradesh are endowed with fascinating vibrant colours and myriad patterns, characteristic of tribe culture. It signifies their aesthetic taste and zeal for embellishment. The Monpas who live north of the Bomdila range, adhere to Buddhism, observed in the venerated Tawang monastery. Thus the traditional costume of the Monpas of Arunachal Pradesh is shaped by Tibetan culture. Besides, they also cover themselves with woolen coats and trousers, to shield themselves from the cold.

It is typical of tribe lifestyle, to use animal body-parts in their daily life, be it as their food, or in the making of their dresses or in other regular objects used by them. The Monpas also are no exception. They wear a skullcap made of felt with laces or tassels as adornments. The Monpas women wear a jacket, above a sleeveless chemise. They bind this chemise round their waists with a lengthy and narrow strip of cloth.

Accessories are a must for any woman, be she a tribal or a city-girl. The Monpa females beautify them with silver rings, earrings cut from bamboo-bits and appended with red beads or lovely turquoises. Another popular dress-item is a cap, endowed with a fascinating peacock-feather.

The Hill Miris inhabiting the lower Kamla valley look attractive in their costume. They tie the hair in a knot just above the forehead. Their women wear attractive "crinoline of cane rings" which serves the purpose of a blouse but now it is not seen in the urban areas. The Sherdukpen, inhabiting south of Bomdila in the Tengapanai valleys, bear striking resemblance with their fellow- Buddhist community, the Monpas. The usual apparel of Sherdukpen men folk is a sleeveless silk material, with its two edges, pinned at the shoulder region. The costume is normally knee-long. The hallmark of their dress-code is the gurdam skull-caps smeared with yak`s hair.

The tassels protruding from the gurdam over the face form a slope to glide away rain-water, as their residential-zone is subject to torrential rain, often. The women sect of Sherdukpen, dress themselves in a collarless and sleeveless garment, stretching from the shoulders to the knees. Added to this, a full-sleeved jacket with nice embroidery and waist cloth, called mushaiks, is worn above the patent robe. The hair-style is also interesting. The women often tie their hair into a bun at the back. It is curious to note that Sherdukpen women are adept in weaving clothes with praiseworthy finesse.

The Tangsa tribe, also, dwelling in the Tirap district and Changlang district of Arunachal Pradesh, is a Naga tribe. These robust, middle-length people cater to the Burmese costume-style. The Tangsa men wear green lungi, proficiently seamed in with matching yellow, red and white yarns. A sleeveless shirt, acts as the upper garment. Tangsa women put in a very attractive looking woven petticoat, along with a linen blouse to top it. Miji women, living in the West Kameng and East Kameng districts, exhibt simplicity as well as refinement in their costume.

The ankle-long white cloak gives the Miji women an immaculate look. And the final touch is given by an ornate red jacket. Big-sized silver earrings and resplendent necklaces, commonly decked with jade, perfectly augments the beauty. A strip of silver chains is occasionally, worn around the head by the wealthier Miji women. One will be awe-struck to learn that these tribal women know the art to extract bio-chemical cosmetics from pine-resin.

The intricate design and colour-abundance of the costume of the Apatanis is indeed captivating. Tattoo-drawing and the attaching of conspicuously big nose plugs called Yaping hullo are the major highlights of this group. It is said, that this peculiar costume-pattern evolved from the strategy of safeguarding, devised by the beautiful Aptani women. They were, since old times, keen, to appear unimpressive to the men of other tribes, to ensure safety. The tattoo done by the women involve broad blue stripes painted from the forehead down to the tip of the nose, and five vertical lines, drawn under the lower lip in the chin.

The women arrange their tresses into a ball, called Dilling on the head-top. A brass skewer, known as Ading Akh, is often passed through the Dilling, in a horizontal direction. By custom, the Aptani men, make a knot of their hair just above the forehead. The local name of this hairstyle is as Piiding and the bras rod used in the creation of this knot is known as Piiding Khotu.

The men also like to apply tattoo or Tiippe on their chin. The tattoo-sketch resembles the shape of a 'T' under the lower lip. So, going for make-up in their own unique manner was included in the heritage-laws of the Aptanis. The Adi tribe is a chief tribal community, staying in the Himalayan hills of Arunachal Pradesh, *i.e.*, in the temperate and sub-tropical regions within the districts of West Siang, East Siang, Upper Siang, Upper Subansiri, and Dibang Valley. The topic of the costume of the Adi, instantly gives glimpses of the galae, a poly-utility garment, used by both the genders.

A galae, which is tied around the loins, comes down in loose hanging down in narrow form. In accordance with the geographical circumstances of the region, men secure themselves with helmets made from cane, bear and deer skin. Senior women, already married, embellish themselves with yellow necklaces and coiled earrings. But, the presence of beyop, an ornament compiled of five to six brass plates, stuck under their petticoats, signify the unmarried status of a young girl. Tattooing is a common feature among the older women. Therefore the costume of the plethora of tribes, thriving for ages in the hills and forests of Arunachal Pradesh are enchanting.

The costume of each of the tribes, namely, Monpa, Sherdukpen, Tangsa, Adi, Aptani, and so on, illuminate the mind with their ever-glorious aesthetic appeal. In fact it is the rare tribal artistry and indigenous caliber that makes Arunachal Pradesh, stand on the high pedestals of fame and reputation.

WEST BETNGAL

Costumes of West Bengal mirror the state's multi-ethnic way of life. From the use of traditional fabrics, designs and motifs to the assimilation of western attires and styles within the Bengalis' cultural domain, the apparels of West Bengal display fine works of creativity and sophistication. For the men in West Bengal, the traditional garment is the "dhoti" and the "panjabi". The graceful icon of elegance that symbolises the quintessential Bengali woman is the saree. Indian sarees can be draped in various ways. Dhotis are lengthy pieces of fabric spun in cotton or silk worn by the Hindus. Previously, dhotis were prevalent only in white though at present coloured dhotis are also in vogue. The dhoti is tied at the waist and wrapped around like a loin cloth passing in between the legs. It is suitably matched by a panjabi, worn atop, also made of silk or cotton. The panjabis are loosely fitted garments, reaching close to the knees and are available in a wide variety of colours.

The "lungi" is another variation of the dhotis worn by men in West Bengal. It is also wound around the waist and is often plaid. Over the years, the traditional dhoti and panjabi have lost much of their appeal and the 'pyajamas' are in vogue. While western attire has overtaken the dhoti's popularity as regular wear, the combination of dhoti and panjabi is an irreplaceable ingredient during traditional festivals and occasions like the Durga Puja and wedding ceremonies. In the rural areas, though, the dhoti is worn by the men as regular attire. In Bengal, the saree is wrapped around the waist and the remaining portion is swathed over4 the shoulder. In the olden days, women had to cover their heads with the ends of their saree or "pallu" as a mark of respect for the family elders. However, such conventions have subsided slowly with the passage of time. They are worn with immense dignity and perfection particularly during Social occasions and festivals. Sarees are worn over petticoats or long skirts tied at the waist with cords which help in keeping the saree tightly fastened about the waist. The exquisite beauty of a saree is further enhanced when it is accessorised suitably with a blouse. At present, blouses are available in multitudes of fashionable patterns which when teamed with a saree does wonders to the attire. The salwar kameez dupatta is nowadays in the same way popular among the Bengali women as the sarees. "Salwars" are loosely fitted trousers worn with a "kameez" or long tunic.

During wedding ceremonies however, the Bengali women usually resort to the traditional Banarasi sarees in shades of red coupled with a golden veil to cover their heads. Ornamented with glittering stones and detailed thread work, sarees are characteristic of the refined Bengali woman of today. In West Bengal, sarees are primarily woven in cotton and silk. These sarees have been named chiefly after their weaving techniques. The traditional weavers or "tantis" of West Bengal are reputed worldwide because of the quality of fabric spun and their elaborate thread work. In the various districts of West Bengal like Murshidabad, Malda, Nadia, Birbhum, Bankura and Hooghly, different varieties of sarees are woven with supreme efficiency and dedication. Bengal silk is famous for its sophisticated quality and texture.

Earlier, the cultivation of mulberry was common in almost every corner of Bengal. However, at present it is concentrated mostly in the districts of Birbhum, Murshidabad and Malda. The town of Baluchar located in Murshidabad is famed for the incredible threadwork on silk called "Baluchari". The Baluchari sarees are noted for their elaborate designing in the pallu and borders with prominent motifs of a specific kind known as "kalka". These motifs are woven with silver zari and often display tales from the Indian Puranas. The kalka motif can be observed in the "Garad" and "Korial" sarees as well, which are variants of the Baluchari and are woven in silk.

Jamdani sarees of West Bengal are extremely popular. They are available in a variety of colours and are favoured by the modern Bengali woman because of its light texture. In the district of Nadia, the rural community of Shantipur is well-known for the better quality of "Shantipuri Jamdani" sarees that display delicate thread work. The districts of West Bengal are also home to the very prevalent "Tangail" sarees. The Tangail sarees are characterised by their use of diverse colour patterns which produce a novel effect called "meenakari".

Some of the most prevalent motifs used in these sarees are lamp and lotus imageries. Another variation of the Jamdani saree is the "Dhaniakhali Jamdani". It is available in brighter shades and is characterised by extended wide borders, often referred to as "maatha" or "beluaari paar". This variant of Jamdani is affordably priced and hence used commonly by the women in West Bengal. It is interesting to note that the Dhaniakhali Jamdani gained popularity due to their utilisation in dhotis for men.

Apart from these traditional handlooms, West Bengal is well-known for its delicate and fine thread work known as"kantha". The kantha embroidery is a supreme work of art and requires utmost concentration and meticulousness. Initially, it referred to the needlework done on coloured patchwork coverlets put together from redundant apparels. These quilts were to serve as covers during the winter. However, now the kantha stitch has been incorporated for use on designing clothing garments like sarees and has gained immense popularity. West Bengal is also home to plenty of tribes who display enormous variety with reference to their costumes. The men of the Magh tribe, for instance, cover their heads with a special form of headgear commonly referred to as"goungpoung" during the festive season. This is accompanied by the"prakha angyi" which is a fitted coat wrapped over the shirt. Body art or tattoos are quite popular among them as well as the Mahli tribesmen of West Bengal.

The costumes of West Bengal are suitably accessorised by delicately designed jewellery which is indigenous to its rich culture. Silver and gold along with alloys of zinc and precious stones are mostly used for jewellery production. While traditional designs are still in vogue, recent trends dictate a preference towards lighter accessories. In weddings, mostly, women adorn their foreheads with a thin string of small gold chain often strewn with pearls and precious stones. This is the"tikli". Gold chokers decorated with gems and diamonds are commonly worn by the women of West Bengal in social ceremonies. The women also embellish themselves with a variety of bangles and bracelets like the"mantasha" and also the"ratanchur". The tribal jewellery of West Bengal has also achieved immense popularity because of its exclusivity. A supreme example here would be the"dokra" artworks. Over the years, different civilizations have left their mark upon the culture of West Bengal which finds its manifestation in the varied costumes and accessories of the people of the State. With the progress of the passage of time, a shift towards western trends has been noticed. Yet, such cross-cultural influences have by no means demeaned the worth of the traditional attires.

ANDAMAN AND NICOBAR ISLANDS

Grown amidst the remote surroundings and forests of the islands of Andaman and Nicobar islands, the aboriginal tribes of this virgin land, un-invaded by civilization, go naked. The Sentinelese tribe till today, wears nothing. However, the predominant community of the Jarwas, flaunt themselves in necklaces, crafted from shells and barks of trees, waistband, armband etc. Major changes has entered the lifestyle and culture of the Car Nicobar islanders, who no longer restrict themselves to the traditional costumes of coconut -leaf petticoats and other similar costumes. They now have adopted modern clothes. Same about the Onges, who after years of no-dress culture, now drape themselves in the costume of the land. The Shompen people cover themselves only from their waist. However, the Hindus, Sikhs and Christians, living on the islands, exhibit themselves in their traditional costumes of sari, salwars, skirt-blouse, Dhoti, Kurtas, Pajamas, pants, trousers, shirts and so on. Costume-patterns of Andaman andNicobar islands are on the tide of change. It is interesting to see the sea-shell ornaments and natural products like leaves of trees, forming the costume of a place. Costumes of Andaman and Nicobar Islands are in harmony with the blue romance of the sea and the sylvan ambience.

4

Food and Indian Social System

INTRODUCTION

Indian food owes its evolution to umpteenth factors. One of the foremost reasons is Indian culture and its diversity. Food has always been an essential factor to determine a country's history and culture. The assortment of the scrumptious recipes of Indian food is simply awe inspiring. It is often said that 'Variety is the spice of life.' This proverb is ideal to describe Indian food. The populace of the sub continent is as varied as its topography. The North Indians have their own culinary practices while the eating habits of the South Indians differ completely. The East Indians love their non vegetarian foods while the West Indians are renowned for their desserts.

This multiculturalism in India has, thus, led to the evolution of different styles of cooking. The history of Indian food dates back to the Harappan civilization. Several ancient texts discuss the eating habits of the sages. Historical data are also available on the culinary practices of the Indus Valley Civilization. When one talks about Indian food vegetarian foods top the list. Interestingly the history of Indian vegetarian food dates back to Buddhist era. Vegetables in Indian food are therefore an indispensable part. Besides this the history of Indian food also provides a glimpse to the different regional cuisines. The Indian food industry has grown in leaps and bounds. Indian is a land of connoisseurs of food. People here not only love to eat but they derive immense pleasure in offering food to others. The contemporary ages have seen the emergence food companies like Bharti Enterprises, Dabur,

Britannia Industries, Mother Dairy, Hindustan Unilever, Amul, Mahashian Di Hatti, Parle Agro and several others. Besides the food manufacturers the hospitality industry with its ever increasing number of restaurants has also added a boom to the Indian food industry.

Indian food is the recipient of international fame because of its unique preparations and who could deny the variety that is rustled up regularly even in the households. The food culture of India not only offers spicy, mouth-watering treats but it also serves some of the most delicious desserts. The popularity of Indian food has indeed popularised the Indian beverages, non alcoholic drinks, can be additive simply for their flavours.

Influences On Indian Food is also immense. Whether it is the religious influence on Indian food or the Culinary Influences by Indian invasion, Indian food has witnessed lot of changes. India has been continuously invaded by forces that were diametrically different from its own culture. But the magnanimous sub-continent has accepted them and welcomed their culture, art and food habits. This is one of the reasons why India such a range of dishes. Aryans, Buddhists, Chinese, Parsi, Portuguese, British and, of course, Mughlai cuisines are the major sources of influences on Indian food.

The region of India can be divided into East, West, Central, North and South. Amazingly each of these regions has their separate specialities. Indian Regional Cuisines: These cuisines include Indian vegetarian food, Indian sweets, Indian chutney and Indian beverages. Indian pickles and Indian snacks are also part of the regional cuisines.

While the Indian foods are delectable the process of preparing them can be appallingly easy. These Indian State Recipes are also quite healthy. Preparations like idli, dhokla, lentils and others can be easily classified as health foods. During festivities special preparations are made. These Indian festival foods are immensely delicious. One may often wonder about the secret behind such scrumptious Indian food! Well the mystery lies with the Indian spices. A host of spices are used in different dishes to add flavour to the preparations. The various ingredients Of Indian Food further spice up the dishes.

A lot of fruits, flowers and leaves, besides the Indian spices, are used even in day to day cooking to make them tasty. Nuts, coconuts, curd, saffron, tamarind and others are some of the oft used ingredients in Indian food preparations.

In India one will come across a deft chef in every household. Another interesting fact is that culinary skills in India are not restricted to women. In fact in ancient times the 'bawarchi' or cooks in royal houses were primarily men. This tradition of Indian Chefs continues even today. As far as the hospitality industry is concerned several Indian chefs have achieved international recognition. Such assorted range of cuisines and recipes makes India a dream come true for the food epicureans.

HISTORY OF INDIAN FOOD

The history of Indian food has experienced extensive immigration and intermingling through many descents. The Indian subcontinent has benefited from numerous food influences. The diverse climate in India, ranging from deep tropical to alpine, has also helped to broaden the diaspora of food ingredients that are readily available in India. Food has become a marker of religious and social identity in India with varying taboos and preferences, which has also bounded these groups to innovate widely with the food sources that are deemed good enough.

History of Indian food is the saga of the travel of the Indian food. History unfolds that around 7000 BCE, sesame, eggplant, and humped cattle were domesticated in the Indus Valley. By 3000 BCE, turmeric, cardamom, black pepper and mustard were harvested in this country. Many Indian recipes first emerged during the initial Vedic period, when India was still heavily forested. Agriculture complemented game hunting, and forest produce. In Vedic times, a normal diet of an Indian consisted of fruit, vegetables, meat, grain, dairy products and honey. The history of Indian food was greatly influenced by the ancient Indian civilizations of Harappa and Mohenjodaro. The Dravidians or inhabitants of these civilizations were urban and not agrarian. They had huge granaries to store grain, houses with a drainage system, pathways or roads and public baths. They sowed the seeds of Ayurveda, or Life Sciences, which is the foundation of Indian cuisine. This system was derived after studying the physical needs, mental need, and needs of our psychology and spirituality.

The people of Mohenjodaro and Harrapa were pushed to the South part of India by the invasion of the Aryans who came from Europe or Asia Minor. It is not very clear where the Aryans originated from but Aryans are to be found only in Europe, Persia and India. The Harappans, probably ate mainly wheat and rice and lentils, and occasionally cows, pigs, sheep, goats, and chicken. Rice and chicken possibly came from Thailand, and wheat and sheep from West Asia. Some of the wheat was made into stews or soups, and some into flat breads called chapattis.

Around 300 BC, under the Mauryans, a lot of Hindus felt that animal sacrifices added to one's karma and kept him from getting free of the wheel of reincarnation. Animal sacrifices became less popular, and although people did not give up eating meat entirely, they ate much less of it, thus many Indians became vegetarians. In the Gupta period, around 650 AD, Hindus began to worship a Mother Goddess. Cows were sacred to her, and so Hindus stopped eating beef. Around 1100 AD, with the Islamic conquests in northern India, most people in India stopped eating pork as well, because the Koran forbids it. Eating sheep, goats or chicken was still prevalent but due to various religious reasons most of the people in India became vegetarians.

The vegetarian food that Indians ate was mainly wheat flatbreads or a kind of flatbread made out of chickpeas, with a spicy vegetarian sauce, and yogurt. Extensively the vegetarians ate rice, yogurt and vegetables. A lot of spicy peppers grew in India and they were extensively used to make bland food tasty. During the Aryan period the cuisine of India concentrated on the fine aspects of food. The Indian cuisine then greatly contributed to the development of mind, body and spirit. The history of Indian food holds this account of changing tradition and food habits. Mongolians came up with the influence of hot pot cooking and introduced dishes mainly maid of milk products and meat. Persians introduced kebabs, fereni and halva.

The Turkish influence brought about preparations made of eggplant, meat and cheese. Greek influence on Indian food brought about different kinds of soups, desserts and sweets. Greek drinks also became popular in India. Chinese influence on Indian food has been the major one, popularising dishes like Chowmein, Choupsey, Momo and diverse types of tea with majestic aroma and flavour.

Arabs brought about different kinds of dry fruits and flat breads among the Indians. Next the Portuguese introduced Indian Vindaloo dish and others. The British influence has been another major one, besides the Chinese. Indian Ketchup and tea were the basic imported tastes in India. Later the British rule brought about many more delicious dishes and preparations into Indian cuisine.

The Mughals were great patrons of cuisine. Lavish dishes were prepared during the rule of Jahangir and Shah Jahan. The Nizams of Hyderabad state meanwhile developed and mastered their own style of cooking with the most notable dish being the Biryani, often considered by many enthusiasts to be the finest of the main dishes in India.

The history of Indian food tells the tale of the influences on Indian food which further supported Indian food to attain today's chic contour. One of the greatest influences on Indian cuisine occurred in the 2nd century B.C. The powerful and popular Emperor Ashoka once popularized a vegetarian cuisine. Even today a majority of Indians are vegetarian.

The two other individuals that helped make India vegetarian are Mahavir and Buddha. Ashoka was also the first statesman in recorded history that had an environmental department in his administration. This department set environmental laws, posted these laws on stone billboards and had an environmental enforcement program.

The history of Indian food further unfurls the verity that the concept of bar â€" b que, of the ancient era in Indian food further received a contemporary silhouette with the renaissance of medieval era in Indian food habit that it ushered in. This also paved the way to the development of the modern era in Indian food habit.

INDIAN STREET FOOD

The most authentic cuisine of India is the Indian street food, which can be bought only for a few rupees from the myriad makeshift or portable stalls found in the Indian cities and town. The street vendors offer hot fresh, lip smacking snacks, which are very filling. These foods are popular mainly because they are available at half the price of any restaurant food. Take-out food, junk food, snacks, and fast food are synonymous with street food and all of these can be purchased on the foot path without entering any building.

The Indian Street Food vary from region to region.The typical North Indian street food is Chaat -a generic name for all tangy,spicy not very nutritious delicacies. The tangy flavour comes from the use of lemon, pomegranate seeds, black salt, tamarind, and various chutneys.Chaat can be prepared with fruits like guava,banana,papaya,apple etc.

Use of paapri,which is crisp pancakes made from fried flour with some out of yoghurt,potatoes sauteed with black cumin powder with some amout of "meetha and khatta chutney" (sweet and sour pickle) with a dash of coriander becomes the lip smacking Paapri Chaat. The Pani Puri also called golgappa in some places in India is another street delicacy.Panipuris are hollow crisp balls made from dough, and filled as-you-eat with a spicy concoction of water and potatoes, topped by a choice of sweet or spicy chutney.

Aaloo Tikki are patties made up of mashed potatoes mixed with a variety of spices and deeply fried in oil and served with sweet and spicy chutney. Poori-Subzie(or Bhaajee) is another variety of North Indian street food available mostly in North India, especially in Uttar Pradesh. The curry is usually prepared of potatoes or in some cases a mixture of chick peas and potatoes in gravy and poories which are made from refined flour(maida)or aata fried in oil.

The "Chai faen" is tea with a roasted biscuit called faen(because it resembles the shape of a fan) is also very popular in North India especially in Uttar Pradesh in cities like Agra and Mathura. The biscuit is also called "khaaree biscuit" in other parts of the country. Then there is the ever-famous tandoori tikkas (marinated meat grilled in a clay oven). They are steamed, grilled and fried.

In the Eastern part of the country a typical street food is the Chop which is a version of potato patties, dipped in flour batter and again deep fried.They are served with onion, cucumber slices.It is usually prepared and consumed as an evening snack. Jhal muri which is basically a mixture of puffed rice(muri) with oil, onion and spices is also very popular in Kolkata. The roll is another variety of fast food found in Kolkata. It is actually parathas with a variety of filling which can vary from chicken to egg to paneer for the vegetarians.This road side food is very filling and popular amongst college students and office goers.

Coming to the Western part of the country is the Vada pav which originated in Maharastra and is the cheapest food that can be found in the sophisticated Mumbai metropolis.It is a masala vada sandwiched between two buns. It is often referred to as the "poor man`s burger". Masala Chai or spiced tea is also found here. Pav Bhaji is another such concotion which had its humble beginnings as street food but is now also available in restaurants. Pav Bhaji is essentially dry buns with a topping butter combined with a mish mash of hot cooked vegetables along with raw onions. It can be made more tangy by adding lime juice and is quite filling.

Another street food of Maharastra is pav-sample. The sample is Sambhar and the pav or the bread is to be had with the sambhar. An extra dish of sambhar is referred to as sample. Although widely used in Maharashtra in roadside eateries, sambar is not native to the local culture. 'Sample' could also mean a plate of curry called 'Usal', which is a water based preparation of cooked sprouted lentils.

The term 'sample' means anything that goes conveniently with pav (usually implying a liquid nature). Maharastra is also famous for it Bhelpuri. It is a mixture of puffed rice with oil, spices, chopped potatoes,onion,corriander leaves,green chillies and tomatoes and topped with sweet chutney, dash of lime juice, rock salt, normal salt and a hint of red chilly powder. Sevpuri which is prepared from hotgrams(bhujia) and chutney is another speciality of Maharastra. In the Southern part of India, in Kerela there is the thattukada which is a covered cart or van with stoves and utensils. They offer thattu dosa a light rice-flour crepe fried in coconut oil and served with coconut chutney. Other street food include omelettes spicy pork fry, and parottas (like naan, but beaten and mixed with oil). In Tamil Nadu there is the thalluvandi"s similar to Kerala's "thattukada"s popularly called "Kaiyendhi Bhavans".

Street food which is found all over India and not restricted to the regions is the samosa Although the type of samosas may vary from region to region but the idea of eating samosas with tea is almost same at every region. Samosas are deep fried pastry filled with potatoes. A deep fried sweet dipped in syrup of North Indian origin, is the jalebi which is now found in more or less all parts of the country. In the South it is called jangiri. It is generally very cheap and easily available throughout India. In Indian cities, street vendors also sell a variety of drinks like Lassi which is a yogurt drink and can be found in plain salty, sweet, or fruit flavoured. The other variety of drinks are the Sherbet and Jaljeera.

These popular street food have to be eaten as soon as they are prepared and hence do not make them caterable foods. It has a local flavour and even foreigners love to gorge on them making the road side eateries a class in itself. Their cheap cost and instant availability has made them world famous. However the cleanliness and the hygienic content of these foods is often questioned.

INDIAN BEVERAGES

India, has since the medieval ages, been extolled as that country, which perhaps possessed the most Oriental treasure that any man could possibly comprehend. As such, Persian, Arabian or Turkish invasions into the country, with the

Europeans also joining in, in the form of Alexander the Great, had begun to foray into India, in anticipation that something might be gained and seized back home.

However, with the significant advent of Islamic rulers unto the India soil, it is also an acknowledged fact now that, they indeed had fallen in love with everything 'Indian', thus beginning to influence Indian culture and ethnicity profoundly. As such, the ancient Indian panorama was gradually changing into something that can be referred to as 'Muslim India', during the medieval period. Besides the everyday to rarefied influences, the culinary and gastronomical part was so much charmed under these Muslim arrivals, that India had acquired a distinctive genre of Islamic cuisine and other food part, during this time period.

And of food is being discussed, beverages or any liquid drink can never remain far behind. Indeed, beverages in India had too acquired its authoritative and punching a status, especially during the Mughal Empire. As such, Indian beverages have, with the cultural amalgamation of Islamic and Hinduism, Buddhism with Sikhism, presently moves in a much promising direction, with everything cool and chilled served in the lips. Somaras or Soma served as a much prized historical beverage in India, which was made as a part of a sacrificial ritual, by pressing the plant between stones, mixing the juice with milk and filtering it through sheepskin. It was however strictly not an alcoholic drink, since less time was involved between manufacture and consumption.

The most traditional Indian beverages comprise Garam-Chai, Lassi, Chach, Sharbat, Thandai, Shikanjami, Kanj, or even sweetened milk with ground nuts. During the olden days, refreshed sweetened warm milk (un-pasteurised, un-homogenised) was known to have been drunk in the morning and as a night-cap at bedtime. Chaach (Buttermilk) was consumed during lunch and dinner. Young women were of the habit to drink sweetened warm milk with turmeric powder, in order to possess a translucent, shimmering skin. The contemporary restaurants, however, prepare their own version of masala milk. Depending upon the season, coconut water, unfermented coconut sap (Neer), fermented coconut sap (Toddy), tempered mango juice (Aam Panna) are quite widespread as beverages in India. The Mughals are acknowledged to have introduced the concept of Sharbat (sweet fruit/flower fragrant beverages) amongst the pan-Indian populace, moving finally from royal household.

The British Raj were the foremost to introduce the class as well as the mass to get hooked on to 'tea' time, ensuing in the most legendary and admired Indian beverages recognised as 'Garam Chai' or 'Masala Chai'. In Punjab, the cold beverages under popular demand incorporate: Lassi, Shikanjami and Kanji. Thandai is yet another popular cold beverage in Rajasthan and Uttar Pradesh. Jal-Jeera is a popular street beverage in the whole of the country.

India has remained legendary, rising to top chart for its mouth-watering, refreshing, cheap and easy to make beverages. Literally drunk with a savouring tongue, until the last drop, the beverages available in India have formulated the most choicest selection of interesting drinks that are reflective of the indigenous culture. Beverages imply those flavoured drinks, suitable for a hot, humid scorching day, when nothing seems at peace with oneself, making them apropos in human consumption. It can be any drink prepared in highly unlike manners in order to satisfy a quenching, yearning thirst. Since alcoholic drinks have always been prohibited by health professionals and medical practitioners, especially in many ethnic cultures in India, Indians have successfully developed a multitude of non alcoholic beverages in its own right.

Tea or Chai is a North Indian beverage made from leaves, twigs or buds of a tea bush called Camellia Sinensis. Indian tea processing procedures includes fermentation, heating and drying. Herbs, flowers, fruits and other spices are being added as an added appeal. Chai is known throughout many countries. It comes in different flavours and strengths. Some of the Indian teas are the Darjeeling Tea, Assam Tea and Nilgri Tea. Most people use tea as a natural hair conditioner, skin vitaliser and a cure for arthritis. To make an Indian tea, it's helpful to understand the basics. Tea can blindly be looked at as a staple beverage all through India; the finest varieties are however grown in Darjeeling and Assam. It is generally concocted as masala chai, wherein the tea leaves are boiled in a mix of water, spices such as cardamom, cloves, cinnamon and ginger, and massive quantities of milk to produce a thick, sweet, milky concoction. Umpteen varieties and flavours of tea are prepared to suit dissimilar tastes all over the country.

Another popular beverage, coffee, is largely dished out in South India. One of the finest varieties of Coffea arabica is grown in stretches of Mysore, Karnataka, and is marketed under the trade name "Mysore Nuggets". Indian filter coffee, or kaapi, is also especially popular in South India. Other beverages incorporate nimbu pani (lemonade), lassi, chaach, badam doodh (almond milk with nuts and cardamom), sharbat and coconut water. India also possesses numerous indigenous alcoholic beverages, including palm wine, fenny and Indian beer.

There also exists the much-liked bhang, prepared using cannabis and typically consumed, especially in North India, during Holi and Baisakhi. However, the practice of drinking a particular kind of beverage with a meal, or termed as "wine and food matching" (the process of coupling food dishes with wine to only enhance the dining experience), is not however traditional or familiar in India. Although the Indian beverages are popular, the populace prefers to consume drinking water with their food, because water does not ever outshine the smack of the food. In fact, it is customary to offer drinking water to guests in any Indian household before serving any hot or cold drinks.

Beverages in India possess that 'something special' about the drinking concoction or mix, which is mostly introduced and instilled in the drink. Any given beverage, possesses an interrelation with the culture of a particular society. Although water is not considered as a beverage in the Indian scenario, beverages can be both alcoholic or non-alcoholic. In case of alcoholic beverages, base of the drink is alcohol, where as, in case of non-alcoholic beverage, alcohol is less than 0.5 per cent by volume. Carbonated drinks mostly serve as flavoured water concoctions. Hot drinks refer to coffee and also the chocolate flavoured drinks. India with its varied cuisine and a la carte menu in terms of solid astronomical delight, also has proudly developed a multitude of beverages to be consumed by its all and sundry habitants. Mango, the choicest summer fruit, grows in most parts of India. This fruit has so many varieties existing and growing in the soil, that all those varieties further taste differently. In summer, one always holds the pleasure to enjoy popular Indian beverages prepared out of mango.

Mango Shake and Mango lassi are the two most popular amongst these mango beverages. Mango Shake is an excellent fruity beverage on any blistering and sultry day in the yearly singeing summer of India. Thick mango pulp is also used along with milk, cream and sugar. Frozen pulp of mango however guarantees better consistency compared to fresh pulp. Usually, a shake is garnished with cracked or crushed dry fruits, to lend both a visual and psychological impact. Coconut powder and rose essence is used to top up the garnishing in any Indian mango beverage. One just needs to taste it to enjoy the real flavour of this drink. Mango can also be replaced sometimes with banana or other seasonal wonders. Mango Lassi is as popular as Mango Shake. In Lassi, the base is yogurt rather than milk. Mixing the pulp of mango in yogurt along with sugar and further in a blender, ensures a complete vision of Indian beverage. The Thickness of the beverage can be made more or less as par one's personal palate. Water is mostly used to make the lassi less thick.

A version of Lassi without mango is another favourite Indian beverage. It comes in two variants, comprising sweet or salty options. Most of the dairy product manufacturers commercialise lassi in these variants. It is an outstanding drink, especially during the regular summer months in India. Peach Melody tastes excellent, implying a fruit cocktail based on rock solid and savoury orange juice. Other ingredients of this concoction include peach and ice-cream.

Aum Kheer is another beverage in India made out from mango. Aum Kheer also serves as a great treat during summer.

Sweetened milk makes a great creamy base and additional flavour is added in the form of cardamom. This drink is simply splendid after a spicy dinner before retiring to bed. Choco-Coffee Shake, another admired beverage, serves as refreshing summer drink, concocted from chocolate and coffee. Tea and coffee are indeed most common beverages in India. Liked in both the hot and cold variations, they are served in umpteen varieties all across India.

Strawberry milk shake is especially popular in south India. Frozen and fresh strawberries and milk is used for this shake, to dish out a memorable beverage, suiting Indian tastes; strawberry milk is yet once more, an excellent summer drink. Banana Berry Smoothie made with fruits like banana, strawberry and raspberry, makes one go weak in the knee, each time he/she is served with it in a chilled glass. Yogurt and milk add creamy richness to the smoothie. The shake also serves more as a health food rich in potassium, antioxidants and calcium. Whether to beat the heat of oppressive Indian summer or just to savour the taste, Indian beverages do possess a worldwide appeal. Tasty, refreshing, easy to make and at the same time cheap, Indian beverages have efficiently carried off a number of celebrations. Thandai (nut milk) Lassi, a drink prepared from curd Nimbu Paani (fresh lime juice) Aam Panna (drink prepared from mango juice), Jal Jeera are some of the typical North Indian beverages.

These drinks are popular on festive occasions and served for entertaining guests. Beverages are also served at Indian weddings, amidst much fanfare. Chaach is a traditional Gujarati beverage and in some places consumed instead of drinking water and is the vernacular term for butter milk. Sharbat is yet another traditional Indian drink that was popularised by the Mughal rulers and is prepared from fruits or flower petals. The Coromandel Coast variation of tea, a mixture of coffee and tea is also a grossly admired beverage in India. However this is only the tip of the iceberg as the Indian beverages can be found in their endless variety and subtlety, perhaps still in an unripened stage, maturing towards futuristic prospects.

INDIAN STATE RECIPES

Indian Food is varied, diverse and distinct as its different state and culture. Regions in India have their traditional and distinctive style of cooking. Moreover, the diverse cuisine of the regions offers a huge option to vegetarians as well as non vegetarians of the country. Indian State Recipes are amazing as each particular state is a treasure house of exclusive cuisine. The states of India identify their food depending on the environment and climate conditions. People accustom to the surroundings and adopt their foods. India can be distinguished into five major areas: North Indian Recipes, South Indian Recipes, West Indian Recipes, East Indian Recipes and Central Indian Recipes. The North Indian Recipe is characterised by the use of large quantities of ghee or clarified butter.

On the other hand, among the Indian State Recipes, South Indian Recipe, tamarind is used in a large quantity just as to the hot climatic condition. A transformation occurs in the eating style of the people much variety so that they can accustom to the prevalent climatic and geographic condition. Moreover, Indian snacks and soups have an exhaustive list. In Indian states Spinach and vegetable soups are garnished with freshly crushed peeper, jeera and salt and served hot. Indian Snacks refer to dhoklas, handvi, muthias, pan cakes in salted and deep fried varieties.

Indian State Recipes also refer to the cooking ingredients. There is a different mediums of oil is used for each state in India. In Bengal, mustard oil is preferred as compared to the South Indian where coconut oil is used. Other states of India prefer using groundnut oil. Spices, condiments and vegetables are used in the Indian cuisine just as to the taste. In the northern part of Indian, there is absolutely no dearth of variety for a creative gourmet. North India introduces Indian to splendid exotic recipes. North Indian Cuisine comprises the Mughlai cuisine of Delhi. The touch of royalty of the Mughals that are added to the food is also reflected. North Indian cooking includes the generous use of spices, sausages, dry-fruits and butter. Food roasted in tandoors preparing Tandoori Chicken and the delicious Seekh Kebab is among the tasteful dishes. Kashmiri Cuisine offers fabulous aromatic banquet consisting of over 36 delectable dishes. The state of Jammu and Kashmir is blessed with the tradition of Wazwan. The cooking style of the state is based on heavy uses spices, condiments and curds. Rista, Tabak Maaz, Rogan Josh are the dishes echoing the awesome cuisine of this state.

The Awadh style of cooking is popular in the city of Nawabs, Lucknow. One of the favourites is 'Dum Pukht' method. Punjabi Recipes complete the aromatic palate of the northern part of India. The dishes such as Makki di Roti with Sarson ka Saag and Punjabi Lassi provides an impressive experience. Punjabi food is rich in butter and ghee and is prepared with lot of spices. South Indian Cuisine is prepared on the basis of the hot, humid climate. The southern states have an added advantage as they lie in the coastal region. The state has abundance of fresh fruit, vegetables and rice. Cooking pattern in the four states of the south zone such as Andhra Pradesh, Karnataka, Kerala and Tamil Nadu, are almost the same. Rice is the staple diet for all in this zone as compared to wheat in the north.

Most of the South Indian states practice vegetarianism. Rice, lentils, grains and vegetables are consumed with chutneys, pickles and papaddams (papads). Among the non vegetarian recipe, exotic sea food becomes the gourmet of sea food. Indian State Recipes introduces the rich variety such as Tamil Recipes including Chettinad cuisine and Andhra Pradesh Recipes offers Hyderabadi cuisine. Indian State Recipes varies in the eastern region. The eastern part largely comprises of fish and sea food which is cooked in mustard oil. There is a use of thickening agents like cashew or poppy seed paste. Bengal is renowned for sweet dishes and many of the popular North Indian sweet dishes originated from here. East India cooking is a blend of vegetarian and non-vegetarian food. West Bengal is known all over for the interesting and varied fish, rice and sweet recipes. In certain parts of Bihar influence of Buddhism is apparent and thus most of the population practices vegetarianism. Orissan Recipes is another example of rich culinary of the eastern region. Western Indian

Cuisine is also a blend of vegetarian and non vegetarian food. The staple diet of this region is rice, Jowar, Wheat, and bajra. In Gujarat, influence of Jainism is widespread, thus Gujrati Cuisine reflect the vegetarian touch. However, Goan Recipes and Maharashtra cuisine ensures that the fish and other sea food is the invariable part of the meal for the non-vegetarians. Maharashtra is famous for bhel puris, Gujarat offers dhoklas and Rajasthani Recipes introduce bati choorma and the spicy vindaloo curries Madhya Pradesh Recipes is however the mix of both sweet and salty dishes. The central part of the country does not have a distinct cuisine of their own, but they have absorbed the best of the food cultures from the neighbouring states. This proves that the diverse Indian state recipes make Indian culinary the most versatile cuisine in the world.

NORTH INDIAN RECIPES

Indian cuisine is ancient and has a 2500-3000 years old history. However, the recipes of the country have changed over the years. Indian State Recipes become unique by the use of many different herbs and spices. India presents a wide selection of different recipes. Different states of the country have its own cooking styles and tastes. Consequently, North Indian Recipes offer wide assortment of food including both vegetarian and non vegetarian. Food occupies a vital position of Indian culture. These recipes are structured just as to the religious beliefs and foreign invasions.

The North Indian Recipes, a couple of main courses are served. They are usually doled out along with different pickles, chutneys and of course different types of Indian bread, "roti". In addition to that recipes of north India take in various dessert preparations. Punjab, for instance, provide a huge assemble of vegetarian and non vegetarian recipes. Punjabi cuisines occupy a prominent position for its healthy, protein enriched food quality. The Punjab recipe is of cooking food in slow fire in order to retain the rich flavour. Punjabi breakfast consists of layered paranthas including breads, stuffed with spiced, mashed potatoes or grated, spiced radish eaten with dahi and tasty mango pickle for pep and pungency. Creamy milk is offered so as to complete the Punjab Cuisine. Among the North Indian Recipes, Punjabi cooking is exquisite and preparation such as Sarson-Ka-Sag—buttered mustard greens, flavoured with aniseed and asafoetida eaten with Makki-Ki-Roti the crisp, fresh corn bread. Punjabi cookery is the universal favourite item which is spicily stewed chick peas. They are dipped in green chillies and onions, and Bhaturas fully, leavened deep fried breads, and Dahi Baras lentil dumplings in creamy yoghurt. Baigan-ka-bharta is made by the egg plant smoked on fire and then cooked with hot spices and tomatoes. Punjab is well-known for the in-house pickles of assorted with small size cut vegetables. The long green chilli marinated in oil and garlic pickles are the delicious preparations. The delicious Karhi is another example of elite North Indian Recipes. The combination of protein rich pulses cooked with onions, tomatoes and red-eyed beans, rice and traditional breads, yoghurt whipped with chick pea flour and chick pea dumplings contribute a lot of the recipe of the northern region. The food of Kashmir, on the other hand can be plain or spicy. The recipe of the region includes spices like cinnamon, cardamom, cloves and saffron. Kashmir recipes originate on the people's love for food. Different varieties including Mutton, chicken or fish are of prime importance in a Kashmiri meal.

North Indian Recipes also depend on the local variety. In areas with a pastoral tradition, milk and its products are used in cooking. Himachal Pradesh is one such state in northern India that concentrates on mostly vegetarian dish. They use tubers like potatoes and turnips as well as Green vegetables. The common Himachali cuisine includes rice, lentil broth, dish of vegetables and bread. Pure vegetarian dishes are also well admired among the recipes of the northern India. The vegetarian dish includes dum-aloo—roasted potatoes in curd-based gravy, and chaman- fried paneer (cottage cheese), in a thick sauce. Sweets also complete the north Indian recipes.

EAST INDIAN RECIPES

Indian State recipes are structured on the basis of history, geography, economical status and culture of the state. The recipes are so designed that help the inhabitants to get accustomed to the climatic condition. East Indian Recipes are mostly spicy and comprise of non vegetarian cooking. Food habits of each region of eastern India represent how the cuisine of the state has evolved over centuries under the influence of various cultures and regimes which controlled over the years.

East Indian Recipes is also influenced by the closeness of the region to the sea. In addition to that the states receive plenty of rain. This rice and fish form the staple diet. Fish is cooked in different styles in the eastern part of the country. The states such as West Bengal, Assam, Bihar, Orissa have developed a strong likeness for fish. There is wide variety of cookery of fish, besides fish curry, fish is prepared smoked, grilled, fried, or into pakoras (patties), stuffed into green coconuts and now into burgers too.

East Indian recipes make food delectable Wheat is also the staple food of the eastern India. East Indian Recipes include the cooking of vegetables, pulses and pickles. Bihari recipe is a culmination of both vegetarian and non vegetarian preparations. Bihari cookery comprise of 'chhonkna' (tadka) with 'panchforan' (a mix of five seeds—saunf, sarson, methi, ajwain and mangraila). In addition to that 'bhoonjana' to food items, implying light frying is also done. Thus food preparation becomes very spicy and colourful. Mustard oil is used as a medium of cooking in Bihari recipe. Furthermore, Bihari cuisine has imbibed the cooking aspects of the Gupta, Mauryan, Turk, Afghan, Persian and European style of cooking and at the same time retained a food culture which is distinct to Bihar.

Orissa cuisine is easy to prepare, simple and delicious. Sea food as well as other vegetables is prepared with expertise. The Orissan Delight has become preferred in all over the world. West Bengal has a very distinct and rich culinary tradition. Bengali recipe is the use of five basic spices which includes zeera, kalaunji, saunf, fenugreek and mustard seeds. East Indian Recipes can be termed as a mixture of sweet and spicy flavours. Among the East Indian Recipes, north—eastern food has striking touch. Assamese cuisine Thekera Dia Maasor

Tenga (Sour Fish Curry with 'Thekeraa'), Kamrupi Biriyani and Vegetable Fry, Masor Jhol (Conventional Fish Curry) and Xoriohor Maasor Jhol (Fish Curry with Mustard), are the favourite of the Assamese people. Sweet dish delicacies complete the recipes of the eastern region. The Bengali sweets are popular all over the world. The preparation of the rasogolla was invented by Nobin Chandra Das. Other sweets prepared in the eastern region include gulab jamuns, sondesh, chum chum made of milk and cottage cheese.

SOUTH INDIAN RECIPES

The specialty of the South Indian Recipes among the Indian State Recipe is that the foods are boiled in different ways. In addition to that the impressive taste of the cookery of the southern region, develop on mixing the ingredients well. Moru or buttermilk is used essentially in cooking. Mulagtanny is a soup which is one of the vital ingredients for cooking of the southern region. The food cooked in the southern part of the country is generally light and appetizing. Besides, rice, spicy curries including vegetables and Sambhar complete a South Indian Dish.

The idli and dosa finds significance in the South Indian Recipes. They are quick Indian recipes and thus preferred by all. A wide variety of Dosas are available such as vegetable dosa, palak dosai, mung dal dosa, methi carrot sprinkled dosa. The recipe of preparing dosa is simple yet intriguing. The dimension of the dosa spans upto document spreads those measures to almost five feet. It is prepared by mixing equal quantities of rava and rice flour. Idlis are also available in different types including Kanchipuram idli, pepper idli, peas idli, dry fruit idli, spinach idli, Lacha idli and Tuvardal Idli. Preparation of idli includes a fermentation process, idlis are easy steamed recipes. It is preferred as a diet food which is full of nutrition.

Among the South Indian Recipes, Sambhar is one of the favourite South Indian curry. It is served with idli and dosa. It is prepared from Indian lentils and vegetables. Moreover, freshly grated coconut is added to sambhar to improve its taste. In addition to that a special masala is added to toor dal with certain vegetables to prepare a delicious sambhar. Sambhar is accompanied with boiled rice, Idli and dosa as they serve a nourishing food menu. The south Indians cooking furthermore is the grouping of chillies, mustard, coconut oil and various other spicy seeds to conjure up mouthwatering dishes. Vegetarian recipes require more garnishing and appetizing opportunities. The variety in raita or curd based dishes are also popular. A wide assortment includes boondi raita, cucumber raita, onion and tomato raita. A little garnishing of coriander leaves makes the raita attractive.

Payasam is another significant preparation among the South Indian Recipes. Kalan and Olan are typical vegetables served along with kootu. The pickle or oorgai is also falls on the recipes. Coconut oil is the medium of cooking and is a necessary garnishing item. Desserts are prepared in coconut and milk mixes and condensed to create the taste. The brown banana of Kerala is boiled in jaggery which makes a wholesome snack. Nei appam is a soft item made in pure ghee, the aapam is another sweet which is made of rice powder with a steamed effort. Modakam or koikatta is usually prepared as a coconut jaggery stuffing in the rice flour. Chutneys are made from coconut crushing and garnished in oil, kadipatta, and rai seeds. The rasam is an excellent cure for chills and fever. Jackfruit is a popular produce in the South and the vegetable is a specialty.

CENTRAL INDIAN RECIPES

Central Indian Recipes are such that they will impress every gourmet heart. The states Madhya Pradesh and Chhattisgarh present an immense culinary effect in the whole of India. Cuisine of Central part of the country consists of both sweet and salted dishes. Though, central region of the Indian sub continent have no distinct cuisine of their own, yet they have ingested the food cultures from the neighbouring states. Hence, choice of food in Chhatisgarh and Madhya Pradesh is quite similar. Food pattern in the central zone has a wide assortment. In some regions magnificent dishes are prepared from wheat and meat, while other regions in the Central India prepare delicacies from rice and fish. Madhya Pradesh offers a great culinary experience to the foodies. The amalgamation of popular food cultures resulted in the exclusive outcome of Central Indian Recipes. The delicacies prepared are in vegetarian and non -vegetarian dishes. Central Indian Recipes are combination of sweets and salty dishes. Most of the recipes are influenced by the recipes of other states.

The recipes of Central India are a considerable blend of spicy, matchless and delicious food items. In addition to that the recipes of Central India have evolved by imbibing share of various ingredients by different foreign invasions of rulers and travelers. Thus cooking in central part of the country becomes appetizing and steaming. The staple foods of the people in the central Indian states are wheat, Jowar and maize. Moreover, the meals are also inclusive of protein rich lentils. The most common Central Indian recipes is Arhar dal. People of these states in Central India cook vegetables in variety of styles. In addition to that dairy based dishes are more prepared in Gwalior and Indore districts.

Other familiar food dishes of the region consists Cashew Barfi, Jalebi, Khurma and Moong Dal Ka Halwa (Lentil Pudding) Central Indian recipes, as a result is a combination of various exotic dishes. Despite being heterogeneity, the unifying factor lies in the usage of various spices and herbs that make each dish delectable and thus the Indian of the central region became widely accepted all over the country. The recipes of Central India are thus acknowledged has interesting and delectable dishes of the country.

WEST INDIAN RECIPES

West Indian Recipes are the combination of nutrients vegetarian diet. The food is cooked in an inimitable flavour with simplest ingredients for making the dishes tastier. The cookery of the region is influenced by different lifestyle and the availability of ingredients. Most of the Western region is arid and the non availability of water creates an impact on the cooking style in the desert areas, and instead of water milk, buttermilk and clarified butter are used as the thickening medium. However, there is diversity in the western food preparation. The coastal areas of Maharashtra include fish in their menu and the cooking is less spicy. Gujarati recipe is strictly vegetarian, Gujarati food is crisp spicy and fried. The Gujarati thali includes farsans, sweetmeats and a variety of sweet and sour chutneys and pickles. Gujrati cooking is all about mixing of the sweet with the salted thus making it unique. Food recipes are chosen depending on the climatic conditions. In the drier regions, cookery of Gujarat comprises of different kinds of pulse preparations.

An exclusive preparation of wheat flour mixed with spinach, green chillies, a dollop of yogurt and a pinch of salt and sugar, are eaten with a hot and sweet shredded mango pickle, Chhundo. Methia Masala, a dry powder made from fenugreek seeds, chilly powder and salt freely sprinkled over raw vegetables and salads are another specialty of Gujarat. Kadhi is another savoury curry made of yoghurt. West Indian Recipes include the preparation of Khaman Dhokla, Doodhpak, a sweet, a salty steamed cake, thickened milk confectionery and Shrikhand, flavoured with saffron, cardamom, dessert made of yoghurt nuts and candied fruit.

Rajasthan Cooking, among the West Indian Recipes is influenced by its dry climate. Dried powdered lentils and beans from indigenous plants are used. Gram flour is used as major ingredient and with this ingredient various Rajasthan Food such as 'khata', 'ghatta ki sabzi' and 'pakodi' are prepared. Rajasthani recipe includes cooking of Bajra and corn, the staple grains, is used to make rotis, 'rabdi' and 'kheechdi. Various chutneys are also provided in order to complete the taste. The locally available spices like turmeric, coriander, mint and garlic make Rajasthani incredible. West Indian Recipes also include Indian vegetarian curry recipes which is prepared with sautéed onion and tomato. The spice or masala include a dhani-jeera powder, turmeric, pepper, dried mango powder for a sour effect. The sweet delicacies in Rajasthan are prepared of sweetness. Sweets like Jodhpur and Jaisalmer are famous for their 'laddoos', Pushkar is famous for 'malpuas', Bikaner for its 'rasgullas', Udaipur for its 'dil jani', Jaipur for its 'mishri mawa' and 'ghevar'.

INDIAN DESSERTS

Indian desserts are a perfect delight in every season. Not only do they satisfy the taste buds but also energize the body. It is a perfect excuse to stay on the dinner table after having a heavy meal. India offers an assortment of desserts. Desserts in India are very tempting and mouth watering. Indian mithai seems difficult to resist. A sumptuous meal is always incomplete without sweet dish like gulab jamun or kulfi or gajjar ka halwa. Desserts can be divided into two broad categories. One major category is the milk based dessert such as Rasbari, Peda, Burfi and so on. The second category of Indian dessert includes flour based sweets such as Lal Mohan, Malpuwa, Halwa and Ladoo.

Indian desserts have always been an integral part of Indian food. Every celebration in Indian subcontinent is unfinished without the servings of sweets and desserts. Preparing dessert with milk is considered to be among the predominant feature of Indian sweets. They are eaten usually after heavy meal and consist of sweet food but sometimes of a strongly-flavoured one, which include cheeses. The popularity of desserts served and prepared in India has gained popularity throughout the world. Sweets and desserts have are preferred throughout South Asia. Popular Indian deserts such as Rassagullla is common throughout South Asia.

Kulfi, Gajar Ka Halwa, Kheer, Shrikhand, Ras Malai, Gulab Jamun and Burfi are some of the India Desserts that are well-liked in an Indian table. Most of the desserts have originated as a local favorite and are typical to only an ethnic group in the country. However, desserts in India have an influence of various cultures those have come to India over the years through invasions or as a visitor. The word Dessert is a French term that has been derived from the word 'desservir' which means "to clear the table "and" to serve Desserts such as cakes, cookies, fruits, pastries, ice cream, and candies have arrived from the United States. British influence led to the popularity of pudding and pies. However, a popular belief in the Western countries consisted that dessert means fruit and sweet. Thus, the custom of eating fruits and nuts after a meal also became a part and parcel of Indian life.

SEASONAL FOODS

The Charaka Samhita prescribes different food preparations and beverages for different seasons that enabled people to remain healthy in all the seasons. People enjoying good health must have been able to discharge their duties efficiently which must have contributed greatly to the happiness of the individuals, as well as the society as a whole. This is because, these rules were framed keeping in view the changes in weather in different seasons of the year.

In the winter season Charaka prescribes food objects fried in fats and sour and saline in taste and meat of fat animals living near water. He also suggested wine prepared from the juice of sugarcane, preparations of milk, sugarcane, fats, oils, new rice and warm water to drink. In the spring season, just as to him one should eat preparations of barley and wheat and meat of a young one of an elephant, hare, sheep, quail and cuckoo and wine prepared with the juice of sugarcane *i.e.* Sidhu or that with honey *i.e.* madhavi. In the summer season one should eat cool paste groats prepared with parched barley or rice meal mixed with sugar, meat of wild animals and birds, clarified butter, milk, boiled sali variety of rice, wine in a small quantity, mixed with plenty of water. In the rainy season one should take old barley, wheat and sali rice and the meat of wild animals mixed with juices of fruits and wine prepared with honey or arista *i.e.* a tincture of medicines.

In the autumn season one should take the meat of quails and cuckoos, hare, young one of an elephant, preparations of wheat barley and rice. One should avoid the use of curds, fats, oils and meat of animals living near water. Thus the food of the rich must have varied just as to the suitability of the preparations for different seasons. The poor people must have eaten whatever food objects they could afford but there must have been some changes just as to seasons. As for example they probably ate groats mixed with unrefined sugar and water in summer and boiled hot wheat or barley mixed with jaggery in winter.

INDIAN BEVERAGE

Indian beverages comprehend a significant portion of the Indian food part. In fact, a traditional Indian meal, complete with every course, is considered incomplete without sherbet. The umpteen recipes, fruits, even vegetables employed to serve a sherbet is absolutely blissful. The humid Indian summers can be turned into a chilled atmosphere, by a mere drinking of sherbets. The sweet, salty, tangy or chilli taste of Indian sherbets, topped with ice, brings a serene effect to the mind. An even more interesting fact that stands out is that, one needs not necessarily burn out a huge sum of money to drink one; the sherbets can be prepared at home, with readily available ingredients. The variety of sherbets made in a strict Indian desi-style, lends the cool drink its definitive edge, strictly concocted to make people smile amidst sultriness. The fruits used like, raw mango, melon, lemon, watermelon or even a drink prepared with tamarind and asafoetida, makes Indian sherbets illustrious worldwide.

INDIAN SPICES

In contemporary India spices are used to rustle up scrumptious delicacies. However the Indian spices are more than just ingredients to add flavour and aroma to foods. In fact from times immemorial these had been associated with magical spells and herein lies the Oriental charm of the spices. Indian spices like cardamom, ginger, mint, parsley, etc were widely used for this purpose. However, magic need not necessarily refer to the supernatural always. A mouth-watering dish or a healing herb can also create a magical spell and the Indian spices perfectly serve these purposes.

The Indian spices play an important role in its economy as well. The Indian climate supports the growth of an array of spices and as a result the nation produces 75 types of spices out of the 109 listed with the International Organization for

Standardization (ISO). Even in the ancient and medieval ages the Indian spices played a significant role in strengthening its economic condition. The history of Indian spices narrates a long story of trading with the ancient civilizations of Rome, China, etc. With changing times, however, the spice trade grew in leaps and bounds and the Spices Board of India was set up to administer the spice trading. States like Kerala, Punjab, Gujarat, Manipur, Mizoram, Uttar Pradesh and several others are the hubs for growing spices. Besides exporting, these spices are also being used within the country for flavoring foods and in medicines, pharmaceutical, perfumery, cosmetics and several other industries.

Besides serving as culinary ingredients, Indian spices have medicinal properties too and are, hence, good for health. In addition to this spices are well known as appetizers and digestives and are considered essential in the culinary art all over the world. Some of them have anti-oxidant properties while others have preservative properties and are used in some foods like pickles and chutneys, etc. Some spices also possess strong anti-microbial and antibiotic activities. Different parts of the spice plants are used to add flavour to the dishes. For instance, both the seeds and the leaves of the coriander plants are used as spices. Hence Indian spices are used in the forms of dried seeds, leaves, flowers, barks, roots, fruits and certain spices are grinded and used in the powder forms. At times a handful of spices are grind together and a paste is made to spice up Indian cuisines. As far as seeds are concerned these used in their original forms to enhance the flavors of certain food items. The seeds are also the fruits of that particular plant but because of their tiny size they are referred to as seeds.

Some common seeds which are used as spices are Ajowan, Anardana, Aniseed, Caraway, Celery, Celeriac, Coriander, Cumin, Indian Dill, Fennel, Fenugreek, Mustard, Poppy Seed, etc. Leaves of some plants are used as a flavoring agent. These leaves have a distinctive flavour and when added with some other food they lend their flavour making it more tasty and delicious. Various leaves are used all over the world for culinary, medicinal and many other uses. Some of the commonly used spices which come under the leaf category are: Basil Laurel Leaves, Tejpat, Curry leaves, Peppermint Leaves, Mint Origanum, Parsley, Sage Savory, Rosemary Leaves and others.

Other types of spices can be derived from the flowers and fruits of a certain plants. Some common flowers which are used as spices are Rose, Caper, Rhododendron, Juniper, Kokam, Mace and Nutmeg, Vanilla, etc. Similarly the roots or parts of roots, of many plant species have become specialised to serve as spices. The following spices are basically roots used as spices and condiments: Galangal, Garlic Ginger, Horse Raddish, Onion, Stone Leek, Lovage, Shallot, Sweet Flag and Turmeric.

Some spices constitute the bark of a plant. These barks are highly flavoured and impart taste to a certain food item. Some spices do not come under any category of seed, fruit etc but yet belong to the family of spices. They are also used to impart flavour and taste to the food. Some common miscellaneous spices are Black Pepper, Long Pepper, Chabika, Clove, Amchur, Asafoetida, Karpoor, Arrowroot, Musk Mallow and others. Besides these the Indian spices are also used in Ayurvedic medicines; as preservatives and perfumes. It does not matter in what forms these are used as the Indian spices are sure to cast a magical spell on whoever uses them.

SWEETS

An Ayurvedic meal is completed with deserts or sweets and is usually served with the main course rather than at the end. Ayurveda suggests sweets if eaten at the end of the meal may cause congestion and sinus problems. Therefore it should be eaten before meals or with meals. In India, sweets are integrally related with ceremonies, festivals and auspicious moments. Sweets aggravate Kapha and therefore people with Kapha dosha and also diabetes and high cholesterol should restrict its consumption. It is a nutritious dish and malnourished and poorly built people are encouraged to have sweets. The important sweet dishes are, Almond kheer is a popular sweet dish, which is delicious and at the same time very nutritious. Date kheer is usually served hot and the saffron and cardamom in thepreparation helps it to digest it easily. Rice kheer is a common Indian desert cooked on all auspicious occasions. Roasted vermicelli kheer is a delicious sweet dish prepared with a special type of ingredient vermicelli, which is locally called sewai. Carrot halwa is a sweet dish usually prepared during the winter season and is very nutritious. Sheera should be served warm and for people with Kapha prakriti, add a pinch or two of ginger.

VEGETABLES

Vegetables are the indispensable ingredient of Indian food. The vegetables were present in the Indian cuisine since the Vedic era. The first vegetables mentioned in the Rigveda are the lotus stem (visa), and the cucumber (urvaruka). Vedas also refer to several others, like lotus roots (shaluka), the bottle-gourd (alabu), the water-chestnut (saphaka, mulali), two other aquatic plants (avaka and andika), and the bittergourd (karivrnta or kara-vella).

The Buddhist and Jain canonical literature6 refers to yams (aluka), two convolvulus roots (etaluka and kadambu), and several leafy vegetables. Kautilya in his Artha-shastra refers to the rajdhana or ksiri (now kauki, Manilkara kauki) and to the cucumber as chidbhita Most of the vegetables are mentioned in the Ramayana. The great epic speaks of the surana or elephant yam (vajrakanda), the pindaluka (possibly the sweet potato, the bottlegourd (kalasaku), the sleshmataka and lasora (both Cordia species that bear fruits which can be cooked or pickled), karira (Capparis decidua, with edible sour berries), and sudarshana or vrspani (unidentified).

After 1500 AD various vegetables of Indian food originated in foreign nations. These vegetables have become inseparable from the Indian cooking. Potato, tomato, papaya and the chilli all are essential to Indian cuisine. Moreover, vegetables like cabbage, cauliflower, lettuce, long orange carrots French or sword beans, haricot or navy beans (rajmah) and the winged beans have been introduced. The major vegetables of India are those which are raised by ploughing, namely cereals, pulses and oilseeds. All these food grains find references in Sanskrit Vedic literature. The collective term for vegetables was shaka, which comprised six kinds. These were ripened vegetables, leaves, tubers, roots, flowers and pods (shimbi). In addition to that there are other entries that include green leafy vegetables such as aroids, melons, pumpkins and gourds. In Ayurveda, certain vegetables, such as, gourds, brinjal, cucumber and radish reduce pitta and kapha.

In Indian cooking, the place of vegetables is not restricted to side dishes. Vegetables are turned into appetizers, snacks, soups, main dishes, relishes, pickles, conserves, desserts, sweetmeats, breads and beverages. Just about any vegetable can be cooked in all these forms, using different ingredients and techniques. Vegetables served as side dishes with an Indian meal are cooked in just about every way conceivable to man. Indian vegetable dishes are easy to cook and require some spices to enhance the flavour of the savour. Some spices, such as turmeric, cayenne pepper, ginger powder and mango powder are often added with or after the vegetables, because they burn so easily.

The heat is then reduced and the vegetables are cooked in their own moisture and vapour. Finally the heat is increased and the vegetables go through a second stir-frying, to get nicely browned and develop a beautiful shiny glaze. Sometimes a little oil or ghee is added to the vegetables at the end, to increase the glaze. Vegetables cooked thus have a roasted flavour and very soft texture, though the pieces hold their shape. Some vegetables, such as potatoes, yams, plantain (green banana) and beetroot are often cooked prior to stir-frying. This is done to preserve the full robust aroma of fried spices, as these vegetables require a lot of water and time to cook and prolonged moist cooking robs the spices of much of their fried flavour.

Vegetables in Indian food find their mention in Sanskrit and other literatures as well. Ancient literatures show the ways of preparation of many vegetables. The Manasollasa uses the generic term pude for a delicacy of mixed fried vegetables folded into a turmeric leaf and then steamed; Chavundaraya's Lokopakara mentions thirty-one vegetables in one chapter on cooking, and Mangarasa's Supa Shastra has a long chapter on the cooking of vegetables.

FOOD IN INDIAN CULTURE

Food, which indeed played a great role in Indian tradition, also stood as an emblem of the concept of racial synthesis in Indian culture. Wheat did not form part of the dietary of the Rigvedic Indians as it is not mentioned in the Rigveda and it continued to be considered an exotic object up to the present day. Barley or yava seems to have been the staple food grain of the Aryans. Rice seems to have been the staple food grain of both the Proto-Australoids and the Dravidians.

By the time of the compilation of the samhitas of the Yajurveda, wheat or godhuma and many varieties of rice, and lentils or masura had become part and parcel of Indian dietary. The Satapatha Brahmana calls wheat the second best of the food objects. Its introduction in the Aryas dietary might have been due to the contract of the Aryans with the Dravidians, who had been using wheat as far back as 2500 B.C. if not earlier. Early Aryans used meat of oxen, barren cows, and goats for preparing non-vegetarian dishes but they most probably used fish as a food object only when they came in contract with the Proto-Australoids and the Dravidians.

The early Aryans used clarified butter as the frying medium. Only the non-Aryans used oil for frying. But the lawgivers later permitted the use of oil if clarified butter was not available. Of the fruits the Inter Samhitas and the Brahmanas mention three varieties of jujube, namely badara, kuvala and karkandhu, bilva or aegle marmelos, kharjura or phoemisilvestris, mango and amalaka or myrobalari were also prevalent. The authors of the Sutras also mention udumbara *i.e.* Indian fig, saphaka or trapabispinsa, jambu or rose apple and mango.The excavations at some Neolithica and Caleolithic sites in the Deccan and at Harappa suggest the widespread use of dates, melons, pomegranates, lemons and coconut fruits by the people associated with these cultures. Sugarcane and bananas were important Indian crops even in the times of the sutras. It is known that their origin is from South-east Asia *i.e.*

Australia. It is also known that in later times all these fruits formed part of Indian dietary. Thus it is clear that there was a synthesis even in this category. The common vegetables used by early Aryans were cucumber or urvaruka, lotus stalks or bisa, roots of lotus or saluka and bottle gourd or alabu. From the sutras it is known that leafy vegetables were also cooked and formed part of the diet of the Indians but respectable people avoided garlic, onions and leeks. Of these it seems that the Aryans included bottle gourd or alabu as a result of their contact with the Proto-Australoids. Of the beverages the common drinks of the early Aryans were soma and sura, but masara is mentioned in the Yaurveda and was the beverage used by the Dravidians. The description clearly shows that even in the proto-historic times the food of Indians reflected the synthetic feature of Indian culture.

IMPORTANCE OF FOOD IN INDIAN CULTURE

Since ages food in Indian culture has played a great role. Importance of food in Indian culture is immense. Ancient Indians realised that all lives in this world are depended upon food. For this reason we find a whole hymn in praise of food in the Rigveda. They regarded food as the source of all life hence they called it Prajapati or Lord of all creatures. In the Taittiriya Upanishad food is equated with Brahma for it is stated that all beings take birth from food, after being born they subsist on it. In the same work it is stated that one should not deprecate food for it is the vital force and the body is fixed on the vital force. An eater of food becomes great in progeny, cattle, and in the luster of holiness and in glory.

It is stated in the Prasna Upanishad that God created food and all the individuals, vigour, rituals and activities depend on food. In the Taittiriya Upanishad food is called a panacea because all creatures depend on it. It is, therefore stated that one should collect plenty of food and should not discard food. They realised that not only worldly possessions depended on food but the ultimate aim of human existence namely salvation also depended on purity of food.

It is stated in the Chhandogya Upanishad that it is food,

which enables a man to use all his faculties. It is only food that enables him to see, to hear, to act and to acquire knowledge hence one should worship food. When there is purity of food the mind becomes pure, when the mind is pure then follows firm remembrance of the real self. Food was considered as an important means of developing good qualities in an individual. It is therefore, equated with truth and right-order in a passage of the Taittiriya Brahmana. It is stated that after the food is served in a plate the eater should sprinkle water round it and say, "I sprinkle thee, that are satya or truth with rta or right order" it is done in the morning and "I sprinkle thee that are rta with satya" it is done in the evening. He then offers five bites on which ghee is sprinkled to the five modes of prana namely prana, vyana, apana, samana and udana preceded by the word `Om` and followed by svaha.

RASA IN INDIAN FOOD

Indian Food has been constituted depending on the percepts of Ayurveda. Ayurveda is the science of life as a whole and has much influence on the choice and style of food in India. This ancient Indian science of life the parameters of Indian food include taste (rasa), aftertaste (vipaka), potency (virya) and guna or property (hot-cold, heavy-light, and oily-dry). The realm of Indian Food is composed as all the components included turn their effect on the hormonal balance (dosha) of a human body.

Rasa in Indian Food is an indispensable part of the cuisine of the country. Rasa or taste is the keystone of Indian dietetics. It is mentioned that there are six rasas namely: sweet (madhura), sour (amla), salty (lavana), pungent (katu), bitter (tikta) and astringent (kasaya). Ayurveda cites that each of these tastes consist a combination of two of the five basic elements. The five essential elements in the universe are earth, water, fire, air and ether, and these pairs when combined have essential effect on the human body. It is being observed that among the different Rasa in Indian Food, the sweet taste or madhura, constitutes a combination of earth and water. The science of body, the sweet taste helps in building of body tissues. Moreover, these body tissues are themselves made from earth and water. The dosha kapha is also made up of earth and water, and it is believed that a sweet-tasting substance will strengthen this dosha. Whereas, this sweet-tasting substance weakens the dosha pitta which is made from the single element fire and the dosha vata is made from air and ether. A sour substance made of earth and fire is another vital portion of the Rasa in Indian Food.

This sour (amla) Rasa also similarly strengthens the kapha and pitta doshas, but weaken vata. It is also observed that the final outcome depends on the interaction of the elements which is present in the six tastes and in the three doshas in the body. Another fundamental idea inferred or derived from this specific instance is that of after taste or vipaka. This Rasa in Indian Food is left just after digestion. Further, the six original mouth tastes are reduced to just three after the process of digestion. Moreover, sweet and salt tastes both become sweet. Pungent, bitter and astringent tastes of another Rasa in Indian Food together turn into a pungent vipaka. Whereas, sour taste remains sour and a sweet vipaka strengthens kapha attributes, a pungent aftertaste vata qualities, and a sour vipaka will boost pitta characteristics.

RELIGIOUS INFLUENCE ON INDIAN FOOD, INDIAN CUISINE

India is a land of diversity. Her countless landscapes, different languages, magnificent festivals and multi-ethnicity reflect the culture and tradition of this land. Indian cuisine is also as diverse and wonderful as the colourful country. From the northern tip of Kashmir to the southern state of Kerala, and from the western ghats of Gujarat to Nagaland in the east, India's food habits are as variant and colourful as the people of India. However, a particular pattern exists among all this diversity. Apart from India, the traditional religious Indian cuisine has also gained popularity across the globe. Religious influence on Indian food has bechanced due to the invaders, immigrations and intermingling of different people from the pre Christian era. The presence of diverse climatic condition has also helped to broaden the sets of ingredients present in the cuisines. In India, food has become a marker of different religious and social identity. Every religion present with varying taboos and preferences, such as Hindus do not consume Cows, Muslims do consume beef and Jain population do not eat roots or subterranean vegetables. This eating habit further supports the fact that Indian cuisine has witnessed a heavy influence of religion.

The main religious influence on Indian food is of the Hindu religion. The Hindu influence on Indian cuisine is immense. The Hindus are mostly vegetarians for ethical reasons and this has They consume a vast range of different vegetables like tomatoes, cauliflower, spinach, green beans and potatoes to make different lavish dishes. They include several other vegetables like cluster beans, beetroot, eggplant, cucumber okra, and white radish. Brahmins are one of the highest castes in Hindu religion. They are strict vegetarians and do not consume meat, fish or egg. However, Brahmins of the eastern coastal regions are non vegetarians.

Another religious influence on Indian food is by the Muslim community. The Muslim influence on Indian cuisine contoured the Indian cuisine while offering it that desired shape with blessed aroma and flavour. The Muslim culture has introduced the lavish Mughlai cuisine to Indian culinary culture. Biryani, the rice-pulao with the mixture of meat and several meats roasts kebabs, flavoured with Indian herbs and spices are some of the famous dishes. Due to the Muslim influence on Indian food, these dishes are always served with almonds, pistachios cashews and raisins. Muslims introduced semolina, phirni, leavened breads and the famous tandoor style of cooking. In Muslim cooking culture, meats can also be cooked in tandoors marinating them in yogurt and spices.

Apart from Hindu and Muslim religion, Jainism community also has religious influence on Indian food. The Jain influence on Indian cuisine popularized the non veg items. In this community, people are influenced by the non-violence or ahimsa. Due to this they are strictly against consuming non-vegetarian food. They take the food that falls under the non-injurious food like rice, lentils, wheat, oil seeds and beans. They do not consume root vegetables, alcohol, honey and meat and also do not waste any food items. Basically their food concept is based on eating after sunrise in the morning and eating before sunset in the evening. They believe in fasting on certain days and offering food to poor people. They eat only those vegetables and fruits which become ripe on the tree. Another important religious influence on Indian food is the Christian religion.

Christian influence on Indian cuisine offered Indian cuisine that touch of contemporaneousness which later reshaped Indian food style to a great extent. This religion is the third largest religion in India. Soups, salads and grilled pork chops marinated in spices and chillies are the famous recipes among Indian Christians. Dishes like sausages, pudding, cutlets, biscuits and jams are famous Christian food items. Alcoholic drinks such as whisky, wine etc and spicy tea were some of the major drinks came to existence in India due to this religion. The magic of Indian cuisine lies not only in the taste and tang but in its diverse pattern which marks Indian cuisine as the motley of several traditions, as the potpourri of various religion.

INDIAN SNACKS

Indian snacks are some of the tastiest and fulfilling preparations popular all across the country. The food consumed in between meals for satiating short-lived hunger are usually categorised under snacks. The Indian snacks are usually delicious and mouth watering preparations consumed in different times of the day, such as in the late afternoon, evening or late night. Savories like samosas, aloo tikki, vada pau are easily prepared and commonly served Indian snacks. Indian snacks are comprised of recipes, which have been passed on for generation together in Indian homes. Young and old alike love the crispness and tempting tastes of Indian snacks. The popularity of Indian snacks grew because of its easy process of preparation and that they can be prepared at any time. It is thought to be ideal to serve the appetizing Indian snacks before coffee or tea. Bhajias or Pakoras can be prepared in both vegetarian and non-vegetarian forms. Sometimes only fried forms of besan with onions can make lovely bhajias, at times chicken or vegetable puree is added to make it fulfilling. Chaat is a popular type of Indian snacks and vendors literally crowd the streets selling all kinds of delicious variations of chaats. Bhelpuri is a type of low fat, nutritious and delicious snacks found in India.

It is just a mixture of puffed rice, sauces, dried chats and other spices. Chivda is a Marathi snacks and is popular for its properties to be crispy and crunchy that can be easily stored for a long time in airtight container. Similarly Vada Pav can be said to be a principle dish of Maharashtra that is presently a popular Indian snacks across the nation. Breadcrumbs along with some delicious mixture of curry make the sumptuous Vada Pav. Steamed Momos is an important input in the list of Indian snacks that has evolved from northern India. Sikkim is the land of momos, however momo has now become a loved Indian snacks among all ages. The low amount of oil and spices used in this preparation has made it loved among all age group. Dhokla or the steamed gram flour snack has come straight from the heart of Gujarat and is served with Tamarind and Mint-Coriander Chutneys. Indian snacks has unlimited variations and the Indian chefs are never tired of experimenting with the traditional dishes to discover some more tantalising tastes.

A variety of tasty Indian snacks have become a regular preparation in households, these Indian snacks are offered while welcoming guests in the evenings. Indian snacks are used as tidbits, which are nibbled between the meals. Sometimes used as starters in the parties, Indian snacks are popular all over the world owing to its mouth-watering tastes and easy method of preparation.

INDIAN FOOD INDUSTRY

In the World, India is the second largest producer of food after China. The country has achieved the potential of being the biggest with the food and agricultural sector. Indian Food Industry is considered to be occupying about two thirds of the total Indian retail market. Food and food processing technologies are developing gradually. In addition to that modern skills and equipment have taken place in industries such as Canning, Dairy and Food Processing, Specialty Processing, Packaging, Frozen Food, Refrigeration and Thermo Processing.

India is an agriculture based country. The country is concentrated in the production of various types of fruits and vegetables which indeed contours the structure of the Indian food industry. Among the sub-sectors of Indian Food Industry, fruits and vegetables industry have achieved the second largest producer of vegetables in the world next to China and accounts for about 15 per cent of the world's production of vegetables. Vegetables are typically grown in India in field conditions.

The current production level in the Indian subcontinent is over 71 million MT and the total area under vegetable cultivation is around 6.2 million hectares. Vegetables such as potato, tomato, onion, cabbage and cauliflower report for around 60 per cent of the total vegetable production in the country. These fruits and vegetable industries manufacture health food as well as health food supplements are rapidly improving segment of this industry, which is gaining vast popularity amongst the health conscious population of the country. Meat and poultry is one of the fastest growing segments of the agricultural sector in India at present. In this industry, the production of eggs and broilers has been rising at a rate of 8 to 10 per cent per annum. India is the fifth largest egg producer and the eighteenth largest producer of broilers in the world. Fisheries also have gained popularity as a major Indian Food Industry.

India is the third largest producer of fish in the world. Milk and milk products have also gained popularity. India is the largest producer of milk in the world. In India both the production and consumption of milk and its derivatives are traditionally high in the country. Amul is regarded to be the largest food product business in the country Plantation

Industry is among the prominent Indian Food Industry. There are about 9500 spices from medicinal and aromatic plants that are produced in the country. India is the largest producer, consumer and exporter of spices and the major spices being produced include black pepper, cardamom, ginger, garlic, turmeric and chili. In the Indian food industry, the consumer product groups like confectionery, chocolates and cocoa products, Soya-based products, mineral water, high protein foods are also on a high rise.

They form the most promising sub-sectors of Indian food industry. Beverages are also included in the industries. Besides these, grain processing and Grain-milling has a position. Inspite being one of the major food producers in the world, India is credited for less than 1.5 per cent of international food trade. Furthermore, the Indian food industry sales turnover is Rs 140,000 crore (1 crore = 10 million) annually as at the start of year 2000. The Indian food industry has the highest number of plants approved by the US Food and Drug Administration (FDA) outside the USA.

INFLUENCES ON INDIAN FOOD

The cuisine of India is rich and is recognised all over the world for its subtle characteristic. Indian culinary is considered to be one of the most diverse cuisines of the world. It is enriched with various influences both by invasions and by religion. These influences have brought about wide assortment of dishes and cooking techniques in the Indian society. Consequently, Indian cuisine varies from region to region and reflects the ethnicity of the country. Influences on Indian Food have brought about an essential change in the concept of food. Indian cuisine has also influenced cuisines across the world.

The religious beliefs of India as well as the culture of the country played an influential role in the evolution of modern cuisine. Influences on Indian Food proves that every bit of India's diversity has had been improving and changing. Cuisine across India evolved with the cross-cultural interactions among the subcontinents. Thus, flexibility developed in the Indian Culinary. The cooking of India can tell much about the people of the country. It indicates that Indian cuisine is the fusion of various religious beliefs. Religion had shaped the Indian cooking since the commencement of several religions. Religious Influence on Indian Food introduced the perception of vegetarianism and Non vegetarianism. Hindus followed the cuisine as laid down by the Aryans, whereas with the coming of the Mughals the Muslims started to prepare food just as to their techniques.

The Muslim tradition is evident in initiate the cooking of Mughlai food, kababs, rich Kormas and nargisi koftas, rogan josh, and preparations from the clay over or tandoor like tandoori rotis and tandoori chicken. The Christians came as missionaries and they added a different flavour to the cooking style of the Indians. Jains are the sect of Hindus but their eating style varied from that of Hindus. Jainism is a religion that believes in non-violence and thus refrained from eating any kind of meat or root vegetables. They consume food that grow on trees and are ripe. Influences on Indian Food augmented the Indian Cuisine.

Thus a number of religions exist in India. There were two major cultures that have contributed to the Indian cooking, that include the Hindu and the Muslim traditions. Each new religion settled in the country and brought with them their own culinary practices. Indian cuisine was a blend of different contribution. In addition to that the Portuguese, the Persians and the British made important contributions to the Indian culinary panorama. Indian cuisine is also augmented by the influence varied religions. India on its journey went through a long history of invasions. These different cultures, that have entered the country created the spectacular palette of foods.

Influences on Indian Food can be traced with the various Indian invasions. Aryans, Mongols, Persians as well as Chinese people invaded India since the ancient times. was the defining factor of Indian cuisine is its creative use of spices. These invasions also had set up specific culinary experiences for different region and in this present moment different regions have distinct cuisines of their own. Moreover in the colonial period European cooking style was introduced to India. It can be rightly put that religion and invasions shaped the Indian Food. Influences on Indian Food include the coming of the Aryans and in this period the cuisine the Great Hindu Empires concentrated on the detailed aspects of food and to understand its essence and how it contributed to the development of mind, body and spirit.

Mongolians brought to India the concept of hot pot cooking. Persians were the rulers who introduced elegant dining style and brought with them rich food with dry fruits. The Chinese introduced stir fries to Indian along with sweet taste of food. Portuguese were the initiator of vegetables such as tomatoes, chilli, and potato, which in the later years became the main components Indian cuisine at present.

HINDU INFLUENCE ON INDIAN CUISINE

India is a land of extensive religion. Religion played a prominent role in shaping Modern Indian Food. Thus Indian Food was classified by religion and region. A certain dimension of cooking was added in the Indian cuisine through various intermingling of people, travellers and invaders from all over the world. However, the foremost factor aspect in the medieval period that defined the food habit was the religious practices in the country.

Indian Culinary was highly influenced by religions. The concept of food from the normal dinner to extravagant ceremonies has its root in the traditions described by the ancient Hindu text, the Ayurveda. The Hindu influence on Indian Cuisine, food was assigned with certain parameters as dictated in the Ayurveda. The parameters of taste (rasa), aftertaste (vipaka), potency (virya) and guna or property (hot-cold, heavy-light, oily-dry and so on) are common to every Indian food. These parameters together effect the hormonal balance (dosha) of the body.

Historical evidences show that before the invasion by the Moghuls, the Indian food was shaped by the Hindu belief. The Hindu Philosophy, eating and spiritual advancement are intertwined. Hindu influence on Indian Cuisine suggested Vegetarianism, and especially avoiding of beef. Hindus believe that each food has its own negative or positive energy. The choice of food determines the character of a man. Foods such as ghee, ginger, honey, limes, almonds, rice, turmeric, and green chilies are considered positive and cooling, while foods like garlic, onions, salt, eggplant, tomatoes, sugar, and red chilies are considered negative and have a heating effect. Indian cooking at present is effected by the distinguishing qualities of foods discussed by the Hindus.

Hindu Philosophy, food is the resource for nutritional and medicinal qualities. Different foods, herbs, and spices are also categorized by Hinduism for their therapeutic use and tasteful aspect. Hindu influence on Indian Cuisine enhances the energetic aspects of food. In the Vedic period the first known recipes originated and it is believed that the Hindus also started following those cooking style.

One strong Hindu influence on Indian Cuisine is the venerable practise of vegetarianism. People belonging to the certain part of the Hindu community follow a strict vegetarian diet. Historically, it is said that vegetarianism is an Aryan philosophy and food was considered to be part of cosmic cycle. In addition to that Hindus pay regard to animals like cows and bulls thus refrained from consuming meat. But, the Hindus are known to eat meat in the ancient eras.

The great epics Mahabharat and Ramayana, also finds evidences of consuming meat by the kings and heroes. Vegetarianism evolved in the country as the Hindu religion was greatly influenced by ideals of non-violence and better Karmas. India is a diverse land in every aspect such as religion, language, to ethnicity and Hindu influence on Indian Cuisine has again strengthened the diversity. The whole country follows different regional food habit and cooking style.

The Hindu influence have developed both vegetarianism and non- vegetarianism food habit. Hindu philosophy can be regarded as the origin of modern Indian cooking. Though, each region has distinct cuisines of their own, yet India is basically united by its devotion to Hinduism for all these thousands of years. Large majority of Indians follow the Hindu philosophy of cooking and eating to this present-day.

INDIAN FESTIVE FOODS

India is a cosmopolitan country and enjoys different religions living together. The country is also the background of various cultures. All the religious beliefs celebrate their own festivals. Indian culinary is associated with Indian festival. Each particular religion has their distinct dish to mark the celebration. The Indian food is influenced by varied religious beliefs and the festival cuisinc depends on the popular faiths. Indian Festive Foods have become popular in the other countries too.

India celebrates its religious festivals almost all the year round. These festivals offer a great opportunity to enjoy the traditional delicacies. These dishes are cooked using the traditional recipes. Moreover, these traditional recipes have been passed on from generations to generations. Each festival brings ceremonious food. In addition to that, these special recipes provide a great opportunity to discover and taste the delicacies of Indians. Major festivals of India such as Diwali, Holi, Eid or Christmas prepare sweets which receives attraction among the Indian Festive Foods. Every festival in India has a different approach towards food, for example Holi offers an opportunity to enjoy some of the best sweet delicacies. Among the Indian Festive Foods, a wide diversity in cooking is experienced. Diwali is one of the grand festivals celebrated all over the country. It is one of the major Hindu festivals and is celebrated for five- days. Besides being a bright festival, Diwali, this festival also follows the custom of offering sweets to the deities who are worshipped and sharing those as blessings. Diwali Delicacies include sweets which are prepared traditionally. The dish also includes food such as delicious rawa laddoos to ghathia and other mouth watering delights.

Christmas Delicacies also form a significant part of the Indian Festive Foods. Christmas is a celebration of a gala feast. Christmas cakes and cookies are included in the delicacies. A taste of delightful cakes, snacks and cookies are offered in this festival. Ramzan Eid Delicacies is enjoyed by the Muslim community as well as by the other communities. This is one of the Indian Festive Foods that provide marvelous dishes. The

EID delicacies include mutton korma, badami ghosht, badami phirni, sheer korma or seviyan. Other Indian Festive Foods comprise of Durga Puja Delicacies, Navratri Delicacies, Makar Sankranti Delicacies, Holi Recipes Delicacies. All these are major Hindu festivals and special emphasis is laid on the sweets. Pongal Delicacies and Onam Delicacies reflect the taste of southern part of India. Pongal the harvest festival of Tamil Nadu and offers two main dishes such as 'Sweet Pongal' and 'Salt Pongal' along with other dishes of rice and 'Avial', which is a concoction of vegetables.

The grand feast of Onam is served in a special manner. 'Onasadhya', is an impressive spread of delicacies which is served in Banana leafs. Other delicacies such as curries, 'pappadams' (round crisp flour cakes), 'achaars' (pickles) and 'payasams' and 'prathamans' as desserts as well as fruits are also served as a part of the dish. Indian Festive Foods are available in variety and it is reflected in the special Navratri cuisine. The culinary delights include special courses which are strictly vegetarian. Specific ingredients and vegetables are used that vary from one region to another. However, dishes prepared with milk, curd; fruits and nuts.

INDIAN REGIONAL CUISINES

India is a country with different states that have been demarcated just as to language, culture, tradition and most importantly geography. These factors influenced the cuisine of the Country too, besides religion and foreign invasions. Intrinsic culinary traditions are thus being restructured by the ever changing political and socio-economic landscape. Though, such contradictions, the basics of an Indian meal are similar. Indian Regional Cuisines reflect miscellaneous taste.

With a 3000 year old religious heritage, India is a home to many religions such as Buddhism, Hinduism, Sikhism, Islam, Jainism, Christianity, Zoroastrianism, and the Bahai religions. All these faiths demonstrated on the choice of food. Vegetarianism and non vegetarianism also originated from these beliefs. This dictated in the choice of culinary in the sates of India and thus became the Indian Regional Cuisines.

The Jains are restricted from eating garlic or any kind of living thing. Besides, Jainism other religious beliefs do not abstain from eating meat. However, different religions have different restrictions on the type of meat. Such as Hindus, Parsis, and Sikhs abstain from eating bee and Muslims regard eating of pork going against their religious belief. Indian Regional Cuisines is thus myriad, different religions and culture intermingles and produces the taste of India. Apart from the religious beliefs, foreign invasions have also played a vital role in deciding the culinary of a particular state. The Punjab was situated in Pakistan. Though, the Punjabis have their own distinct cuisine, as with any other Indian state and region, yet much of their cuisine has been influenced by the refugees who fled to India.

It is here in Punjab products like milk and ghee, parathas stuffed with radishes and pomegranate seeds, mustard greens, corn bread, complete the richness of dishes. Kashmir on the other hand is a Muslim dominated state. It is, therefore, a region reflects Mughal influence. Various Muslim dishes are enjoyed in the region which involves meat and cream dishes. Gujarati Cuisine is another example of miscellany. Among the Indian Regional Cuisines, Gujarati cuisine refers primarily vegetarian cuisine. This region is solely influenced by the religious faiths of Hinduism and Jainism. The authentic Gujarati Thali includes Roti, daal or kadhi, rice, and sabzi or shaak, which is a dish made up of different combinations of vegetables and spices.

Gujarati cuisine varies widely in flavour and heat and is the example of variations. Orissa cuisine is presented with affluent usage of spices and local ingredients. According to history, in the 17th and 18th Century, during the Bengal Renaissance, Oriya cooks were influenced by the cooking style of West Bengal. Another example of the richness in Indian Regional Cuisines is presented through the West Bengal Cuisine. The cuisine of West Bengal has been developed through different rulers through the ages. Historical records put forth that, the ancient inhabitants of Bengal were the Dravidians and later Aryans were located in Bengal during the Gupta era. Moreover, Bengal had experienced the authority of the Muslim rulers and the British rulers. In addition to that this region was the abode of different culture including Jews, Afghans and Chinese, the Dutch and the French. All these had a great impact on the cooking style of Bengal. Food habits in the state changed with the Anglo Indians and the Christian Community.

A wide assortment in Indian Regional Cuisines is seen in the southern part of the Country. Kerala is situated in South India and presents a separate taste of its own. The richness in spices adds flavour to the dishes. Furthermore, the region is inhabited by the occupied by the Syrian-Christian community, along with Chinese traders and Jewish settlers. Kerala is thus a region to produce cosmopolitan taste. Thus the state produces archetype Syrian Christian dish.

WEST BENGAL CUISINE

West Bengal cuisine, Indian food, has been developed and embellished through lots of sources as Bengal had different rulers through the ages. The ancient inhabitants of Bengal were the Dravidians and later Aryans located in Bengal during the Gupta era. Bengal had experienced the jurisdiction of the Muslim rulers and the British rulers and later on, the inhabitation of Jews, Afghans and Chinese fortified the Bengal cuisine culture. During the time of British dictatorship, the Dutch and the French had established colonies in west Bengal and they had a great impact on Bengal's culinary habits as well as that of the Anglo Indians and the Christian Community. The process of baking which is now extensively used was unknown before the British period. West Bengal has included Chops and Cutlets, which are originated from the British, in the Bengali food list.

West Bengal cuisine involves the use of huge variety of spices like "Pachforon", " tej pata"(bay leaf), "jeera", "mouri"(snafu), "kala jeera", "jayfol", "joyitri", "shorshe" (mustard seed),"jafran"(saffron), "groom moshla" which is a mixture of "elaichi"(cardamom), "darchini"(cinnamon) and "long"(clove), "posto"(poppy seeds).

The cuisine of West Bengal has its wide ramification which enlists "bhaja", "bora", "dal", "pora", " shukto"," "torkari", "labra", "ghonto", "chanchra", "chochhori", " bhapa", "bhate", " bhorta", "bhuna", "chechki", "dalna", "kalia", "kofta", "kasha", "korma", "polau", "jhal","jhol", "curry", "biriyani", "chutni" etc.

Bhaja and Bora: Bhaja comprises anything fried like alu bhaja (fried potato) etc and Bora is a kind of food which needs to dip into batter and then it is fried. Dal in West Bengal cuisine includes different types of cereals like mung dal, arhar dal,mushur dal, matar dal etc. Pora is a preparation which needs to be roasted over wood, charcoal, coal fire or sometimes directly on the flame. The pora is mixed with oil, chopped onion, chopped chilli, coriander leaves and salt to taste. This special dish dominates the West Bengal cuisine.

Shukto is another most sought after food in West Bengal. It`s a bittersweet dish eaten in summer in West Bengal. It`s a balance of bitter and sweet taste and is a soupy mixture of various vegetables. Torkari in West Bengal cuisine is a general preparation, which is made in West Bengal and is generally with "ruti" and "luchi". Torkari is originated from Persia. In Persia it means "uncooked vegetables", but in West Bengal it is a dish of cooked vegetables. Labra in West Bengal cuisine has gained importance. It`s a preparation of mixed vegetables with "Panch foron". Ghonto is prepared with different kind of finely grated vegetables like potatoes, banana, coconut, cabbage, pumpkin, green peas etc and is cooked with "foron" and ginger. Then ghee and bori are added to make it more tasty. Some non-veg ghontos are cooked with the fish head among them "murighonto "is famous for its taste in Bengal.

Apart from these dishes like Chanchra, a dish which needs the ingredients like different vegetables, fish oil and fish portions, Chochori,(a combination of varieties of vegetables and leefy green stalks. These are cut into stripes and foron, mustard oil and poppy seeds are added for flavour), also offers quite a distinct dimension to West Bengal cuisine. Spicy and zesty, tasty and nutritious West Bengal cuisine has indeed a lot to offer to the epicure. Whether it is the taste of the Bhape (a cooking process which involves steaming fish with oil and spices like paste of poppy seeds, chilli, paste of mustard seeds, salt etc and is wrapped in banana leaf), or the tang of the Bhate (It literally means "steamed with rice". Any kind of vegetable or even dal is first boiled with rice and then mashed and mixed with chopped onion, chillies, salt and mustard oil) or be it the very tang of Bhorta. (a dish which involves boiling of any kind of vegetable and mashing it and then adding onion, spices and mustard oil) or the flavour of Bhuna (Originated from Urdu, Bhuna involves the slowly cooking of meat in oil with rich and aromatic spices, without water) West Bengal cuisine is there to pamper almost every palate. Apart from the mentioned main courses the following dishes are also popular in West Bengal.

- *Chechki*: Chechki is food in which vegetables and sometimes the peels of vegetables are used. It's cooked with panch foron or kala jeera; chopped onion and garlic are added to enhance its flavour and taste.
- *Dalna*: This is a preparation of vegetables or egg. The touches of garam masala and ghee give the gravy an awesome taste.
- *Kalia*: Its gravy, mainly the preparation of fish, cooked with lots of mustard oil, onion paste, garlic paste and a sprinkle of garam masala.
- *Kofta*: Ground meat or vegetable croquettes bound together by spices and sometimes eggs, served alone or in savory gravy.
- *Kasha*: Kasha comprises the cooking of mutton or chicken with rich spices like paste of onion, ginger and garlic, turmeric, jeera paste, dhaniya paste and salt to taste. Then garam masala is added to the gravy to make it aromatic.
- *Korma*: Korma is an Urdu term which means "braised with onion". Meat or chicken is cooked in a mild onion and yoghurt sauce with ghee.
- *Polau*: Polau is cooked with fine aromatic rice. Kaju, kismish, ghee, jayfol, jayitri, choti elaichi, bari elaichi are mixed and fried before boiling. It's a sort of rich and scented dish of rice.

- *Jhal*: Jhal suggests the meaning "spicy and hot". This is one of the favourites of the Bengali people. It is a preparation which needs to be cooked with light sauce and chilli along with several spices.
- *Jhol*: It's a stew of fish or vegetable. It's lightly cooked with ginger, jeera, dhania powder, chilli powder and sometime coriander leaves are added for extra taste.

West Bengal cuisine remains incomplete without the mention of chutney. Chutney styles are strikingly different in various parts of West Bengal, each standing out with their innovativeness.

West Bengal is well known for their affection for sweets and a large variety of sweets. No meal in West Bengal is complete without the sweets. In a word West Bengal cuisine is somewhat incomplete without the sweetness of Rosogolla, Pantua, different types and flavours of Sandesh, Chomchom, Misti doi, Dorbesh, Raghabshai, Chhanar Jilepi, Kalo jam and Shor bhaja. West Bengal is also famous for its various occasions and tradition of making "pithas" which are made from rice or wheat flour, mixed with sugar and coconut. Bhapa Pitha, Pakan Pitha, Puli Pitha, Chandra Puli, Gokul, Pati Sapta, Chitai Pitha, Muger Puli and Dudh Puli are some of the cherished pithas of West Bengal.

5

The Caste System in India

A VERY BRIEF OVERVIEW

An increasing number of international companies and banks are investing in the countries of South Asia, particularly in India. This may have positive consequences for those countries. However the Dalit Solidarity Network UK believes it is increasingly important that foreign investors look carefully at their recruitment and employment policies in South Asia. Especially in India, there is a distinct and all-pervasive system of discrimination based on caste.

The United Nations and its agencies refer to it as "discrimination based on work and descent". What it means is that people who are born into specific groups, trades or castes are unable to escape from the stigma of their background or their origins. Hence those born as leatherworkers, barbers, agricultural workers or manual scavengers (toilet cleaners) will remain in those employment sectors all their lives. Sometimes people escape from the system by moving to the large towns or cities, but overall the system remains heavily in place. "Dalit" is a term which has had increasing currency in recent years. Literally, it means "the oppressed". It encompasses peoples who used to be called "untouchables", or "Harijans"; who are often also referred to as "Scheduled Castes", because the way they are referred to in the constitution of India. "Adivasi" is a term which refers to those who are members of "Scheduled Tribes".

That is, individuals who are racially distinct, as indigenous peoples, in contradistinction to the Caucasian peoples who invaded and settled India centuries ago. There is legislation stemming from the Indian Constitution which outlaws caste discrimination. The Chair of the committee which wrote the constitution of the Republic of India was Dr. Ambedkar. He was a highly educated Dalit who was admitted into Gray's Inn and was called to the Bar. He also completed his second Doctoral studies in the London School of Economics and his thesis was subsequently published as 'The problem of the rupee'.

Ambedkar became an all-India figure and the undisputed leader of the Dalits. He used this vantage-point successfully to question with blunt and militant doggedness the claim of Gandhi to represent all of India and especially the Dalits. He died in 1956 having served as India's first Law Minister. Under the constitution, the Republic of India is empowered to "promote with special care the educational and economic interests of the weaker parts of the people, and, in particular, of the Scheduled Castes and the Scheduled Tribes, and shall protect them from social injustice and all forms of exploitation".

To achieve this aim, the State has used a two-fold approach: the provision of legal safeguards against discrimination; and a "Reservation Policy" in the State sector and State Supported Sector Subsequently, there has been further legislation, which has introduced penalties for specific examples of caste discrimination. These include the 1989 Prevention of Atrocities Act, the 1993 Protection of Human Rights Act, and the 1993 Employment of Manual Scavengers Act. However, these laws are far from effective.

The Reservation Policy allocates 17% of public sector jobs to Scheduled Castes, and a further 8% to Scheduled Tribes. This approximately reflects their respective percentages in the population as a whole. Since the inception of the Reservation Policy following independence in 1947, there has been a significant increase in the number of Dalit and Adivasi government employees, but this is for a population of between about 250 million Dalits and Adivasis (167 million Dalits, and 86 million Adivasis, in 2001). 60 years after Independence, the raw percentages in government employment and public sector undertakings now do very roughly reflect the percentages of the population which are Dalit and Advasi. Because the Reservation Policy does not extend to the private sector recruitment is not done according to quota systems.

Therefore, it is not possible to get comparative figure for the proportion of Dalits and Adivasi employed in the private sector, nor—most importantly—the seniority of jobs they hold. This is unfortunate, because the private sector, in relation to the State Sector and State Supported Sector, is rather a big player. 76% of the workforce is engaged in the private sector and only 24% is employed in the State Sector and the State Supported Sector.

The present context is also that the State Sector and the State Supported Sector are shrinking, while the private sector is expanding. It is estimated that 90% of the Dalit and Adivasi workforce is engaged in menial jobs in the Private Sector (mainly agriculture and private industry). In practice, they have very little-and sometimes no—protection against discrimination. It remains extremely difficult for the 25% of the population referred to by the government as Scheduled Castes and Scheduled Tribes, to overcome the discrimination they face. This is a negative situation, both in terms of human rights, and in terms of economic potential. An object in the New York Times recently described the typing competition, in English, the journalist had with an eight-year-old Dalit girl in a village "about an hour's drive – and ten centuries – from Bangalore, India's Silicon Valley". The eightyear- old, he said, "left me in the dust, to the cheering delight of her classmates". It is important to examine the potential which is being lost because of the caste system.

The United Progressive Alliance government in New Delhi is committed to exploring the expansion of the reservation system, into the private sector. According to a recent object in the Indian Express, the state government of Maharashtra is already preparing such legislation. Foreign investment in India is high, and increasing, not the least because it is viewed as a stable country with a high growth rate. Economically, India is a "happening" country. The caste system has specific effects, when it comes to recruitment of workers for industries which are being developed with outside capital and technological know-how. To respond to this situation DSN-UK, a member of the International Dalit Solidarity Network, is proposing a set of employment principles for foreign investors in South Asia. After a series of consultations spread over a year with the private, public, and charities sectors, we have finalised what we shall call the Ambedkar Principles, and are pleased to be launching them formally on the 20 July 2006.

HISTORY OF THE INDIAN CASTE SYSTEM

POSSIBLE GENETIC ORIGIN

The origin of the caste system as it is today is still obscure. There is significant disagreement regarding whether or not castes are genetically distinct, and whether genetic differences between groups might partly explain their origin. A 1995 study by Joanna L. Mountain et al. of Stanford University concluded that there was "no clear separation into three genetically distinct groups along caste lines", although "an inferred tree revealed some clustering according to caste affiliation".

A 2001 genetic study, led by Michael Bamshad of University of Utah, found that the genetic affinity of Indians to Europeans is proportionate to caste rank, the upper castes being most similar to Europeans, whereas lower castes are more like Asians. The researchers believe that the Indo-European speakers entered India from the Northwest, admixing with or displacing the proto-Dravidian speakers. Subsequently they may have established a caste system and placed themselves primarily in higher castes. The study concludes that the Indian castes "are most likely to be of proto-Asian origin with West Eurasian admixture resulting in rank-related and sex-specific differences in the genetic affinities of castes to Asians and Europeans.". Because the Indian samples for this study were taken from a single geographical area, it remains to be investigated whether its findings can be safely generalized. A 2002-03 study by T. Kivisild et al. concluded that the "Indian tribal and caste populations derive largely from the same genetic heritage of Pleistocene southern and western Asians and have received limited gene flow from external regions since the Holocene." A 2006 genetic study by the National Institute of Biologicals in India, testing a sample of men from 32 tribal and 45 caste groups, concluded that the Indians have acquired very few genes from Indo-European speakers.

According to a 2006 study by Ismail Thanseem et al. of Centre for Cellular and Molecular Biology (India) "the vast majority (>98%) of the Indian maternal gene pool, consisting of Indo-European and Dravidian speakers, is genetically more or less uniform", while the invasions after the late Pleistocene settlement might have been mostly male-mediated.

The study concluded that the "lower caste groups might have originated with the hierarchical divisions that arose within the tribal groups with the spread of Neolithic agriculturalists, much earlier than the arrival of Aryan speakers", and "the Indo-Europeans established themselves as upper castes among this already developed caste-like class structure within the tribes." The study indicated that the Indian caste system may have its roots much before the arrival of the Indo-Aryan immigrants; a rudimentary version of the caste system may have emerged with the shift towards cultivation and settlements, and the divisions may have become more well-defined and intensified with the arrival of Indo-Aryans.

A study conducted by the Centre for Cellular and Molecular Biology in 2009 (in collaboration with Harvard Medical School, Harvard School of Public Health and the Broad Institute of Harvard and MIT) analysed half a million genetic markers across the genomes of 132 individuals from 25 ethnic groups from 13 states in India across multiple caste groups.

The study concludes, based on the impossibility of identifying any genetic indicators across caste lines, that castes in South Asia grew out of traditional tribal organizations during the formation of Indian society, and was not the product of any mythical Aryan Invasion and subjugation of Dravidian people.

HINDU SCRIPTURES

The caste system as we know today is not from the classical Hindu system. According to classical Hindu system, the society was divided into four "Varnas" (classes or categories), purely based on profession.

- *Brahmins*: The clergy, teacher, religious authority
- *Kshatriya*: The warriors, administrators, political authority
- *Vaisyas*: The merchants, farmers, the business persons
- *Shudras*: The servants, laborers

The Varna system was originally evolved for the classification of human duties in a healthy society. The system allowed free movement within the Varnas. So a Brahmin's son can be a Khatriya or Vaisya or a shudra.Simillarly a shudra's son can be a brahmin or a vaisya. The caste system practiced today is not mentioned anywhere in any of the Hindu scriptures.

Although the Hindu scriptures contain some passages that can be interpreted to sanction the caste system, they also contain indications that the caste system is not an essential part of the Hindu religion, and both sides in the debate are able to find parts in scriptures that support their views. The most ancient scriptures—the Shruti texts, or Vedas, place very little importance on the caste system, mentioning caste only sparingly and descriptively (*i.e.*, not prescriptive). Indeed, the only verse in the Rigveda which mentions all four varnas is 10.90, the Purushasûkta.

The other varnas, the Brahmâ (*i.e.* Brahmins) and Râjanya (*i.e.* Kshatriyas) are mentioned separately in some other verses in the Rigveda (*e.g.* RV 10.80.1) and the other Vedas, and rarely in the Upanishads. Some—definitely including most Smriti texts—have interpreted these as prescribing the division of society in the four varnas. A hymn from the Rig Veda seems to indicate that one's caste is not necessarily determined by that of one's family:

- *Rig Veda*: I am a bard, my father is a physician, my mother's job is to grind the corn.

In the Vedic period, there also seems to no discrimination against the Shudras (which later became an ensemble of the so-called low-castes) on the issue of hearing the sacred words of the Vedas and fully participating in all religious rights, something which became totally banned in the later times. Later scriptures such as Bhagavad Gita and Manusmriti state that the four varnas are created by God. However, at the same time, the Gita says that one's varna is to be understood from one's personal qualities and one's karma (work), not one's birth. Some scholars believe that, in its initial period, the caste system was flexible and it was merit and job based.

One could migrate from one caste to other caste by changing one's profession. This view is supported by records of sages who became Brahmins. For example, the sage Vishwamitra belonged to a Kshatriya caste, and only later became recognized as a great Brahmin sage, indicating that his caste was not determined by birth. Similarly, Valmiki, once a low-caste robber, became a great sage. Veda Vyasa, another sage, was the son of a fisherwoman. Vasishtha was a shudra and he became sage later.

Manusmriti, dated between 200 BCE and 100 AD, contains some laws that codified the caste system. The Manu Smriti belongs to a class of books that are geared towards ethics, morals, and social conduct—NOT religion. The content of these texts reflects the thinking of philosophers (like Manu) belonging to that age regarding issues pertaining to ethics, morals and social conduct. In this non-religious text (the Manu Smriti), the sage Manu explains that society is like the human body, where all body parts are required to function optimally in order to ensure the optimal function of society as a whole. *He divided this metaphoric body into 4 main constituent parts*: Head, Arms, Torso, Legs. The head of a body is required for thinking, planning, and decision making. Thus the metaphoric head of society (the Brahmins) were also responsible for these things. The arms of a body are responsible for protection of the body. Thus the arms of society were the Kshatriyas who were responsible for protection of the society. The torso of the body is responsible for consumption, production, and to hold society together as a whole. Thus, the Vaishya class was likened to the torso and constituted of the peasants, farmers, merchants, etc. Finally, the legs of a body are what carry the entire body altogether without which the body can make no movement or progress. These legs are the hardest physically working part of the body. The Shudra class of laborers was likened to the legs and was responsible for most physical labour jobs.

In this way, the entire body of society was complete and functional. No part of the body (society) was intended to be superior to another, just as all parts of the human body are equally important for optimal function. There was no hierarchy intended. This societal superiority/inferiority interpretation was a product of our flawed human nature which is to belittle those whom we believe are doing more menial work than we are. It was the tendency to think "Well, I'm a Brahman, and you're just a Shudra so I'm better or higher than you are" that caused the belief that Brahmans are the highest and Shudras are the lowest. Again, an unintentional twisting of the original caste system which was nothing more than. Furthermore, the caste a person belongs to was traditionally inherited not genetically. However, it should be noted that these castes were not permanent and inherited only. Study of the Gita and other ancient texts allows one to understand that an individual's "caste" is largely determined by his character and nature.

This is reflected in the Gita when Krishna explains to Arjun that the moment he ceases to perform the duties of a Kshatriya, he will no longer remain one. Also, in his book, "The Holy Science" (less commonly known as "Kaivalya Darshanam"), Swami Sri Yukteshwar Giri explains that an individual's caste is largely determined by the nature of one's Chitta (the deepest, purest conscious state of the unliberated soul). The nature of one's Chitta (and essentially any desire other than that for unity with God) is expressed in the desires and tendencies of man. Therefore, one ignorant of spirituality and able to comprehend only the physical world would be in a dark state of mind prevalent in the Kali Yuga that would correspond with the Shudra caste. As one's spiritual awareness grows lifetime upon lifetime, his natural caste (as opposed to the caste assigned by default from birth) climbs "upward" (spiritually, not socially or materialistically—and no, this does not imply that Brahman's are superior to anyone, just as a saint does not consider himself to be superior to anyone else, simply because he's in the later stages of spiritual evolution)

EMERGENCE OF RIGID CASTE STRUCTURES

Megasthenes, the Greek ambassador to Chandragupta Maurya's court in India classified people of India into seven classes: philosophers, peasants, herdsmen, craftsmen and traders, soldiers, government officials and councilors. In its later stages, the caste system is said to have become rigid, and caste began to be inherited rather than acquired by merit. In the past, members of different castes would not partake in various activities, such as dining and religious gatherings, together. In addition, the performance of religious rites and rituals were restricted to Brahmins, who were the designated priesthood. The "Pandaram" priests are an example of an order of Dravidian tamil priests, based in Nepal and South India.

The Pandaram maintain the same tradition as the Brahmin priests, including the use of the Sanskrit language (traditionally reserved for the Brahmins) for the rituals. While they are not generally as well trained as the Brahmin priests, they are highly respected within their community and are addressed with reverence. According to the Manusmriti, every caste belongs to one of the four varnas (Brahmin, Kshtriya, Vaishya, and Shudra). However, there have been many disputes about the varna of many castes, such as castes being considered Kshatriya by some scholars, while described as Shudra by others. While texts such as the Manusmriti attempted to rationalize ambiguous castes by placing them in varna-sankaras (*i.e.* mixed varna), the fact remains that Indian society was, and is, composed of numerous geographically diversified but endogamous groups. With many occupational groups practicing endogamy within a particular region, as well as numerous sub-divisions within the four main castes, a more complex system of subcastes and jâtis is evident. The jatis have broken up into clans like Agarwal, Iyer, etc.

Mobility Across the Castes

The view of the caste system as "static and unchanging" has been disputed by many scholars. For instance, sociologists such as Bernard Buber and Marriott McKim describe how the perception of the caste system as a static and textual stratification has given way to the perception of the caste system as a more processual, empirical and contextual stratification. Other sociologists such as Y.B Damle have applied theoretical models to explain mobility and flexibility in the caste system in India. According to these scholars, groups of lower-caste individuals could seek to elevate the status of their caste by attempting to emulate the practices of higher castes. Some scholars believe that the relative ranking of other castes was fluid or differed from one place to another prior to the arrival of the British.

The distinctions, particularly between the Brahmans and the other castes, were in theory sharper, but in practice it now appears that social restrictions were not so rigid. Brahmans often lived off the land and founded dynasties. Most of the groups claiming Kshatriya status had only recently acquired it. The conscious reference to being Kshatriya, a characteristic among Rajputs, is a noticeable feature in post-Gupta politics. The fact that many of these dynasties were of obscure origin suggests some social mobility: a person of any caste, having once acquired political power, could also acquire a genealogy connecting him with the traditional lineages and conferring Kshatriya status.

A number of new castes, such as the Kayasthas (scribes) and Khatris (traders), are mentioned in the sources of this period. According to the Brahmanic sources, they originated from intercaste marriages, but this is clearly an attempt at rationalizing their rank in the hierarchy. Many of these new castes played a major role in society. The hierarchy of castes did not have a uniform distribution throughout the country. Flexibility in caste laws permitted very low-caste religious clerics such as Valmiki to compose the Ramayana, which became a central work of Hindu scripture. According to some psychologists, mobility across broad caste lines may have been "minimal", though sub-castes (jatis) may change their social status over the generations by fission, re-location, and adoption of new rituals.

Sociologist M. N. Srinivas has also debated the question of rigidity in Caste. In an ethnographic study of the Coorgs of Karnataka, he observed considerable flexibility and mobility in their caste hierarchies. He asserts that the caste system is far from a rigid system in which the position of each component caste is fixed for all time. Movement has always been possible, and especially in the middle regions of the hierarchy. It was always possible for groups born into a lower caste to "rise to a higher position by adopting vegetarianism and teetotalism" *i.e.* adopt the customs of the higher castes. While theoretically "forbidden", the process was not uncommon in practice. The concept of sanskritization, or the adoption of upper-caste norms by the lower castes, addressed the actual complexity and fluidity of caste relations. Historical examples of mobility in the Indian Caste System among Hindus have been researched. There is also precedent of certain Shudra families within the temples of the Shrivaishava sect in South India elevating their caste.

HISTORICAL ADVANTAGES OF THE CASTE SYSTEM

Historically, the caste system offered several advantages to the population of the Indian subcontinent. While Caste is nowadays seen by instances that render it anachronistic, in its original form the caste system served as an important instrument of order in a society in which mutual consent rather than compulsion ruled; where the ritual rights as well as the economic obligations of members of one caste or sub-caste were strictly circumscribed in relation to those of any other caste or sub-caste; where one was born into one's caste and retained one's station in society for life; where merit was inherited, where equality existed within the caste, but inter-caste relations were unequal and hierarchical. A well-defined system of mutual interdependence through a division of labour created security within a community.

- Preservation of order in society through the use of institutional stratification of social groups.
- Integration of foreigners and invading forces into Indian culture by assigning a caste to them (a process that historian Jawaharlal Nehru referred to as "Indianization"): India has faced repeated invasions from outside the region, dating back to the Macedonian invasion by Alexander the Great. Most invaders were swiftly assimilated into ancient Indian society by assigning them specific castes. Examples include the Kambojas, believed to be of Indo-Scythian descent, who were retroactively assigned a social position in the Manusmriti.
- The Varna system, with its normative interpretation as a division of labour, had and continues to have a heavy bias towards spiritual evolution. The deep religious proclivities and the urge for spiritual uplift had induced the people to search for simpler and effective ways to achieve the spiritual goal which led to innovations like the Bhakti movement which had a powerful impact on the socio-cultural-spiritual life of the people even at mass level without distinctions of caste or class or other social differences. It is these deeply run cultural roots which caused an abiding following for Hinduism even in the face of unrelenting assaults by other religions and had in fact continued to influence the lives of people even after their conversion to other faiths. Thus, the caste system can be said to have preserved ancient cultural values in Indian society.
- The caste system played an influential role in shaping economic activities. The caste system functioned much like medieval European guilds, ensuring the division of labour, providing for the training of apprentices and, in some cases, allowing manufacturers to achieve narrow specialisation. For

instance, in certain regions, producing each variety of cloth was the speciality of a particular sub-caste.

- Philosophers argue that the majority of people would be comfortable in stratified endogamous groups and have been in ancient times. Membership in a particular caste, with its associated narrative, history and genealogy would instill in its members a sense of group accomplishment and cultural pride. Such sentiments are routinely expressed by the Marathas, for instance.

BRITISH RULE

The caste system had been a fascination of the British since their arrival in India. Coming from a society that was divided by class, the British attempted to equate the caste system to the class system. As late as 1937 Professor T. C. Hodson stated that: "Class and caste stand to each other in the relation of family to species. The general classification is by classes, the detailed one by castes.

The former represents the external, the latter the internal view of the social organization." The difficulty with definitions such as this is that class is based on political and economic factors, caste is not. In fairness to Professor Hodson, by the time of his writing, caste had taken on many of the characteristics that he ascribed to it and that his predecessors had ascribed to it but during the 19th century caste was not what the British believed it to be. It did not constitute a rigid description of the occupation and social level of a given group and it did not bear any real resemblance to the class system. However, this will be dealt with later in this thesis. At present, the main concern is that the British saw caste as a way to deal with a huge population by breaking it down into discrete chunks with specific characteristics. Moreover, as will be seen later in this document, it appears that the caste system extant in the late 19th and early 20th century has been altered as a result of British actions so that it increasingly took on the characteristics that were ascribed to by the British. One of the main tools used in the British attempt to understand the Indian population was the census. Attempts were made as early as the beginning of the 19th century to estimate populations in various regions of the country but these, as earlier noted, were methodologically flawed and led to grossly erroneous conclusions. It was not until 1872 that a planned comprehensive census was attempted. This was done under the direction of Henry Beverely, Inspector General of Registration in Bengal. The primary purpose given for the taking of the census, that of governmental preparedness to deal with disaster situations, was both laudable and logical. However, the census went well beyond counting heads or even enquiring into sex ratios or general living conditions.

Among the many questions were enquiries regarding nationality, race, tribe, religion and caste. Certainly none of these things were relevant to emergency measures responses by the government. Further, neither the notion of curiosity nor planned subterfuge on the part of the administration suffices to explain their inclusion in the census. On the question of race or nationality it could be argued that these figures were needed to allow analyses of the various areas in an attempt to predict internal unrest. However, there does not appear to have been any use made of the figures from that perspective. With regard to the information on religion and caste, the same claim could be made but once again there does not appear to have been any analyses done with the thought of internal disturbance in mind. Obviously there had to be some purpose to the gathering of this data since due to the size of both the population and the territory to be covered, extraneous questions would not have been included due to time factors.

Therefore, there must have been a reason of some sort for their inclusion. That reason was, quite simply, the British belief that caste was the key to understanding the people of India. Caste was seen as the essence of Indian society, the system through which it was possible to classify all of the various groups of indigenous people according to their ability, as reflected by caste, to be of service to the British. Caste was seen as an indicator of occupation, social standing, and intellectual ability. It was, therefore necessary to include it in the census if the census was to serve the purpose of giving the government the information it needed in order to make optimum use of the people under its administration.

Moreover, it becomes obvious that British conceptions of racial purity were interwoven with these judgements of people based on caste when reactions to censuses are examined. Beverly concluded that a group of Muslims were in fact converted low caste Hindus. This raised howls of protest from representatives of the group as late as 1895 since it was felt that this was a slander and a lie. H. H. Risely, Commissioner of the 1901 census, also showed British beliefs in an 1886 publication which stated that race sentiment, far from being: a figment of the intolerant pride of the Brahman, rests upon a foundation of fact which scientific methods confirm, that it has shaped the intricate grouping of the caste system, and has preserved the Aryan type in comparative purity throughout Northern India.

Here is a prime example of the racial purity theories that had been developing throughout the 19th century. Here also is the plainest explanation for the inclusion of the questions on race, caste and religion being included with the censuses. Thus far this thesis has dwelt almost entirely with British actions to the exclusion of any mention of Indian actions and reactions. This should not be taken to mean that the Indians were passive or without input into the process. Any change within a society requires the participation of all the groups if it is to have any lasting effect. The Indian people had a very profound effect on the formulation of the census and their analysis. However, Indian actions and reaction must be considered within the context of Indian history and Indian culture in the same way that British actions must be considered within British cultural context.

For this reason, it has been necessary to postpone consideration of Indian reactions and contributions to the British activities until the next part of this thesis which will then be followed by a more in depth examination of the development of British attitudes. Finally, the results of the combination of both Indian and British beliefs will be examined with a view to reaching a consensus on how they affected the compilation of and conclusions reached through the censuses. The word caste is not a word that is indigenous to India. It originates in the Portuguese word casta which means race,breed, race or lineage. However, during the 19th century, the term caste increasingly took on the connotations of the word race. Thus, from the very beginning of western contact with the subcontinent European constructions have been imposed on Indian systems and institutions.

To fully appreciate the caste system one must step away from the definitions imposed by Europeans and look at the system as a whole, including the religious beliefs that are an integral part of it. To the British, viewing the caste system from the outside and on a very superficial level, it appeared to be a static system of social ordering that allowed the ruling class or Brahmins, to maintain their power over the other classes. What the British failed to realise was that Hindus existed in a different cosmological frame than did the British. The concern of the true Hindu was not his ranking economically within society but rather his ability to regenerate on a higher plane of existence during each successive life.

REFORM MOVEMENTS

There have been cases of upper caste Hindus warming to the Dalits and Hindu priests, demoted to outcaste ranks, who continued practising the religion. An example of the latter was Dnyaneshwar, who was excommunicated from society in the 13th century, but continued to compose the Dnyaneshwari, a Dharmic commentary on the Bhagavad Gita. Other excommunicated Brahmins, such as Eknath, fought for the rights of untouchables during the Bhakti period.

Historical examples of Dalit priests include Chokhamela in the 14th century, who was India's first recorded Dalit poet, Raidas, born into Dalit cobblers, and others. The 15th century saint Ramananda also accepted all castes, including untouchables, into his fold. Most of these saints subscribed to the Bhakti movements in Hinduism during the medieval period that rejected casteism.Nandanar, a low-caste Hindu cleric, also rejected casteism and accepted Dalits. Many movements in Hinduism have welcomed Dalits into their fold, the foremost being the Bhakti movements of the medieval period. Early Dalit politics involved many Hindu reform movements which arose primarily as a reaction to the tactics of Christian Missionaries in India and their attempts to mass-convert Dalits to Christianity under the allure of escaping the caste system (unfortunately, there is Caste system among Indian Christians among large parts of Indian Christians).

In the 19th century, the Brahmo Samaj under Raja Ram Mohan Roy, actively campaigned against untouchability. The Arya Samaj founded by Swami Dayanand also renounced discrimination against Dalits.Sri Ramakrishna Paramahamsa founded the Ramakrishna Mission that participated in the emancipation of Dalits. Upper caste Hindus, such as Mannathu Padmanabhan also participated in movements to abolish Untouchability against Dalits, opening his family temple for Dalits to worship. While there always have been places for Dalits to worship, the first "upper-caste" temple to openly welcome Dalits into their fold was the Laxminarayan Temple in Wardha in the year 1928 (the move was spearheaded by reformer Jamnalal Bajaj).

Also, the Satnami movement was founded by Guru Ghasidas, a Dalit himself. Other reformers, such as Mahatma Jyotirao Phule also worked for the emancipation of Dalits. Another example of Dalit emancipation was the Temple Entry Proclamation issued by the last Maharaja of Travancore in the Indian state of Kerala in the year 1936. The Maharaja proclaimed that "outcastes should not be denied the consolations and the solace of the Hindu faith". Even today, the Sri Padmanabhaswamy temple that first welcomed Dalits in the state of Kerala is revered by the Dalit Hindu community.

The 1930s saw key struggles between Mahatma Gandhi and B.R. Ambedkar, most notably over whether Dalits would have separate electorates or joint electorates with reserved seats. The Indian National Congress was the only national organisation with a large Dalit following, but Gandhi failed to gain their commitment. Ambedkar, a Dalit himself, developed a deeper analysis of Untouchability, but lacked a workable political strategy: his conversion to Buddhism in 1956, along with millions of followers, highlighted the failure of his political endeavours. India's first Prime Minister, Jawaharlal Nehru, based on his own relationship with Dalit reformer Ambedkar, also spread information about the dire need to eradicate untouchability for the benefit of the Dalit community.

In more contemporary times, India has had an elected Dalit president, K. R. Narayanan, who has stated that he was well-treated in his community of largely upper-caste Hindus (24 July 2002). Another popular Harijan includes Babaji Palwankar Baloo, who joined the Hindu Mahasabha and was both a politician and a cricketer. He was an independence fighter. In addition, other Hindu groups have reached out to the Dalit community in an effort to reconcile with them, with productive results. On August 2006, Dalit activist Namdeo Dhasal engaged in dialogue with the Rashtriya Swayamsevak Sangh in an attempt to"bury the hatchet".

Also, the"Pandaram" are an order of Dravidian Tamil Hindu priests (a task traditionally reserved for the Brahmins) based largely in Nepal and parts of South India. These Pandaram priests maintain the same tradition as the Brahmin priests, including using Sanskrit for the rituals.

They perform religious ceremonies from weddings to death rituals. They are highly respected within the tamil community and are addressed reverentially. Also, Hindu temples are increasingly more receptive to Dalit priests, such as Suryavanshi Das, the Dalit priest of a notable temple in the midst of Patna, the capital of Bihar. Discrimination against Hindu Dalits is on a slow but steady decline. The results of Bhakti Movements are clearly visible. Numerous Hindu Dalits have achieved affluence in society, although vast still remain poor irrespective of caste. In urban India, discrimination against Dalits is largely disappeared, but rural Dalits are struggling to elevate themselves. Government organizations and NGO's work to emancipate them from discrimination, and many Hindu organizations have spoken in their favour.

CASTE AND SOCIAL STATUS

Traditionally, although the political power lay with the Kshatriyas, historians portrayed the Brahmins as custodians and interpreters of Dharma, who enjoyed much prestige and many advantages. Fa Hien, a Buddhist pilgrim from China, visited India around 400 AD."Only the lot of the Chandals he found unenviable; outcastes by reason of their degrading work as disposers of dead, they were universally shunned... But no other part of the population were notably disadvantaged, no other caste distinctions attracted comment from the Chinese pilgrim, and no oppressive caste'system' drew forth his surprised censure." In this period kings of Sudra and Brahmin origin were as common as those of Kshatriya varna and caste system was not wholly prohibitive and repressive.

The castes did not constitute a rigid description of the occupation or the social status of a group. Since British society was divided by class, the British attempted to equate the Indian caste system to their own social class system. They saw caste as an indicator of occupation, social standing, and intellectual ability. Intentionally or unintentionally, the caste system became more rigid during the British Raj, when the British started to enumerate castes during the ten year census and codified the system under their rule.

The Harijans, or the people outside the caste system, had the lowest social status. The Harijans, earlier referred to as untouchables by some, worked in what were seen as unhealthy, unpleasant or polluting jobs. In the past, the Harijans suffered from social segregation and restrictions, in addition to extreme poverty. They were not allowed temple worship with others, nor water from the same sources. Persons of higher castes would not interact with them. If somehow a member of a higher caste came into physical or social contact with an untouchable, the member of the higher caste was defiled, and had to bathe thoroughly to purge him or herself of the impurity. Social discrimination developed even among the Harijans; sub-castes among Harijans, such as the dhobi and nai, would not interact with lower-order Bhangis, who were described as"outcastes even among outcastes". Sociologists have commented on the historical advantages offered by a rigid social structure as well as its drawbacks. While caste is now seen as anachronistic, in its original form the caste system served as an instrument of order in a society where mutual consent rather than compulsion ruled; where the ritual rights and the economic obligations of members of one caste or sub-caste were strictly circumscribed in relation to those of any other caste or sub-caste; where one was born into one's caste and retained one's station in society for life; where merit was inherited, where equality existed within the caste, but inter-caste relations were unequal and hierarchical.

A well-defined system of mutual interdependence through a division of labour created security within a community. In addition, the division of labour on the basis of ethnicity allowed immigrants and foreigners to quickly integrate into their own caste niches.

The caste system played an influential role in shaping economic activities, where it functioned much like medieval European guilds, ensuring the division of labour, providing for the training of apprentices and, in some cases, allowing manufacturers to achieve narrow specialisation. For instance, in certain regions, producing each variety of cloth was the speciality of a particular sub-caste. Additionally, some philosophers have argued that the majority of people would be comfortable in stratified endogamous groups, as they were in ancient times.

It is believed that the relative ranking of other castes was fluid or differed from one place to another prior to the arrival of the British. Sociologists such as Bernard Buber and Marriott McKim describe how the perception of the caste system as a static and textual stratification has given way to the perception of the caste system as a more processual, empirical and contextual stratification. Other sociologists such as Y.B Damle have applied theoretical models to explain mobility and flexibility in the caste system in India. According to these scholars, groups of lower-caste individuals could seek to elevate the status of their caste by attempting to emulate the practices of higher castes. Flexibility in caste laws permitted very low-caste religious clerics such as Valmiki to compose the Ramayana, which became a central work of Hindu scripture. There is also precedent of certain Shudra families within the temples of the Sri Vaishnava sect in South India elevating their caste.

The following is a list of changes in varna cited in Hindu texts:

- Manu eldest son [Priyavrata] became king, a Kshatriya. Out of his ten sons seven became kings while three became Brahman. Their names were Mahavira, Kavi and Savana.
- Kavash–ailush was born to a Sudra and attained varn of a Rishi. He became mantra-drashta to numerous Vedic mantras in Rig-Veda 10th Mandal.
- Jabala's son [Satyakama] born from unknown father became Rishi by his qualities.
- [Matanga] became a Rishi after his birth in low Varna.

According to some psychologists, mobility across broad caste lines may have been "minimal", though sub-castes (jatis) may have changed their social status over the generations by fission, re-location, and adoption of new rituals. Sociologist M. N. Srinivas has also debated the question of rigidity in Caste. In an ethnographic study of the Coorgs of Karnataka, he observed considerable flexibility and mobility in their caste hierarchies. He asserts that the caste system is far from a rigid system in which the position of each component caste is fixed for all time; instead, movement has always been possible, especially in the middle regions of the hierarchy.

It was always possible for groups born into a lower caste to "rise to a higher position by adopting vegetarianism and teetotalism" *i.e.* adopt the customs of the higher castes. While theoretically "forbidden", the process was not uncommon in practice. The concept of sanskritization, or the adoption of upper-caste norms by the lower castes, addressed the complexity and fluidity of caste relations.

The fact that many of the dynasties were of obscure origin suggests some social mobility: a person of any caste, having once acquired political power, could also acquire a genealogy connecting him with the traditional lineages and conferring Kshatriya status. A number of new castes, such as the Kayasthas (scribes) and Khatris (traders), are mentioned in the sources of this period. According to the Brahmanic sources, they originated from intercaste marriages, but this is clearly an attempt at rationalizing their rank in the hierarchy. Khatri appears to be unquestionably a Prakritised form of the Sanskrit Kshatriya. Many of these new castes played a major role in society. The hierarchy of castes did not have a uniform distribution throughout the country.

MODERN STATUS OF THE CASTE SYSTEM

In some rural areas and small towns, the caste system is still very rigid. Caste is also a factor in the politics of India. The Government of India has officially documented castes and sub-castes, primarily to determine those deserving reservation (positive discrimination in education and jobs) through the census. The Indian reservation system, though limited in scope, relies entirely on quotas.

The Government lists consist of Scheduled Castes, Scheduled Tribes and Other Backward Classes:

- *Scheduled castes (SC)*: Scheduled castes generally consist of "Dalit". The present population is 16% of the total population of India (around 160 million). For example, the Delhi state has 49 castes listed as SC.
- *Scheduled tribes (ST)*: Scheduled tribes generally consist of tribal groups. The present population is 7% of the total population of India *i.e.* around 70 million.
- *Other Backward Classes (OBC)*: The Mandal Commission covered more than 3000 castes under OBC Category and stated that OBCs form around 52% of the Indian population. However, the National Sample Survey puts the figure at 32%. There is substantial debate over the exact number of OBCs in India; it is generally estimated to be sizable, but many believe that it is lower than the figures quoted by either the Mandal Commission or the National Sample Survey.

The caste-based reservations in India have led to widespread protests, such as the 2006 Indian anti-reservation protests, with many complaining of reverse discrimination against the forward castes (the castes that do not qualify for the reservation). Many view negative treatment of forward castes as socially divisive and equally wrong.

CASTE SYSTEM AMONG NON-HINDUS

CHRISTIANS

In some parts of India, Christians are stratified by sect, location, and the castes of their predecessors, usually in reference to upper class Syrian Malabar Nasranis. Christians in Kerala are divided into several communities, including Syrian Christians and the so-called "Latin" or "New Rite" Christians.

Kerala

Syrian Christians derive status within the caste system from the tradition that they are converted High caste Hindus such as Namboodiris, Nairs and Jews (Israelites), who were evangelized by St. Thomas. Writers Arundhati Roy and Anand Kurian have written personal accounts of the caste system at work in their community. Syrian Christians, especially Knanaya Christians, tend to be endogamous and not intermarry with other Christian castes.

The Latin Rite Christians were among the scheduled castes in the coastal belt of Kerala, where fishing was the primary occupation. They were actively converted by missionaries in the 16th and 19th centuries. These missionary activities were carried out by Western Latin Rite missionaries who did not understand the significance of the caste system in India; none of the Syrian churches had participated in such activities among the scheduled castes of India because they were aware of the prejudices of the caste system. The government of India later granted this group OBC status. Very rarely are there intermarriages between Syrian Christians and Latin Rite Christians. Anthropologists have noted that the caste hierarchy among Christians in Kerala is much more polarized than the

Hindu practices in the surrounding areas, due to a lack of jatis. Also, the caste status is kept even if the sect allegiance is switched (*i.e.* from Syrian Catholic to Syrian Orthodox).

Goa

In the Indian state of Goa, mass conversions were carried out by Portuguese Latin missionaries from the 16th century onwards. The Hindu converts retained their caste practices. The continued maintenance of the caste system among the Christians in Goa is attributed to the nature of mass conversions of entire villages, as a result of which existing social stratification was not affected.

The Portuguese colonists, even during the Goan Inquisition, did not do anything to change the caste system. Thus, the original Hindu Brahmins in Goa now became Christian Bamons and the Kshatriya became Christian noblemen called Chardos. The Christian clergy became almost exclusively Bamon. Vaishyas who converted to Christianity became Gauddos, and Shudras became Sudirs. Finally, the Dalits or "Untouchables" who converted to Christianity became Maharas and Chamars, the latter an appellation of the anti-Dalit ethnic slur Chamaar. Units of social stratification, termed "castes" by many, have developed among Muslims in some parts of South Asia. Sources indicate that the castes among Muslims developed as the result of close contact with Hindu culture and Hindu converts to Islam. The Sachar Committee's report commissioned by the government of India and released in 2006 documents the continued stratification in Muslim society.

MUSLIMS

Among Muslims, those who are referred to as Ashrafs are presumed to have a superior status derived from their foreign Arab ancestry, while the Ajlafs are assumed to be converts from Hinduism, and have a lower status. In addition, the Arzal caste among Muslims was regarded by anti-caste activists like Ambedkar as the equivalent of untouchables. In the Bengal region of India, some Muslims stratify their society according to 'Quoms'. While many scholars have asserted that the Muslim castes are not as acute in their discrimination as those of the Hindus, some like Ambedkar argued that the social evils in Muslim society were "worse than those seen in Hindu society".

BUDDHISTS

The Buddhists also had a caste system. In Sri Lanka, the Rodis might have been outcast by the Sri Lankan Buddhists due to the absence of ahimsa (non-violence), a central tenet of Buddhism, among their beliefs. The writer Raghavan notes, "That a form of worship in which human offerings formed the essential ritual would have been anathema to the Buddhist way of life goes without saying; and it needs no stretch of imagination that any class of people in whom the cult prevailed or survived even in an attenuated form would have been pronounced by the sangha (*i.e.* the Buddhist clergy) as exiles from the social order." Savarkar believed that the status of the backward castes (*e.g.* Chamar) that performed non-violence only worsened. When Ywan Chwang traveled to South India after the period of the Chalukyan Empire, he noticed that the caste system had existed among the Buddhists and Jains.

JAINS

Jains also had castes in places such as Bihar. For example, in the village of Bundela, there were several "jaats" (groups) amongst the Jains. A person of one "jaat" cannot intermingle with a Jain or another "jaat". They also could not eat with the members of other "jaats".

SIKH

The Sikh Gurus criticized the hierarchy of the caste system. While some castes were widely perceived as being better or higher than others (*e.g.* Brahmins being higher than others), they preached that all parts of society were valuable and that merit and hard-work were essential aspects of life. In the Shiromani Gurdwara Prabandhak Committee, out of 140 seats, 20 are reserved for low caste Sikhs. However, the quota system has attracted much criticism due to the lack of meritocracy, since merit is considered the single most important component of winning a seat. Baha'i Faith has grown to prominence in India, since its philosophy of the unity of humanity attracted many of the lower castes.

CASTE-RELATED VIOLENCE

According to government statistics, there were 110,000 registered cases of violence, murder, rape and other atrocities committed against Dalits in 2005. Independent India has witnessed a considerable amount of violence and hate crimes motivated by caste. Various incidents of violence against Dalits, usually by other backward castes such as Kherlanji Massacre and the killings in 2010 at Mirchpur, have been reported from many parts of India. Many violent protests by Dalits, such as the 2006 Dalit protests in Maharashtra, have also been reported. An exception to the norm is the Ranvir Sena, a caste-supremacist fringe paramilitary group based in Bihar, which committed violent acts against Dalits.

Phoolan Devi, who belonged to the Mallah lower caste, was mistreated and raped by upper-caste Thakurs at a young age. She became a bandit and carried out violent robberies against upper-caste people. In 1981, her gang massacred twenty-two Thakurs, most of whom were not involved in her kidnapping or rape. Later, she became a politician and Member of Parliament.

CASTE POLITICS IN INDIA

B. R. Ambedkar and Jawaharlal Nehru had radically different approaches to caste, especially concerning constitutional politics and the status of untouchables. Since the 1980s, caste has become a major issue in the politics of India. The Mandal Commission was established in 1979 to"identify the socially or educationally backward" and to consider the question of seat reservations and quotas for people to redress caste discrimination. In 1980, the commission's report affirmed the affirmative action practice under Indian law, whereby additional members of lower castes—the other backward classes—were given exclusive access to another 27 per cnet of government jobs and slots in public universities, in addition to the 23 per cnet already reserved for the Dalits and Tribals. When V. P. Singh's administration tried to implement the recommendations of the Mandal Commission in 1989, massive protests were held in the country. Many alleged that the politicians were trying to cash in on caste-based reservations for purely pragmatic electoral purposes.

Many political parties in India have openly indulged in caste-based votebank politics. Parties such as Bahujan Samaj Party (BSP), the Samajwadi Party and the Janata Dal claim that they are representing the backward castes, and rely on OBC support, often in alliance with Dalit and Muslim support, to win elections. Remarkably, in what is called a landmark election in the history of India's biggest state of Uttar Pradesh, the Bahujan Samaj Party was able to garner a majority in the state assembly elections with the support of the high caste Brahmin community.

CRITICISM OF CASTE

There has been criticism of the caste system from both within and outside of India. Criticism of the Caste system in Hindu society came both from the Hindu fold and Dalit.

HISTORICAL CRITICISM

'NOT Both Buddha and Mahavira severely criticized and opposed the caste system. They preached people to break the bonds of caste system. Many bhakti period saints, including Nanak, Kabir, Caitanya, Dnyaneshwar, Eknath, Ramanuja and Tukaram, rejected all caste-based discrimination and accepted disciples from all the castes. Many Hindu reformers such as Swami Vivekananda believe that there is no place for the caste system in Hinduism. The 15th century saint Ramananda accepted all castes, including untouchables, into his fold. Most of these saints subscribed to the Bhakti movements in Hinduism during the medieval period that rejected casteism. Nandanar, a low-caste Hindu cleric, also rejected casteism and accepted Dalits. Some other movements in Hinduism have also welcomed lower-castes into their fold, the earliest being the Bhakti movements of the medieval period. Dalit politics involved many reform movements; these arose primarily as a reaction to the advent of Christian missionaries in India and their attempts to convert Dalits, who were attracted to the prospect of escaping the caste system. In the 19th Century, the Brahmo Samaj under Raja Ram Mohan Roy actively campaigned against untouchability and casteism.

The Arya Samaj founded by Swami Dayanand also renounced discrimination against Dalits. Sri Ramakrishna Paramahamsa and his disciple Swami Vivekananda founded the Ramakrishna Mission that participated in the emancipation of Dalits. Upper-caste Hindus such as Mannathu Padmanabhan participated in movements to abolish untouchability against Dalits; Padmanabhan opened his family temple to Dalits for worship. Narayana Guru, a pious Hindu and an authority on the Vedas, also criticized casteism and campaigned for the rights of lower-caste Hindus within the context of Hinduism. The first upper-caste temple to openly welcome Dalits into their fold was the Laxminarayan Temple in Wardha in the year 1928; the move was spearheaded by reformer Jamnalal Bajaj.

The caste system has also been criticized by many Indian social reformers. Some reformers, such as Jyotirao Phule and Iyothee Thass, argued that the lower caste people were the original inhabitants of India, who had been conquered in the ancient past by"Brahmin invaders." Mahatma Gandhi coined the term Harijan, a euphemistic word for untouchable, literally meaning Sons of God. B. R. Ambedkar, born in Hindu Dalit community, was a heavy critic of the caste system. He pioneered the Dalit Buddhist movement in India, and asked his followers to leave Hinduism, and convert to Buddhism. India's first Prime Minister, Jawaharlal Nehru, based on his own relationship with Dalit reformer Ambedkar, supported the eradication of untouchability for the benefit of the Dalit community. In 1936, the Maharaja proclaimed that"outcastes should not be denied the consolations and the solace of the

Hindu faith". Even today, the Sri Padmanabhaswamy temple that first welcomed Dalits in the state of Kerala is revered by the Dalit Hindu community.

CONTEMPORARY CRITICISM

Organizations such as the Rashtriya Swayamsevak Sangh have actively criticized the caste system. Some activists consider the caste system a form of racial discrimination. At the United Nations Conference Against Racism in Durban, South Africa in March 2001, participants condemned discrimination based on the caste system and tried to pass a resolution declaring caste as a basis for segregation and oppression a form of apartheid. However, no formal resolution was passed. The alleged maltreatment of Dalits in India has been described by some authors as "India's hidden apartheid". Critics of the accusations point to substantial improvements in the position of Dalits in post-independence India, consequent to the strict implementation of the rights and privileges enshrined in the Constitution of India, as implemented by the Protection of Civil rights Act, 1955. They also note that India has had a Dalit president, K.R. Narayanan, and argue that the practise had disappeared in urban public life.

According to William A. Haviland, however:

- Although India's national constitution of 1950 sought to abolish cast discrimination and the practice of untouchability, the caste system remains deeply entrenched in Hindu culture and is still widespread throughout southern Asia, especially in rural India. In what has been called India's "hidden apartheid", entire villages in many Indian states remain completely segregated by caste. Representing about 15 per cent of India's population—or some 160 million people—the widely scattered Dalits endure near complete social isolation, humiliation, and discrimination based exclusively on their birth status. Even a Dalit's shadow is believed to pollute the upper classes. They may not cross the line dividing their part of the village from that occupied by higher castes, drink water from public wells, or visit the same temples as the higher castes. Dalit children are still often made to sit in the back of classrooms.

Sociologists Kevin Reilly, Stephen Kaufman and Angela Bodino, while critical of casteism, conclude that modern India does not practice any apartheid since there is no state-sanctioned discrimination. They write that casteism in India is presently "not apartheid. In fact, untouchables, as well as tribal people and members of the lowest castes in India benefit from broad affirmative action programmes and are enjoying greater political power."</ref> The Constitution of India places special emphasis cn outlawing caste discrimination, especially the practice of untouchability.

CASTE AND RACE

Allegations that caste amounts to race were addressed and rejected by B.R. Ambedkar, an advocate for Dalit rights and critic of untouchability. He wrote that "The Brahmin of Punjab is racially of the same stock as the Chamar of Punjab. The Caste system does not demarcate racial division. The Caste system is a social division of people of the same race", Such allegations have also been rejected by sociologists such as Andre Béteille, who writes that treating caste as a form of racism is "politically mischievous" and worse, "scientifically nonsensical" since there is no discernible difference in the racial characteristics between Brahmins and Scheduled Castes.

He states, "Every social group cannot be regarded as a race simply because we want to protect it against prejudice and discrimination". The Indian government also rejects the claims of equivalency between caste and racial discrimination, pointing out that the caste issues are essentially intra-racial and intra-cultural. Indian Attorney General Soli Sorabjee insisted that "[t]he only reason India wants caste discrimination kept off the agenda is that it will distract participants from the main topic: racism. Caste discrimination in India is undeniable but caste and race are entirely distinct". Many scholars dispute the claim that casteism is akin to racism. Sociologist M. N. Srinivas has debated the question of rigidity in caste. Others have applied theoretical models to explain mobility and flexibility in the caste system in India. According to these scholars, groups of lower-caste individuals could seek to elevate the status of their caste by attempting to emulate the practices of higher castes.

In her book Democracy and Authoritarianism in South Asia, Pakistani-American sociologist Ayesha Jalal writes, "As for Hinduism, the hierarchical principles of the Brahmanical social order have always been contested from within Hindu society, suggesting that equality has been and continues to be both valued and practiced." In India, some observers felt that the caste system must be viewed as a system of exploitation of poor low-ranking groups by more prosperous high-ranking groups. In many parts of India, land is largely held by high-ranking property owners of the dominant castes, who economically exploit low-ranking landless labourers and poor artisans. Matt Cherry claims that karma underpins the caste system, which traditionally determines the position and role of every member of Hindu society. Caste determines an individual's place in society, the work he or she may carry out, and who he or she may marry and meet. According to him, Hindus believe that the karma of previous life will determine the caste an individual will be (re)born into.

On 29 March 2007, the Supreme Court of India, as an interim measure, stayed the law providing for 27% reservation for Other Backward Classes in educational institutions. This was done in response to a public interest litigation—Ashoka Kumar Thakur vs. Union of India. The Court held that the 1931 census could not be a determinative factor for identifying the OBCs for the purpose of providing reservation. The court also observed, "Reservation cannot be permanent and appear to perpetuate backwardness". However, the Supreme Court later upheld the reservation.

GENETIC ANALYSIS

There have been several studies examining caste members as discrete populations, examining the hypothesis that their ancestors have different origins. A 2002–03 study by T. Kivisild et al. concluded that the "Indian tribal and caste populations derive largely from the same genetic heritage of Pleistocene southern and western Asians and have received limited gene flow from external regions since the Holocene." Studies point to the various Indian caste groups having similar genetic origins and having negligible genetic input from outside south Asia. Because the Indian samples for this study were taken from a single geographical area, it remains to be investigated whether its findings can be safely generalized. An earlier 1995 study by Joanna L. Mountain et al. of Stanford University had concluded that there was "no clear separation into three genetically distinct groups along caste lines", although "an inferred tree revealed some clustering according to caste affiliation". A 2006 study by Ismail Thanseem et al. of Centre for Cellular and Molecular Biology (India) concluded that the "lower caste groups might have originated with the hierarchical divisions that arose within the tribal groups with the spread of Neolithic agriculturalists, much earlier than the arrival of Aryan speakers", and "the Indo-Europeans established themselves as upper castes among this already developed caste-like class structure within the tribes."

The study indicated that the Indian caste system may have its roots long before the arrival of the Indo-Aryans; a rudimentary version of the caste system may have emerged with the shift towards cultivation and settlements, and the divisions may have become more well-defined and intensified with the arrival of Indo-Aryans. A 2006 genetic study by the National Institute of Biologicals in India, testing a sample of men from 32 tribal and 45 caste groups, concluded that the Indians have acquired very few genes from Indo-European speakers. More recent studies have also debunked the British claims that so-called Aryans and Dravidians have a racial divide. A study conducted by the Centre for Cellular and Molecular Biology in 2009 (in collaboration with Harvard Medical School, Harvard School of Public Health and the Broad Institute of Harvard and MIT) analysed half a million genetic markers across the genomes of 132 individuals from 25 ethnic groups from 13 states in India across multiple caste groups. The study establishes, based on the impossibility of identifying any genetic indicators across caste lines, that castes in South Asia grew out of traditional tribal organizations during the formation of Indian society, and was not the product of any Aryan invasion and subjugation of Dravidian people. Some researchers from India, Europe and the U.S. claim that genetic similarities to Europeans were more common in members of the higher ranks. Their findings, published in Genome Research, claimed the idea that members of higher castes are more closely related to Europeans than are the lower castes.

6

Human Rights and Indian Society

INTRODUCTION

EMERGENCE OF CIVIL LIBERTIES MOVEMENTS

In India, the last quarter of the 20th century has been witness to a growing recognition of the place and relevance of human rights. It is axiomatic that this interest in human rights is rooted in the denial of life and liberty that was a pervasive aspect of the Emergency (1975-77). The mass arrests of the leaders of the opposition, and the targeted apprehension of those who could present a challenge to an authoritarian state, are one of the dominant images that have survived.

The involuntary disappearance of Rajan in Kerala is more than a symbol of the excesses of unbridled power.1 Forced evictions carried out in Delhi in what is known as'Turkman Gate' conjures up visions of large scale razing of dwellings of those without economic clout, and of their displacement into what were the outlying areas of the city. The catastrophic programme of mass sterilisation is an indelible part of emergency memory. The civil liberties movement was a product of the emergency. Arbitrary detention, custodial violence, prisons and the use of the judicial process were on the agenda of the civil liberties movement.

WOMEN'S MOVEMENT

The same period also saw the emergence of a nascent women's movement. In December 1974, the Committee on the Status of Women in India submitted its report to the

Government of India preceding the heralding in of the International Women's Year in 1975. The Status Report, in defiance of standard expectations

- Set out almost the entire range of issues and contexts as they affected women. Basing their findings, and revising their assumptions about how women live, on the experiences of women and communities that they met, the Committee redrew the contours of women's position, problems and priorities.
- Gave a fillip to the re-nascent women's movement

The women's movement has been among the most articulate, and heard, in the public arena. The woman as a victim of dowry, domestic violence, liquor, rape and custodial violence has constituted one discourse. Located partly in the women's rights movement, and partly in the campaign against AIDS,3 women in prostitution have acquired visibility.

The question of the practice of prostitution being considered as 'sex work' has been variously raised, while there has been a gathering unanimity on protecting the women in prostitution from harassment by the law. The Uniform Civil Code debate, contesting the inequality imposed on women by 'personal' laws has been resurrected, diverted and re-started.

Representation, through reservation, of women in parliament and state legislatures has followed the mandated presence of women in panchayats. Population policies have been contested terrain, with the experience of the emergency acting as a constant backdrop. 'Women's rights are human rights' has demanded a re-construction of the understanding of human rights as being directed against action and inaction of the state and agents of the state. Patriarchy has entered the domain of human rights as nurturing the offender.

PUBLIC INTEREST LITIGATION

In the late '70s, but more definitively in the early '80s, the Supreme Court devised an institutional mechanism in public interest litigation (PIL). PIL opened up the court to issues concerning violations of rights, and nonrealisation of even bare non-negotiables4 by diluting the rule of *locus standi*; any person could move the court on behalf of a class of persons who, due to indigence, illiteracy or incapacity of any other kind were unable to reach out for their rights. In its attempt to make the court process less intimidating, the procedure was simplified, and even a letter to the court could be converted into a petition.5 In its early years, PIL was a process which

- Recognised rights and their denial which had been invisibilised in the public domain. Prisoners, for instance, hidden amidst high walls which confined them, found a space to speak the language of fundamental and human rights.
- Led to 'juristic' activism, which expanded the territory of rights of persons. The fundamental rights were elaborated to find within them the right to dignity, to livelihood, to a clean environment, to health, to education, to safety at the workplace....The potential for reading a range of rights into the fundamental rights was explored.

Individuals, groups and movements have since used the court as a situs for struggle and contest, with varying effect on the defining of what constitutes human rights, and prioritising when rights appear to be in conflict.

STRUGGLE AGAINST PERVASIVE DISCRIMINATION

Dalit movements have kept caste oppression, and the oppression of caste, in public view. Moving beyond untouchability, which persists in virulent forms, the movement has had to contend with increasing violence against dalits even as dalits refuse to suffer in silence, or as they move beyond the roles allotted to them in traditional caste hierarchy. The growth of caste armies in Bihar, for instance, is one manifestation. The assassination of dalit panchayat leaders in Melmazhuvur in Tamil Nadu is another. The firing on dalits by the police forces when they were seen to be rising their oppression in the southern tip of Tamil Nadu is a third. The scourge of manual scavenging has been brought into policy and the law campaigns; there have been efforts to break through public obduracy in acknowledging that untouchability exists. In the meantime, there are efforts by groups working on dalit issues to internationalise deep discrimination of caste by influencing the agenda of the World Conference Against Racism.

RESISTING DISPLACEMENT INDUCED BY DEVELOPMENT' PROJECTS

There has been widespread contestation of project-induced displacement. The recognition of inequity, and of violation of the basic rights of the affected people, has resulted in growing interaction between local communities and activists from beyond the affected region, and the articulation of the rights and the injuries has been moulded in the process of this interaction. Resource rights were agitated in the early years of protest in the matter of forests; conservation and the right of the people to access forest produce for their subsistence and in acknowledgment of the traditional relationship between forests and dwellers in and around forests. Environmentalists and those espousing the dwellers' and forest users' causes have spoken together, parted company and found meeting points again, over the years. The right to resources is vigorously contested terrain.

COMMUNALISM

The 1980s, but more stridently in the 1990s, communalism has become a part of the fabric of politics. The anti- Sikh riots following Indira Gandhi's assassination was a ghastly reminder that communalism could well lurk just beneath the surface. The Bhagalpur massacres in 1989 represent another extreme communal manifestation. The demolition of the Babri Masjid on December 6, 1992 is an acknowledged turning point in majoritarian communalism, and impunity. The complicity of the state is undeniable. The killing of Graham Staines and his sons in Orissa was another gruesome aspect of communalism. The questioning of conversions in this climate is inevitably seen as infected with the communal virus. The forcible 're-conversion' in the Dangs area in Gujarat too has communal overtones. Attacks on Christians are regularly reported in the press, and the theme of impunity is being developed in these contexts.

NEW MOVEMENTS AND CAMPAIGNS

The professionalising of the non-governmental sector has had an impact on finding public space for certain issues and in making work on the issues sustainable. Child labour, AIDS-related work, the area of devolution and aiding women's participation in panchayat institutions, and battling violence against women have found support and sustainability in funding infrastructure development and support.

These have existed alongside civil liberties groups and initiatives, grassroots campaigns such as the Campaign for the Right to Information based in Rajasthan, the development struggle which has the Narmada Bachao Andolan at its helm, or the fishworkers' forum that has combated, sometimes successfully, the encroachments by the large-scale and capital-intensive into the livelihoods of traditional fishing communities. Movements for self-determination, militancy, dissent and the naxalite movement have provoked various extraordinary measures which have, in turn, prompted human rights groups into protest and challenge. The Terrorist and Disruptive Activities (Prevention) Act (TADA) is an instance.6 The Armed Forces Special Powers Act (AFSPA) continues.

Encounter killings, disappearances and the ineffectiveness of the judicial system in places where 'extraordinary' situations of conflict prevail, characterise the human rights-related scenario. A jurisprudence of human rights has emerged in these contexts. Networking, and supporting each other through conflicts and campaigns, is not infrequent. There are glimmerings of the emergence of, or existence of a human rights community in this. This has had groups and movements working on tourism, forest dwellers rights, civil liberties, displacement, women's rights and environment, for instance, finding a common voice in protesting the nuclear blasts in May 1999, or in condemning the attacks on the filming of 'Water' which had undisguised communal overtones. There has also been a building of bridges across causes and the emergence of an inter-woven community of interests. As the vista of rights has expanded, conflicts between rights have begun to surface.

There has been a consequent prioritisation of rights. The determination of priorities has often depended on the agency which engages in setting them—sometimes this has been environmental groups, at others workers, and yet other times, it has been the court, for instance. In this general setting, we embarked on a mapping of

- Human rights issues
- Responses–state and non-state–to human rights situations
- Conflicts between rights and prioritisation of rights,
- A miscellany of issues including the treatment, and the place of state and non-state violence, and the question of who speaks for whom, and the relationship between the advocate of an interest and the persons or classes of persons affected by the advocacy.

THE STUDY

The mapping exercise involved travel to the states of Maharashtra, Andhra Pradesh, Kerala, Karnataka, Rajasthan, West Bengal, Orissa, Tamil Nadu, Uttaranchal and Delhi. We travelled to Mumbai in Maharashtra, Calcutta in West Bengal, Bhubaneshwar and Konarak in Orissa; Ernakulam, Neyyali, Thrissur, Kottayam, Tiruvananthapuram and Calicut in Kerala; Bangalore in Karnataka; Ajmer District in Rajasthan; Hyderabad, Nalgonda District, Puttur, Chittoor and Tirupati in Andhra Pradesh; Chennai, Poonamallee District, Tuticorin, Tiruchendur (Nadunaalumoolai Kinaru village), Madurai and Chingleput in Tamil Nadu; Dehradun, Almora and Nainital in Uttaranchal.

The work done in documenting a human rights network in Orissa in July 1999 by one of us, and visits to Bhopal and Chattisgarh while researching common property resources in Madhya Pradesh in 1998-99 were also drawn upon. On a visit to Dhaka, human rights groups, lawyers and affected people were met with in May 2000, as part of a regional study on human rights. That experience too has been inducted into interpreting the human rights arena in India. In an attempt to understand the role, and influence, of the courts in the context of human rights, the law reports covering cases from all the High Courts and from the Supreme Court were comprehensively researched from 1994 to 2000. The Annual Reports of the NHRC have also been analysed. We met movement people, campaigners, persons from NGOs, community based groups, civil libertarians, political activists, journalists, academics, government functionaries, panchayat leaders, bureaucrats and lawyers, among others.

We also met victims of human rights violations. As far as possible, we did not predetermine the people we would meet in the states we visited, but allowed a flexibility which would take us from lead to lead. We also attended workshops and conferences which would give us insights into issues, as well as what people thought about them. In Konarak, therefore, one of us attended a Dialogue Among Activists, where arrest, detention and firing on protesters was under discussion among activists working among communities who were resisting their displacement from areas being taken over for projects, particularly mining.

Within a week of the meeting, in December 2000, firing claimed the lives of three tribals in Koraput district when they were protesting mining incursions into their area, standing testimony to the legitimacy of the concern of the activists at the meeting.

Again, one of us attending a planning meeting for conducting a census of the practice of untouchability; this was in January 2001, in Hyderabad, where dalit activists helped a funding agency set the terms of the study. We attended a workshop to discuss how to stall the changes being proposed in the bureaucratic circles, to Schedule V of the Constitution—which would deprive tribal areas of protection from alienation of land to non-tribals. One of us attended the meeting of the Campaign against Death Penalty where campaigners from across the country participated. There were, further, meetings on slums and demolitions, the women's movement in the last

25 years, the International Criminal Court (in Mumbai, and in Dhaka, after Bangladesh had signed on to the statute), juvenile justice, proposed changes in labour law and on strategising for participating in the World Conference against racism. We also organised a discussion-meeting on a Code of Conduct for Corporations, which is in a draft form before a committee set up by the Office of the High Commissioner for Human Rights in Geneva.

In the succeeding sections in this report, it will be our endeavour to set out the issues, responses and conflicts that we encountered, especially during the period of enquiry, viz. May 2000 to February 2001.

A MAPPING OF HUMAN RIGHTS ISSUES

This part sets out the issues which inhabit the human rights landscape in areas of ordinary governance.

CUSTODIAL VIOLENCE

Custody death, torture in custody and custodial rape have been subjects of much concern. Custodial violence has been on the agenda of civil rights groups for over two decades, and reports documenting instances of violence and its systemic occurrence, have been instrumental in the campaigns against custodial violence. Although custody deaths have found an acknowledgment from the state, and the NHRC has issued directions to the states it is difficult to assess if this has resulted in any reduction in the incidence of custody deaths. NHRC reports show a marked increase in the reported cases of custody deaths each year.

This is attributed, by the NHRC, to increased reporting and not to increased incidence of the crime; this, however, needs to be further investigated. The incidence of custody deaths demonstrates more undeniably the brutalisation of the processes of law enforcement by the police and armed forces. However, custodial torture (not resulting in death) is not at the focus of campaigns to reduce custodial violence. There are few places which have taken up the treatment of the victims of torture as victims of torture. The Indian state, in the meantime, has resisted attempts (including that of the NHRC) to have it ratify the Torture Convention.

- To report of the NHRC any death in custody within 24 hours of the occurrence, and
- To videotape the post-mortem proceedings,

In recent reported cases from the Gauhati High Court, it is 15 and 16-year olds who are found to have been victims of state violence, and the defence of the state has been that they were hardened militants.7 Custodial rape has found an expanded definition—in terms of power rape—in the Penal Code, 1860.8 However, these provisions have hardly been invoked.

In the meantime, most often, judicial perceptions of the victim of custodial rape have in significant measure, discredited the victim's version, and blamed the victim resulting in reduction of sentence for policemen convicted of rape to less than the minimum prescribed in law.

From Mathura to Rameeza Bi to Maya Tyagi to Suman Rani—these women have become symbols of patriarchal prejudices. Campaigns in the matter of custodial rape have invoked their name, and they are now names that are etched into the history and legend of the women's movement. In the meantime, the legal dictum that the identity of a victim of rape be not disclosed to protect her privacy has been set in place.

PROJECT DISPLACEMENT

Project displacement, for the construction of large dams or for power projects, for instance, have led to protest movements directly involving the affected people. The NBA has utilised strategies and tactics of protest—including *jal samarpan,* human chains, working on the funders and the contractors to withdraw, participating in the proceedings before, and surrounding, the World Commission on Dams—which have refused to let the issue be drowned out. This has also seen the manufacturing of conflicting forces, such as the pro-dam lobby which is believed to be largely state-sponsored.

Human rights issues that arise include:

- Displacement, per se

- The poverty of rehabilitation, and often, the impossibility of rehabilitation
- The impoverishment that results from displacement
- The non-reckoning of cultural and community identity and of rights.

What constitutes development has come into severe question in this arena. The Land Acquisition Act 1894 has been at the centre of protests. Among the strategies adopted to deal with the coercive nature of the law has been the drafting of alternative legislation. The obduracy of the state in not approving a policy for rehabilitation of the displaced has also been cause for protest.

THE INTERNALLY DISPLACED DUE TO CONFLICTS

The large-scale internal migration caused by political violence has created classes of internal refugees. During the years of militancy in the Punjab, after the anti-Sikh riots in 1984, and the movement of Kashmiri Pandits out of the valley have provided visible evidence of such migration. While the violence that preceded the migration has been squarely addressed in human rights terms, the rehabilitation and return of the migrants after displacement appears to have been only on the margins of the human rights movement.

REFUGEES

India has not ratified the 1951 UN Convention on Refugees, nor has it signed the 1967 protocol. The Indian state has generally resisted visits from the UNHCR to camps where refugees are housed. Activists say that the Indian state has been relatively benign towards refugees.

According to one non-governmental source, in 1999, India hosted more than 2,92,000 refugees; which includes more than 16,000 persons from Afghanistan, 65,000 Chakmas from Bangladesh, 30,000 Bhutanese of Nepali origin, 50,000 Chin indigenous people from Myanmar and about 39,000 pro-democracy student activists from Rangoon and the Mandalay region, 1,10,000 Sri Lankan Tamils of whom 70,000 are in camps and 40,000 outside, 1,10,000 Tibetans and around 7000 persons from other countries. The assassination of Rajiv Gandhi in 1991 has reportedly altered the treatment meted out to the Sri Lankan refugees. According to a fact-finding report of a civil liberties organisation in Tamil Nadu, Sri Lankan refugees fall into three categories: those who are in the 133 refugee camps; refugees who maintain themselves outside the camps; and those who have been identified as belonging to militant groups who were kept in virtual rigorous confinement in the three special camps.

In August 1995, 43 inmates of the Special Camp at Tippu Mahal, Vellore escaped and a one-man commission set up by the state describes the structure and administration of the camps. The refugees were found to be prisoners in these camps and, as even the state appointed commission had remarked, 'admittedly these inmates or most of them are in rigorous confinement in the special camps for five or six years continuously.' The testimony of the two inmates to the fact-finding team also revealed that the camp in Vellore had among its inmates at least 12 disabled persons. The Government of India does not appear to have any policy on how to deal with refugee-prisoners in their camps. The protection of Chakma refugees in the state of Arunachal Pradesh, and their right to have their claim for citizenship considered, was canvassed by a civil liberties group before the NHRC.

The Supreme Court, approached by the NHRC, directed that the threats held out to the Chakmas by the local citizens be dealt with by the state. It also asserted that their applications for being granted citizenship be considered under the Citizenship Act. The difficulties besetting refugees even after long years of residence in a state, with state acquiescence, were in evidence here.

LAND ALIENATION

The loss to communities of right over land is widespread, and various movements to recover control over land and related resources have been active particularly in the past decade and a half, though some movements go back many decades. The issue of tribal land alienation was linked with that of displacement, and the judicial system was used to get an order declaring unconstitutional the transfer of land from a tribal to a non-tribal through the medium of the state (in its land acquisition capacity). Recent efforts to delete this constitutional protection given in Schedule V of the Constitution are being resisted as a denial of basic protection given to tribals, paving the way for their displacement and impoverishment.

The issue of land alienation was one of the primary issues in the struggle for separate statehood for Uttaranchal, and till today is identified as one of the main rights violations occurring in the state. In Kerala, the issue is differently positioned. While the loss of land to the tribal is viewed as a violation of their rights and protection of those rights, the settlers are largely people who are themselves on the economic margins. While groups from within the tribal communities have been demanding restoration of alienated land, and the High Court has supported their stand, other human rights advocates maintain an uneasy silence since the contest appears to be between two vulnerable communities.

RIGHT OVER RESOURCES

The right of the forest dwellers to reside in forests, and for those dependent on forest produce to have access to forests, is contested terrain. Till recently, there were conservation groups which demanded that removing tribals from within forest areas was necessary in the interest of conservation. This stand has softened somewhat, and a more symbiotic relationship between the forest and the dweller recognised as possible.

The problems are now spoken of in terms of over-population, and over-grazing, in the forest area. State policy is, however, widely perceived as being inimical to the continuance of the forest dweller within the forest. 'Settling' of rights and interests is therefore met with deep suspicion, as is happening in Madhya Pradesh. Activists have therefore been mobilising the grassroots in MP, it was through a padayatra over a period of six months-to resist the conservation projects which may end up pauperising the dwellers, and, further, may denude the forest too.

There have been attempts in the early '90s to prepare a new Forest Bill that will contain within it the interests of conservation, and of the people. Efforts such as this have stalled the legislation proposed by the state which groups and movements see as being opposed to rights—including the right to livelihood, to culture, to security, to shelter, among others—even, while the alternative bills have hardly ever been adopted. An activist identified the problem of land and resources being related to how possession and ownership of land are perceived.

There are three kinds of property he said:

- Private property
- Public property
- Common property

What is held as 'public property' by the state, he said, has been treated as property owned by the state, and not held in trust by the state. It is the notion of common property that has to be resurrected and advanced. The entry of mining interests inιo Orissa has, for instance, brought into the open the problem that is inherent in globalisation when it comes into conflict with local interest.

The unequal, triangular contest between multinational mining interests, the state which binds itself to protecting the multinational interest on Indian territory, and the local dwellers—in the case of mining, it is often tribals—manifests itself as a human rights issue. Aquaculture, which brings in corporations to exploit resources through prawn culture, for instance, has been resisted on grounds of loss of livelihood, long-term destruction of marine life and consequent degradation of the environment. Corporatised aquaculture and shrimp farms have been banned. Deep-sea trawlers have also been banned, and the livelihood and lives of fisher communities salvaged. So, too, with prawn culture. Human rights activists see setbacks to these efforts at preservation of community livelihoods and of the environment in the Aquaculture Bill that has been presented to the Parliament in

2000. The Aruvari Sansad (Water Parliament) in Ajmer district in Rajasthan, which, with the help of the Tarun Bharat Sangh, an NGO, has wrested control over the river, the check dams it has built along it, the revived rivers and the fish that have sprung into being in the river is an uncommon assertion over water and water resources to the exclusion of agencies of the state. The issue of land reforms and the redistribution of land was encountered in Andhra Pradesh. The Peoples War Group, for instance, avers that land reform is at the root of their attacks against the state. The problem of professional land grabbers, and the response of land invasion to take possession of land which should rightly belong to the invading community, was also seen in Andhra Pradesh.

State response has been to treat the attacks, and invasion, as public order, or law and order, problems. The loss of tribal land through land alienation—something that the law limits—has raised other issues in Kerala, for instance. The land had been bought from the tribals by settlers who are themselves economically and socially marginalised. A prolonged legal battle, where the court had directed the return of the land to the tribals, has not seen a solution to the contending interests of two communities, each in need of protection from expropriation.

URBAN SHELTER AND DEMOLITION

There has been a routinising of the emergency visible in the matter of cleaning up of the cities. In 2000-2001, Delhi has seen a spate of demolitions of 'slums'. The slum dwellers have been divided up into eligibles and ineligibles, with the eligibles being given very small plots of land on which they are required to construct houses within six months on a licence basis. The size of the plot ensures that it is only a 'slum' that develops.

The 'ineligibles' are not thereafter considered by state policy. Housing rights activists too do not appear to have been able to identify what happens to the ineligibles when demolition occurs. In Bangalore, housing rights groups have been attempting to demonstrate the effort and money that 'encroachers' expend on the land on which they settle; and that they have worked for their entitlement to alternative plots. In

Bombay, and to a lesser extent elsewhere, there have been attempts to involve the slum dwellers in reconstructing the area in a manner which will let the slum disappear, while they are given places in high-rise tenements in the same area with the rest of the space to be used commercially. In Patna, an order of the High Court in a PIL, requiring the municipal corporation to demolish encroachments, resulted in a demolition spree that an embarrassed court had to step in to stop.

The illegal status of the urban dweller who cannot afford to purchase legality has been aggravated by B.N. Kirpal, J saying: 'Establishing or creating slums, it seems, appears to be good business and is well organised...Large areas of public land, in this way, are usurped for private use free of cost... The promise of free land, at the taxpayers' cost, in place of a jhuggi, is a proposal which attracts more land grabbers. *Rewarding an encroacher on public land with free alternate site is like giving a reward to a pickpocket.*' Unlike South Africa, where the state's obligation to provide shelter before destroying even an illegal habitat was recognised, drawing upon international law, there is no such recognition in Indian law or judicial decisions.

Activists and campaigners therefore face an unenviable, if unavoidable, task of combating the anti-poor stand of the state. Pavement dwelling, and houselessness, was raised in the '80s and, though it may never really have disappeared, it has resurfaced more rigorously since the demolitions have begun in Delhi. Migrant workers living on pavements have been particularly vulnerable to random attacks in areas of militant violence. Newspapers have reported such occurrences in the '90s. This issue affecting migrant labour particularly needs to be addressed. The 'clearing' of pavements by removing hawkers has been a phenomenon visible in most cities. Eviction of hawkers, and of dwellers, is a significant issue, and the demands include recognition not only of shelter, land and monetary compensation, but of livelihood too.

LIVELIHOOD

Apart from issues of rights over resources, and in the

context of displacement and relocation, the death of cotton farmers has, for instance, raised questions about protection of livelihood. Liberalisation has resulted in loss of jobs to large numbers in the workforce, and we hear of deaths among the working classes. This is an area that seems to demand closer attention. The withdrawing of protective labour legislation, which is proposed, such as the 'abolition' part of the Contract Labour (Prohibition and Regulation) Act 1970, or the prohibition of night work for women except where specifically attempted, it is feared, is likely to shrink the rights of workers to a great degree.

Freedom of association is also being re-cast in a new Trade Unions Bill, which labour leaders and activists believe is meant to stifle the powers of labour to group together and be heard. The casualisation of labour which the changes portend are expected to drastically reduce the bargaining power of labour. In 1989, a PIL filed by two social/political activists from Orissa, led to the express recognition of starvation as a violation of fundamental rights. In 1994, the NHRC acknowledged that starvation is a violation of human rights and ordered the state to pay compensation to the families of victims of starvation in Kalahandi in Orissa. In March/April 2001, academics/ researchers from the Delhi School of Economics and the Madras Institute of Development Studies have asked for distribution of buffer stocks that the government has stored in its godowns, to stem the tide of hunger among those with low purchasing power.

The juggling with the public distribution system, and the defining and re-defining of the poverty line and consequently of 'below poverty line' is causing particular concern. The death of 17 protesters chased by the police into the Tamaraparani river, and over 200 injured in the incident has been compared to the killing of innocent persons by the British at Jallianwallabagh 80 years ago. On July 23, 1999, a solidarity procession organised by several political parties proceeded to the Collectorate in Tirunelveli Town in South Tamil Nadu, demanding an early solution of the wage dispute that had been the cause of discontent and agitation among tea workers in the Manjolai Tea Estate. The also demanded the immediate and unconditional release of 652 tea estate workers who had been kept in the Tiruchi jail for six weeks following a demonstration before the same Collectorate on June 7 and 8, 1999. Talks on the labour dispute having failed, the political parties decided to present a charter of demands to the Collector. As the processionists neared the Collectorate, the police attempted to prevent the jeep which had the leaders of the agitation in it from proceeding further.

As the crowd milled around, the events that ensued included a lathi charge by the police, the lobbing of tear gas and the police also opened fire.

A video footage shows an injured person, bleeding, being carried away by four policemen. This injured person remains unaccounted for The police then chased the people down the banks of the river Tamaraparani forcing the people to jump into the water to save themselves from the police force. Photographs graphically reveal the pursuit of the people by the police into the river, even pushing the people back into the water 17 people drowned. There were injuries on the person of the drowned victims, testifying to ante-mortem police brutality.

This episode constitutes a new threshold to police violence and brutality in labour related agitation and protest. The 'clearing' of pavements by removing hawkers has been a phenomenon visible in most cities. Eviction of hawkers, and of dwellers, is a significant issue, and the demands include recognition not only of shelter, land and monetary compensation, but of livelihood too.

SEXUAL HARASSMENT AT THE WORKPLACE

This issue acquired visibility with the decision of the Supreme Court in *Vishaka*. Earlier efforts at having the problem addressed, as, for instance, in the Delhi University, has drawn strength from the guidelines set out in the judgment. It was widely reported, however, that it was still proving difficult to get institutions to adopt the guidelines and act upon it. The Madras High Court, for instance, was reportedly averring that the guidelines did not apply to the court; and allegations of sexual harassment by a senior member of the Registry were given short shrift. The process of setting up a credible grievance redressal mechanism was reportedly being watered down in the recommendation of a committee to the Delhi University.

In Kerala, a Commission of Inquiry was set up after Nalini Netto, a senior official of the Indian Administrative Service, pursued her complaint of sexual harassment against a serving minister of the state cabinet-which is seen as a diversion from a representative investigative and redressal forum.

P E Usha, in Kerala, faced hostility in her university when she followed up on her complaint of sexual harassment. There have been allegations of sexual harassment of women employees by senior persons within institutions working on human rights, and in progressive publications, which too have shown up the inadequacy of the redressal mechanisms.

- Translating the guidelines into norms in different institutions and workplaces;
- Finding support systems for women who are sexually harassed
- Breaking through thick walls of disbelief are reckoned to be the priorities. This has also been introduced into programmes on gender sensitisation for judicial officers.

Sexual harassment accompanied by violence has become a common feature with cases of acid throwing where there is unrequited love, and harassment which has culminated in the murder of a hounded girl.20

RAPE

In the '80s and into the early '90s, was widely discussed, and alternative drafts and definitions essayed.

- The definition of rape
- The meaning of consent in the context of rape
- Marital rape

While following *Tukaram and Ganpat's* case, 21 'power' rape was partially introduced into the law. The definition of rape, consent and the status of marital rape in law has however not been altered. Again, while the campaign's gains are witnessed in the Supreme Court holding that, as a rule, the victim's version should not require corroboration and that it should be given credence

- The trauma of the trial continues,
- The law's sanction to delving into character evidence concerning the victim remains in the Evidence Act22 despite the flood of criticism and protest it has provoke

In Uttaranchal, an issue not uncommon in investigations into, and trial of, rape surfaced. It was reported that women who were raped at Muzaffarnagar are being pressurised not to testify in the criminal cases not only by the police but also by their own community and political leaders, particularly since monetary compensation has been paid.

In 1994, the National Commission for Women (NCW) was asked by the Supreme Court to propose a scheme for establishing Rape Crisis Centres, and for a Criminal Injuries Compensation Board, which could care for victims of crime. This is yet to materialise. In the meantime, the women's movement in Rajasthan has got the administration to provide monetary relief to victims of rape, unconnected with trial and conviction.

Though this has, at least occasionally, resulted in the veracity of the accusation being challenged as having been made so as to obtain the sum in compensation, it is seen as a move to helping the woman recover. Rape as reprisal was symbolised in Bhanwari Devi's experience. Bhanwari Devi, a *saathin* working in Rajasthan in and around her village, was part of a wider network of women who were involved in a state-sponsored programme of empowerment particularly of women and girls.

Her intervention to thwart the practice of child marriage in the community around her is commonly acknowledged as having resulted in the gang rape that was inflicted on her—as punishment, by men of the dominant community who were outraged by her intervention. The acquittal of the alleged rapists, more especially the reasoning of the court, based on caste and hierarchies of belief, accentuates the re-victimising of the woman.

The low rate of conviction for rape, and the protest from women's groups, were held out to justify a proposed amendment to criminal law to provide death penalty for the offence of rape. The conflict between provisions of the death penalty and human rights has surfaced, even if gradually, and the groups we met, as well as the National Commission for Women, have rejected the proposal for death penalty for the offence of rape.

DEATH PENALTY

The civil liberties movement has been consistent in its opposition to the death penalty. For a brief while, there were some parts in the women's movement who supported—either vocally, or by their silence—the imposition of death penalty for rape. This too has been retracted, and death penalty for rape opposed. After the period in the early '80s, when the Supreme Court drew up the 'rarest of rare' rule, there has been a downward slide, particularly discernible in the 1990s.

- Multiple death sentences,
- Death penalty to minors, and
- Death sentence while reversing acquittal are not uncommon

The campaign against execution of two youths in Andhra Pradesh who had been convicted of burning a bus which killed 23 passengers saw concerted action, which resulted in their sentence being commuted by the President. The confirmation of the sentence of death on women is a relatively recent phenomenon. Ramashri's sentence was reduced to life by the Supreme Court, even as the court rejected the right of the NCW to intervene.

The sentence of death imposed upon Nalini, convicted in the Rajiv Gandhi assassination case, has been opposed by human rights groups, along with the sentence of death meted out to three others in the same matter. Death sentence confirmed despite dissent among judges of benches of the

Supreme Court on the sentence that should be imposed is another, disturbing, occurrence. Even doubts about the age of the accused—whether he had been less than 16 years of age and therefore a juvenile—were not sufficient to dispense with death sentence where death was awarded by a majority of judges.

That the young accused was defended by legal aid lawyers and that 'It is reasonable to presume, in such circumstances, that the amicus curiae or advocate appointed on State brief, would not have been able even to see the petitioner, much less collect instructions from him, during the second and third tiers' was noticed only by the minority judge. Dearth of data, and difficulty of access to data is one obstacle to effectively countering the retentionists. In the meantime, the proliferation of death penalty in recent statutes, viz.,

- The Narcotic Drugs and Psychotropic Substances Act 1985 (and as amended in 1988)
- National Security Guards Act 1986
- TADA 1987 (which lapsed in 1995, but trials under which continue)
- Arms Act 1950 (as amended in 1988)
- Indo-Tibetan Border Police Act 1992
- The Scheduled Castes and Scheduled Tribes (Prevention of Atrocities) Act 1989
- Commission of Sati (Prevention) Act 1987
- Section.364 A IPC as introduced in 1993—'kidnapping for ransom, etc.

There has been a deafening silence from the NHRC on the issue of the death penalty.

FAKE ENCOUNTERS (EXTRA-JUDICIAL KILLINGS)

In India, extra-judicial killings by the police or the security forces are called 'encounter killings', meaning that the killing occurred during an armed encounter between the police or security forces and the victim. The killing by the state forces is most often declared to be defensive, cases of attempted murder and other related offences are registered against the victims, and the cases closed without further investigation since criminal cases come to an end upon the death of the accused. Despite being 'unnatural deaths', and the victim having being killed, no investigation ensues to determine whether the death was in fact in an actual encounter, nor whether the use, and the extent of use, of force was justified. This is an acknowledged strategy of the state for eliminating certain kinds of opposition to the state and the established order.

In Andhra Pradesh, for instance, the naxalites have been the targets; in Punjab, it was the militant; in Mumbai, it is those who are alleged to be part of the underworld. Civil liberties groups, journalists and lawyers have consistently challenged this practice over the past two decades. The demand as it has been articulated after recent episodes has been

- For doing away with state violence in the form of killings in fake encounters, and
- That all cases of encounter killings ought to be registered as first information reports (FIRs) and investigated before the case is closed. The practice of registering cases against the deceased and terminating the proceedings even before it begins is being vigorously challenged. The NHRC too has issued directions endorsing this recommended practice, but to little effect. These court, and out-of-court, battles have carried on throughout the '80s and the '90s to the present.

The Committee of Concerned Citizens (CCC), a group of individuals in Andhra Pradesh, has approached encounter killings differently. Addressing both naxalite groups and the state, the CCC has been working at de-escalation of violence. While the naxalite response has taken the CCC to the issue of land reforms as being fundamental in understanding violence of the opposition, the state, it is widely believed, is pursuing the path of unbridled unleashing of the use of encounters.

The numbers killed in encounters have increased in the two years when the process of reconciliation was being negotiated by the CCC, making some of them ask if intervention by the human rights actors was actually prompting the state to escalate the violence. The human rights community has had to contend with the issue of impunity which is immediately seen as arising from thee non-registration and the non-investigation of cases.

INVOLUNTARY DISAPPEARANCES

The Punjab disappearances were brought into the open by two human rights defenders, Khalra and Kumar. Khalra was himself thereafter 'disappeared'. Investigations into these disappearances—which were uncovered when mortuary records in three districts of the Punjab were scrutinised and 'unidentified' and partially identified persons were found to have been cremated without informing the families of the deceased—was handed over by the Supreme Court to the NHRC. The manner in which the matter was reduced to a point where the State of Punjab agreed to pay compensation of ₹ 1 lakh *(without admitting liability)* to the families of 18 persons who had been disappeared and the NHRC's tolerance of this stand of the state, is striking in the *general denial of the phenomenon of disappearances.*

This was after the CBI had found that bodies of several persons had been cremated surreptitiously in the late '80s and early '90s—585 persons who had been subsequently identified had been cremated after being labelled as unidentified. Around 330 of them had been partially identified and over 1200 remained to be identified. The deficiency of compensation as a measure of reconciliation is also evident. Disappearances appear to be a pattern where there is militant resistance to the state. Case law speaks of this phenomenon in the Northeast. In fact, the first major case of compensation for disappearance after being picked up by the armed forces was from the Northeast. On February 27, 2001, newspapers reported that it was alleged in the Lok Sabha, without being effectively countered, that the number of persons missing from the custody of the security forces and the police has risen to 2174 in Jammu and Kashmir; 76 cases had been registered and only one person had been challaned so far.

- Acknowledgment of involuntary disappearances
- Investigation, and seeking to establish what happened to the disappeared so that families and the community can finally know
- Prosecution and punishment, for reasons of deterrence too, and
- Compensation as a measure of atonement are being sought to be worked into the system. It was also reiterated that reconciliation would be impossible to achieve without such acknowledgment, identification of the disappeared and reparation.

That Khalra disappeared even while the matter was being taken to the Supreme Court is a statement on impunity. The theme of impunity was laid out when K.P.S. Gill, the policeman in-charge in Punjab through the waning years of militancy, lashed out in protest when a policeman, Sandhu, committed suicide while facing multiple charges of excesses committed during the years of militancy. The schizophrenic attitude of the process which rewarded him when he killed 'terrorists', and later sought to prosecute him for abuse of power even amounting to murder, stood exposed. Gill

- Blamed the judiciary for having been inactive, or of playing safe, when captured terrorists were brought before it, and
- Held out the threat that if pursued by prosecution, the police would be unavailable to deal with militancy another time.

EXTRAORDINARY LAWS

These have been one of the means of routinising the enactment of laws that are normally promulgated in an emergency or in extraordinary situations. The Terrorist and Disruptive Activities (Prevention) Act 1987 (TADA) was contested for

- Its denial of fair trial standards—*e.g.*, it reduced the tiers of appeal
- The provision regarding making confessions to a police officer admissible in evidence

- The broad contours of the law on what constitutes terrorism, and
- Potential and proven abuse—for *e.g.*, the largest number of TADA detenues were in Gujarat, where militant activity was not present.

The public condemnation of TADA, political opposition to it, the NHRC's spirited intervention and the state's assessment that it was no longer necessary, led to the law not being reenacted when it lapsed in 1995. There have, however, been further attempts to revive the law—as in the Prevention of Terrorism Act recommended in 1999 by the Law Commission, for instance.

Further, state laws in Maharashtra, Andhra Pradesh and, more recently, in Madhya Pradesh and Karnataka—as a measure against organised crime- have brought the TADA back into their states under a hardly disguised identity. Tamil Nadu has also proposed a Prevention of Terrorism Bill along similar lines.

The Armed Forces Special Powers Act 1958 (AFSPA) is another law which provides extraordinary powers. It has been in force in the Northeast for these years. The TADA and the AFSPA survived challenge before the Supreme Court in the '90s. This has caused a serious rethink on the courts as a situs for testing the legitimacy of such extraordinary laws that deny fundamental rights, and breach human rights principles. It is evident that it is only vigilance, and resistance, which is keeping the proliferation of these laws in check.

The arrest and detention of civilians under extraordinary laws, like the TADA, also appears to be routine. It has been alleged, for instance, that villagers in the vicinity of Veerappan, the sandalwood smuggler's beat are routinely subjected to harassment, search and detention. In the negotiations for the release of actor Rajkumar who was taken hostage by Veerappan on July 30, 2000, the release of 51 detainees being held under TADA since 1992 on suspicion of having participated in the murder of policemen was in issue.

Human rights activists claim that many of them were local people who had been roped in as being 'associates' of

Veerappan. When a civil liberties organisation moved the court for release of those so incarcerated, the petition was not entertained.

But during the negotiations, the government of Karnataka showed a readiness to release them in the interests of law and order, and also, significantly, since others released on bail earlier 'have not repeated the offences and they have not involved themselves in any similar offences and terrorist activity have not been noticed recently in the area.'

PREVENTIVE DETENTION

When the Constitution came into being in 1950, preventive detention laws were avowedly intended to be a transient measure. During the emergency, the Maintenance of Internal Security Act 1971 (MISA) was among the more infamous laws which allowed for preventive detention of persons in the avowed interest of maintenance of internal security. There are now a number of legislations which permit preventive detention, in the states and at the centre.

The National Security Act 1980 (NSA) is an instance of the latter. The A.P Prevention of Dangerous Activities of Bootleggers, Dacoits, Drug Offenders, Goondas, Immoral Traffic Offenders and Land Grabbers Act 1986 is an example of the former. Public protest against the continuance of these laws is almost inaudible despite

- The long periods, sometimes up to two years, that a person may be kept in preventive detention
- The tardiness of the procedure prescribed—*e.g.*, the executive may be given up to three months to get the opinion of the Advisory Board which may effectively have a person in custody under executive order up to ninety days
- The range of activities that are allowed to be covered by preventive detention laws that are unconnected with public order or law and order.

Unlike the challenge to the TADA, preventive detention laws have not engaged the human rights community in any sustained manner.

DETENTION

A range of detentions including those that were plainly illegal came to light during the course of our work:

- The incarceration of persons deemed to be 'non-criminal lunatics' (NCLs) or the wandering mentally ill in jails was investigated in a PIL before the Supreme Court. These are persons picked up under the Police Acts of the states, or under police powers in other laws such as the Indian Lunacy Act 1912, or its successor law, the Mental Health Act 1987. They are treated as `nuisances', or bracketed as being dangerous, this providing the rationale for putting them away. The term NCL is in contradistinction to `criminal lunatics', that is, those accused of crime but found to be mentally ill or suffering from mental disorder. For years NCLs were received in jails as places of `safe custody' under the Indian Lunacy Act 1912 and later under the Mental Health Act 1987. In the states of West Bengal and Assam, where the Supreme Court sent Commissioners to investigate, it was found that many of those in jails as NCLs were in fact not mentally ill at all, but had been placed there deviously, to serve some completely unrelated purpose. For instance, a 70-year woman was found to have been put away as an NCL apparently because her landlord was using it as a means of evicting her. We heard resonances of this reasoning from a lawyer-activist in Chennai.
- The Supreme Court declared, in August 1993, that using jails as places of safe custody to house non-criminal mentally ill persons (NCMI) is unconstitutional.36 Apart from the state of Assam, which admitted in an affidavit in the Supreme Court to continuing the practice, the NHRC has intermittently reiterated that NCMI should be housed in places other than jails. It is plain that the practice continues.
- This is an area that has not been widely addressed

within the human rights community. NHRC's recognition of the issue too has been desultory.

- There is evidence in law reports, and activists have admitted to have knowledge of, the practice of hostage taking by the police where the person to be apprehended is not within reach of the police. Relatives of the person sought are then picked up and kept in custody till he surrenders. This appears to have happened with some regularity in Punjab, but we also heard of it in Delhi and Andhra Pradesh, for instance. This breach of the law needs further investigation and response.
- There have been reports of people spending long years in jail, which could have been averted if prisons were not as inaccessible as they are. *Rudul Sah,* the man who spent fourteen years in jail because he had been considered unfit to stand trial, and continued to remain untried despite having been declared fit, is one wellknown instance. Recent instances from Bihar and West Bengal reveal that the neglect that occasions such illegal incarceration continues. The incapacity of a person to follow up on his trial and sentence, and to procure orders in time has been known to keep him in prison long after he was due to have been released. The inability to furnish bail or sureties was reportedly one such reason for the large undertrial population.
- It is evident that systemic changes are imperative if these questions of personal liberty are to be addressed.
- In custodial institutions other than prisons-in 'protective homes' for women, for instance, the problem of custody versus shelter has been raised. Protective homes are established under the Immoral Traffic (Prevention) Act 1956 (ITPA). Since they are the only statutory institutions that can house women for 'protection' as also for 'correction', they act as places of custody, operating within the executive-

magistracy system. We met women in 'protective custody' in the Agra Protective Home, who were witnesses in a case to be tried in Jhansi; they desired to leave and they had been in the institution for nearly two years. But the law would not let them. 'Rescued' women were placed in these institutions, but the purpose of 'rehabilitation' was found to be too inadequate to make the difference.

- Prison jurisprudence since the late '60s recognises that prisoners do not lose all their rights because of imprisonment. Yet, there is a loss of rights within custodial institutions which continue to occur. For instance, it was found that the HIV status of all the women in the Agra Protective Home was public knowledge, and there was no confidentiality attaching to this information. There was segregation within the institutions of those found to be HIV positive, and, for a while, the Supreme Court too endorsed this. The rules governing women in these institutions uncannily resemble prison rules such as those concerning visitors, letters, and even punishment for conduct within the institutions.
- Persons working in this area said that this was an area which called for an injection of human rights experience and perspectives.
- The non-release of persons cured of mental illness from institutions was also reported to be a problem. We repeatedly met the need for halfway homes and support services which could help a person be restored to liberty.
- In Delhi, we heard of persons who had been picked up as being persons of Bangladeshi origin, who were kept in custody in a night shelter till they could be repatriated if they were, in fact, found to belong to Bangladesh and the Foreigners Act 1946 could be invoked to effect this move. There was concern that even the basis of identifying them as possible foreigners was not clear and that dispelling suspicion

of nationality could well be more difficult for the poor and the dispossessed.

It is also found that it is common practice to pick up people for questioning, and not record their presence in the police station till the police is ready to present them before a magistrate—a way of thwarting the constitutional requirement that every person taken into custody be produced before a magistrate within 24 hours. Apart from the illegality of such detention, it also makes difficult proving torture in custody during the period of illegal, unrecorded, detention.

Human rights activists suggest that telegrams be dispatched to the Chief Minister, the Director General of Police, the Superintendent of Police, and the Governor for instance, when information about such illegal detention is obtained, to establish the time of detention. The conditions of persons with mental illness in institutions have been cause for human rights concern. In Gwalior Mental hospital, for instance, it was found that persons with mental illness were left in nakedness; the explanation was that they tore their clothes if they were given them. The press raised the issue. Chaining of mentally ill patients was also a practice, and this was outlawed by an order of the court. One difficulty in ensuring that such violations do not occur, and in getting the law implemented, is access.

The human rights community has not engaged with the problems faced within the walls of custodial institutions. Imaginative answers which will make open institutions of what are now bureaucratic, and closed, institutions is an imperative. The hysterectomy controversy in the early 1990s in Pune represents another aspect of the control and decisionmaking within custodial institutions. The hysterectomy of girls below 18 years of age, who were mentally retarded, raised controversy about the decision made by the professionals. The professionals involved in making the decision neither denied that the hysterectomy was being done, nor did they did see it as a violation. It was justified as being in the best interests of the hygiene of the mentally retarded girl, as making practicable the care of the mentally retarded. The response did not rule out the possibility of sexual abuse when within the institutions, but said it would protect the girls from pregnancy in the event of such an encounter. The persons responsible for the decision responded angrily to the charges of human rights violations. The Medical Council of India, however, distanced itself from this position, and declared the practice as being against their norms. The intervention of the media and the human rights community precluded further hysterectomies from being done.

MISSING WOMEN

There are various situations which throw up the issue of'missing' women. The lopsided sex ratio in many states, and the juvenile sex ratio in even a state such as Kerala (which is held out by planners and economists as the model performer on the population front), is one area where women, and girls, go `missing'. In Orissa, we heard of the phenomenon of'Jhansi' marriages and'Gwalior' marriages. Girls from very poor homes were escorted by a'broker' to be married to men in Jhansi or Gwalior, and he would bring back a bride price of Rs.10,000 to Rs.25,000 to be given to the girl's family.

While some of these marriages had been found to be genuine, the possibility of some of these women being trafficked was not ruled out. Also, what a girl/woman did if deserted or ill-treated was not clear. There was therefore an attempt by activists to keep track of women who had not been heard from for over a period of three months, so that their whereabouts could be verified and their safety ascertained. In July 1999, activists had begun the process of documenting the'missing' woman. In Delhi, we were informed that missing persons reports when women go missing from their marital homes were hardly ever related with unidentified bodies of women who were declared to have committed suicide by drowning, for instance. The paucity of information, and the difficulties in follow up, has kept this issue in the margins of human rights concerns.

HOMICIDE IN THE MATRIMONIAL HOME

Often identified as being dowry-related deaths, unnatural

deaths of women in their marital home has acquired prominence. Like encounter killings, acknowledgment has not led to a reduction in the incidence of such homicide. In Andhra Pradesh in 1990 a civil liberties organisation raised the issue of violation of women's rights as a human rights issue by comparing the number of dowry deaths and the number of encounter killings during one time period—about 2000 dowry deaths, and 300 deaths in encounters.

In Bangalore, a women's group keeps a watch in the Burns Ward of the leading government hospital, and also scrutinises newspapers for reports of deaths of young women, which they then follow up. They also had a'Truth Commission' where a tribunal heard the narratives of the families of girls/women who had been the victims of dowry deaths. The inadequacies of investigation, and the many slips in the judicial process which results in a low rate of prosecution and a lower rate still of conviction, was observed everywhere. The definition of'dowry death' in the Penal Code, based on preponderance of probability and a shifting of onus represents a significant shift in criminal law and jurisprudence. In the meantime, the Dowry Prohibition Act has been hardly at all implemented. Most states still have no Dowry Prohibition Officers.

The maintenance of list of things given and received is still not mandatory. S.498 A, which was brought in to deal with cruelty in the matrimonial home, has suffered criticism as being abused, sending the family of the man to prison till bail is procured. Some women's groups, however, contended that the abuse was only marginal, and that this was the only provision in law which could hold the perpetrator of domestic cruelty accountable. Some also spoke of bringing into law the notions of right to matrimonial home and matrimonial property as other approaches of protecting women on whom cruelty is practised.

DOMESTIC VIOLENCE

In locating domestic violence in the terrain of human rights, one point of view was that it is not the identity of the perpetrator alone which can be allowed to determine whether a victim has been subjected to a human right violation or not: that it is a man or his family who exercises their power to harass, assault and injure a woman, and not the state which is the perpetrator, should then make no difference to the place for this violence in human rights discourse. Also, it is state practice, and endorsement, of patriarchy that keeps such violence in the home, we were told.

- Crime against women cells in police stations
- Counselling centres
- Help lines
- Short stay homes—which, though, are few in number

have been set up in many cities.

There has also been a concerted effort to bring in a law to deal with domestic violence. A Bill prepared, debated and presented to the government by a women's organisation has been adopted by Parliament for discussion, which is a significant step in a non-governmental role in law making. S.498 A was introduced into the Penal Code in 1983. It makes cruelty to a woman within the matrimonial home punishable with imprisonment up to three years and fine. It is a cognisable, non-bailable, offence. Widespread violence against women, and increasing evidence of women dying unnatural deaths in the matrimonial homes provoked the women's movement to demand a change in the criminal law.

The offence is non-bailable, that is a complaint under s.498 A, once registered as an FIR, would result in the arrest of the members of the matrimonial family of the woman. They would have to be granted bail by a court before release, and this could keep them in custody for varying periods of time. In matters of remission of sentence, too, offenders convicted under s.498 A may be excluded.

On the one hand, there have been complaints of the misuse of this provision, and the consequent harassment, often incarceration, of many members of the family complained against. On the other, there is little scope to deny that the incidence of cruelty, including physical cruelty, which leads even to death, is extraordinarily high. This is an issue yet unresolved; the Domestic Violence Bill may have some impact on it. In the meantime, an activist lawyer asserts that the phenomenon of violence and death in the matrimonial home should not need to be linked invariably with the phenomenon of dowry; violence and cruelty are independent entities within many homes. An activist also told us: when a man beats his wife regularly, and the wife gets him soundly thrashed by the police, civil liberties groups are sometimes confused on what stand to take.

SATI

The burning of Roop Kanwar on the pyre of her husband in Rajasthan in 1986, has reintroduced sati into mainstream discourse. Questions of volition, custom and communal pride have been raised justifying the practice. State inaction has been at issue. In 1987, the Commission of Sati (Prevention) Act was enacted making abetment of sati an offence; and the death penalty was introduced as an alternative sentence.

The attempt to commit sati was made punishable with imprisonment for a term up to six months or with fine, or both; this has been contested ever since its inception as punishing the victim. The 'glorification' of sati, where a temple is constructed and a dead woman worshipped bringing in money to the family, has also been made punishable. This last is constantly under contest—as denying the right to practise a religion. Women's groups in Rajasthan see this as a particularly important provision in taking away the material incitement in the commission of sati. The communal violence of much of the protest against this law, and of the practice itself, is a telling statement of the capacity of patriarchy to deny a place for human rights.

CHILD MARRIAGE

Though a law prohibiting child marriage has been in the statute books since 1929, it is still performed in many parts of India. For instance, the practice of performing child marriages on *Akas Teej*, it is reported, has not stopped in Rajasthan. It is widely believed that the gang rape of Bhanwari Devi was intended as a session, since she was active in preventing child marriages. Another aspect of child marriage was revealed when Ameena, a girl of about 12 years, was married to an old man from Saudi Arabia who was to take her out of the country as his bride.

CHILD LABOUR

Apart from the employment of children in work, including those classified as hazardous, it was reported that

- Children continue to be sold into labour. The parents of a young girl from Assam were paid a sum of money for the girl to be brought to Delhi as a domestic worker. Her plight came to light when she ran away from the ill-treatment she suffered, and she was given shelter by a social activist.
- Child workers employed in homes and in commercial workplaces, were subjected to ill-treatment. The chaining of bonded child labour in the carpet industry near Varanasi so that they could not escape was reported. Injuries on the person of domestic child workers in Delhi sometimes resulting in death, have been reported intermittently in the press. In Maharashtra, a civil liberties organisation took the state and a contractor to court when the latter ill-treated, resulting in death, one of the young boys he had brought with him from Tamil Nadu.

These manifestations of violence against the child disguised as child labour calls to be addressed. The vulnerability of the child has also been seen in Delhi, for instance, where child domestic workers have been accused of killing their employers, or in being accomplices to outsiders.

The 'social clause' on child labour does not result in doing away with child labour, we were told, but causes segregation. There were dissenting voices on the ILO Convention on the Elimination of the Worst Forms of Child Labour. The provisions which speak of child prostitution and child pornography as labour are unacceptable, they said. 'These are crimes, not labour,' we were told. Further, when Indian law is so strict that it says that non-payment of minimum wages amounts to bonded labour—a provision that is not found in any international convention—what use is one more convention, we were asked. In 1993, the Supreme Court declared that education is a fundamental right till a child reaches the age of 14 years.

Education for the child has got tangled with the issue of child labour; sending the child to school is projected as a necessary step to ending the practice of child labour. In Andhra Pradesh, an organisation working in the area of education for children has done away with the uncertainties of definition by working on the premise that every child out of school is child labour.

They have therefore arrived at a non-negotiable: that every child must belong in a school. In this view, NFE (non-formal education) centres, for instance, would be a means of perpetuating child labour. So, too, with the adjusting of school timings to accommodate the working child. In the meantime, this 1999 Convention is being canvassed for signature, and ratification by the Indian State.

The convention defines 'the worst forms of child labour' as comprising:

- All forms of slavery or practices similar to slavery, such as the sale and trafficking of children, forced or compulsory labour, debt bondage and serfdom;
- The use, procuring or offering of a child for prostitution, for the production of pornography or for pornographic performances;
- The use, procuring or offering of a child for illicit activities, in particular for the production and trafficking of drugs as defined in the relevant international treaties;
- Work which, by its nature or the circumstances in which it is carried out, is likely to jeopardize the health, safety or morals of children.' This is in consonance with the recent trend among UN organizations (*e.g.*, WHO) to directly involve human rights in standard-setting, and the creating of binding obligations of states in their area of operation.

THE 'NEGLECTED' CHILD

Street children have their peculiar vulnerability. In Bangalore, a study reveals that almost every street child has been sexually violated at some time or another. They are also specially susceptible to drugs. Street children, however, take care of themselves, and often of each other. It does not appear that institutionalising them is an answer to their needs, nor do they seem willing to trade their liberty for a life off the streets. In Bangalore, Bombay and Delhi, we heard of drop-in centres: places where children could drop in for a wash, some sessions, to keep their savings and to discuss their problems with others, if they so chose.

They were, however, reported to be vulnerable to being 'rounded up' and sent periodically into state institutions from where they would need help to emerge, or from where they would 'escape'. Women in prostitution have faced the possibility of their children being forcibly separated from them, following an order of the Supreme Court in *Gaurav Jain v. Union of India.* A 'raid' conducted by Delhi Police in 1990 (a year after the first *Gaurav Jain* order), in which 112 'children' were picked up from the GB Road area was an indication of what such a power being given to the police could mean to the women and their children. The recent changed law on 'children in need of care and protection' even prescribes adoption as an option that may be enforced by the state.

CHILD ABUSE

There has been increasing evidence of child abuse, and more particularly child sexual abuse, being pervasive. The perpetrator is often a near relative or someone close to the family. This adds to the vulnerability of the abused child, and, apart from the confusion and sense of shame which the child experiences, it is also that there is a problem with a refuge which the child can access. The dependence on the family as a support structure in times of abuse breaks down when the offending event occurs in the home. Following what is widely considered as a useful intervention in the Supreme Court in the *Vishaka* guidelines regarding sexual harassment in the workplace, the matter of child abuse has also been taken to the court, and the Law Commission has been inducted into setting the parameters for care and action in cases of child sexual abuse.

THE 'UNWANTED' GIRL CHILD

The declining sex ratio, particularly the declining juvenile sex ratio, even in Kerala which is celebrated in economic writings and in state policy for having achieved a high rate of literacy and negative population growth, has begun to seriously engage, among others, researchers and women activists. The low status of women continues to be reflected in

- The practice of infanticide including in some parts of Tamil Nadu,
- Foeticide,
- Sex-selective abortion which the amniocentesis technology has made common, and
- Mal-nourishment among girl children.

In Usilampatti Taluk, reportedly, the ratio of female: male is 879:1000. Since 1986, the issue of female infanticide has been in focus in this area. More recently, scanning centres have mushroomed in the area, and female foeticide is rampant among those who are able to afford it. We were told that, in Tamil Nadu, there are around 2000 scan centres, most of which are unregistered. A researcher reported his encounter with the sale of girl children by communities in Andhra Pradesh to persons who then placed them for adoption. He drew attention to the astonishing fact that there is, as of now, no law to control, or punish, the sale of children. The involvement of adoption agencies in A.P. in what is allegedly the sale of children has since come to public attention, in April 2001.

PROSTITUTION

The fear of AIDS, it is perceived, has given the issue of prostitution a visibility. This has, however, led to attributing to women in prostitution the trait of being a 'high risk group', even as it has been contended that it is high risk behaviour and not high risk groups that should be targeted. It appears that patterns of funding have impacted on this identification of the prostitute woman as belonging to a high-risk group.

The demand for prostitution to be recognised as 'sex work' has been raised, with dignity of the woman in prostitution as its basis. There are differing perceptions about prostitution—one which sees it as exploitative of women, and another that views it as representing the 'agency' of the women in the profession. There are various shades of meaning given to 'exploitation' and 'agency' which lies in the spaces between these two positions.

Decriminalisation is also proposed, and disputed, on differing understandings of what decriminalising will mean, and do. Most of the people we spoke to on the issue of prostitution, however, felt after a discussion emphasising the difference, that the practice of prostitution should be delinked from the issue of trafficking. In this context, trafficking is seen to be the sale and purchase of women and girls, and, more recently, boys, into prostitution.

While 'voluntariness' is a term with graded meanings, especially since economic compulsions and social exclusion are not uncommon causes for entering into the practice of prostitution, it is the distinctly involuntary nature of trading in human beings that is at the hub of trafficking. Trafficking in minors is a scourge that is commonly referred to as a crime to be curbed. We encountered the issue of organising women in prostitution in two different ways. In Calcutta, a 'samiti' of sex workers are articulating their position, and taking a pro-active lead in matters of preventing the entry of minors into the profession in their area of operation. They also said that, if trafficking be seriously dealt with, they be allowed to, legally, participate in curtailing trafficking—for who else was more likely than the people already in the profession to know when women and girls were bought and sold, they asked.

In Mumbai, a respondent working among prostitute women for over a decade, advocated 'collectivisation' but had a problem with adopting the norm of forming unions of women in prostitution. While she did find that the state was doing very little about trafficking, she was convinced that if sex work were seen as 'real work' under the law, all efforts to curb trafficking would cease. It was also suggested that 'sex work is real work' is a funderdriven agenda, and, that those who do not adopt this line were being deliberately excluded. In Kerala, however, a different perspective emerged where a distinction was drawn between the demand that persons in sex work should get all labour rights and the rights based approach. As a feminist, our respondent espoused the rights based approach.

There was a recognition that most feminist ideologies oppose commercial sex workers coming together; the commercialisation of the body was identified as the problem. Also, most people do not believe in the agency of commercial sex workers, it was explained. There was an opposition to licensing since that would only lead to further exploitation.

The issue has been invisibilised over the years, and with people in high places being involved, it has helped to send it further underground. The *Surinelli* and *Vidhura* cases have however increased confidence to complain; and people are now listening differently.

Another women's activist opposed the use of the term 'commercial sex worker': prostitution is not productive work, she said. But her main problem was that she saw prostitution as reinforcing patriarchy, and that endorsing prostitution as work would fall into the snare patriarchy has set for the women's movement. In the matter of trafficking, it was pointed out that proposals for checking all women travelling on their own, particularly across borders was a move detrimental to the interests of women and could end up curbing their right to free movement and achieve little else.

PRISONS

The conditions in jails; solitary confinement; the refusal to make condoms available in Tihar jail on the ground that homosexuality is an offence in law, and this would be seen as fostering an illegality; the inhuman treatment of prisoners, including their being kept in leg irons, for instance; overcrowding of prisons; the right of prisoners, including undertrials, to vote are issues that have been raised repeatedly over the years. The courts have been the arena of contest. The inadequacy of medical services in prisons, often resulting in the death of prisoners has been much in evidence. Apart from the inconclusive enquiry into the death of Rajan Pillai, when he was in jail, High Courts and the NHRC have been confronted repeatedly with this issue. Statistics in the Annual Reports of the NHRC reveal that there are a much larger number of deaths in judicial custody than there is in police custody.

Given the frequency and seriousness of the complaints about medical services in prisons, it would bear investigation to find out how many of the deaths in judicial custody are, in fact, occasioned by medical negligence. The condition of persons on death row does not appear to have been investigated so far. Nor the effect that execution of prisoners has on their families.

The inaccessibility to legal services that is endemic in most prisons, has been identified as a human rights issue, but has not been resolved yet. There are reports of prison riots which were allegedly caused by the poor conditions in prisons including insufficient provision of food, and the maltreatment, including the brutalising, of prisoners. On November 17, 1999, for instance, a riot broke out in Chennai Central Prison. It left at least nine persons dead, and one more succumbed to injuries on November 19, 1999. There were at least seven prisoners with bullet injuries who were referred to the government general hospital. The figures of those injured and dead in the riots varies, but it appears to be around 100 prisoners. The deputy jailor was killed in the riots.

The simmering discontent seems to have had to do with inadequate food, the meagre water supplied to the prisoners, and the torture meted out to them by the prison staff. The death of a prisoner tortured and killed in the Central Prison in July 1999, which was explained away without an enquiry as being a suicide, seems to have caused resentment and anger among the prisoners. It was the death of Boxer Vadivel, a prisoner believed to have been tortured for over three days between

12th and 15th of November, and the torture of two other prisoners by the Deputy Jailor which sparked off the riots. Jeyakumar was burned alive. The prisoners claimed to a fact-finding team that the rebellion had already come under control when antiriot police were brought in and prisoners were indiscriminately targeted.

For instance, a prisoner who was physically disabled, and could not have posed any threat to the police, was shot at point blank range. The anatomy of a prison riot, and what it means in the context of human rights, and of punishment, calls to be investigated in full, and addressed. Prison riots have been erupting sporadically, leaving little reason to doubt that they are symptomatic of a systemic malaise. The condition of medical care in prisons is woeful, and cases before the High Courts and the NHRC testify to this fact.

The inordinately large number of deaths in judicial custody, as reflected in the figures set out in the Annual Reports of the NHRC, is also an indicator. That prisons are death traps becomes apparent. Overcrowding of prisons, with a large population of undertrial prisoners spending extended periods in jail—a recent press report cites a survey conducted by the State (Jail) Department in Bihar which shows 154 undertrial prisoners in Bhagalpur jail for over 20 years awaiting trial and they are now over 70 years old—only strains the system further. Systemic changes and bold initiatives are imperative. So far, the Supreme Court's directive in 1979 to release undertrial prisoners on personal recognisance bonds, and periodic intervention thereafter by the Supreme Court, has provided ad hoc relief. There is little to indicate that there has been any fundamental re-thinking on this matter.

On the other hand, recent legislation is severe in matters of bail, and persons arrested under the NDPS Act 1985, for instance, regardless of the nature of their participation in the offence, are not entitled to bail. In Mumbai, social workers reported that they have been allowed access to prisoners to help them re-establish, and maintain, contact with their families, and to provide related support services to the prisoners. They admitted to shutting their eyes to human rights violations in prisons (and in lock-ups) since any intervention of that nature would jeopardise even the services they are now able to provide. In Chennai and in Mumbai, the '80s and a part of the '90s saw active provision of legal aid to prisoners; in Chennai, the High Court legal aid board was engaged in this process. In Delhi, legal literacy, literacy, meditation and yoga and legal aid has reached Tihar jail. The setting up of the NHRC appears to have had some impact on the accessibility of prisons, as have the many PILs which challenged the conditions within.

WAGES TO PRISONERS

The work that prisoners do has been devalued in a decision of the Supreme Court in *State of Gujarat v. High Court of Gujarat.* A judge in the case has held that

- Prisoners are not entitled to minimum wages, particularly where they have been sentenced to rigorous imprisonment, and it is part of their sentence to do hard labour
- The non-payment of wages in prison will not amount to a violation of the constitutional dictum on the right against exploitation
- Where they do earn a wage, apart from deductions for their maintenance in the prison, monies may be taken from it to pay to the victim as compensation.

There is a complete negation of the rehabilitative potential of work and wages, and a re-introduction of the purely punitive in this judgment of the court that human rights advocates and activists will have to contest.

SEXUALITY

Discrimination against, and harassment of, those with a sexual orientation different from the heterosexual is being more openly addressed in the past ten years than it was earlier. Yet, coming out openly is still an act of courage. And we were told how homosexual couples were susceptible to arrest and extortion. Just the knowledge that a person is a homosexual would render him vulnerable, they said. The lesbian groups that we met spoke about the difficulty of coming out, and the support services that were needed to help resist, principally, the families. One of the ways of providing that support is in the initiation of 'help lines'.

FREEDOM OF EXPRESSION

The rise of communalism has been accompanied by an assault on free expression. The vandalising of M.F. Hussain's paintings because he had painted a nude Saraswati many years ago; the destruction of the exhibition organised by Sahmat in Varanasi because it depicted Rama differently from how the vandals believed he should be depicted; the protests, and their vulgarisation when the protesters paraded in their underwear in front of Dilip Kumar's house, against the film 'Fire'; the concerted attacks on the filming of 'Water'—all these are instances of intolerance, which have denied free expression, with the implicit—sometimes explicit—support of the state.

The banning of the play on Nathuram Godse following protests and disturbances are part of a pattern. More recently, there have been reports of a government circular that conferences, seminars, workshops...which include participants from abroad require clearance from the government, including the External Affairs Ministry. Human rights are specifically in the list. And it is particularly applicable to people from Pakistan, China, Bangladesh, Sri Lanka and Afghanistan.

DALITS

The practice of untouchability has persisted, and dalit activists and unions have been making efforts to demonstrate its pervasiveness and variety, even whiie they contest its practice. In Andhra Pradesh, in a study done by dalit activists, 46 ways of practising untouchability have been documented. In Kerala, there was collaboration underway between caste groups and dalits in combating caste and brahmanism.

In Gujarat, a study of the practice of untouchability has been recently done. Some groups working among dalits, and including some dalit groups, have been lobbying to place caste as an agenda in the World Conference against Racism. The definition evolving in the conference, which includes discrimination based on descent and occupation is seen as an acknowledgment of caste discrimination. This is an avowed effort to internationalise the issue of caste-based discrimination and oppression. This issue permits an exploration into the relationship between a movement—in this case, the dalit movement—and groups working with dalits and/or dalit issues in terms of their respective politics and priorities. Police firing on a group of dalit villagers in Nadunalumoolaikkinaru in Tamil Nadu in 1991 is believed to have occurred to put down a young leadership that was emerging in the village.

A chain of circumstances from the support given to the villagers by activists, to filing the matter as a case in the Supreme Court, to three committees which investigated the matter, to the awarding and disbursement of compensation to the injured villagers and the court order which prohibited the indicted policemen from being posted in the vicinity appears to have empowered the village. It has also bolstered their confidence that help could well come from beyond the village. In Melavalavur it was a different story. This is a panchayat which is reserved for dalit leadership within the panchayat system. When elections were first to be held

- The dalits were chastised, subjected to a community fine of Rs.2000 and warned to withdraw their nominations.
- In the second round, the administration urged the dalits to file nominations, which they did. The ballot boxes were taken away by the non-dalit villagers.
- The third time around, the administration promised protection and conducted the elections amidst threats and tight security. About a month after the elections, the dalit panchayat leader, Murugesan, and five of his comrades were waylaid when they were travelling in a public bus, and brutally hacked to death on the highway.

This was in June 1997. Since then, another election has nominally installed a dalit as panchayat head. But the village lives in a state of permanent terror. A police outpost has been set up, but in that part of the village from where the threat to the dalits emanates. A memorial has been constructed to the memory of the six dead men. The Scheduled Castes and Scheduled Tribes (Prevention of Atrocities) Act has been on the statute books since 1989. There are however hardly any convictions under this Act. Dalit activists say that there are many loopholes in the law which help offenders slip out of both the Atrocities Act as well as the Penal Code. An activist made particular mention of s. (iii) (iv) and (v) of the Act in illustrating the non-user of this law. Studies on the working of this Act have been started in some states. Manual scavenging, and the disinterest of the state in putting an end to this inhuman practice which involves the carrying of excreta manually, and which additionally aggravates caste-based exclusion has been identified as a priority for action in Andhra Pradesh and Tamil Nadu.

MEDICAL RESEARCH

The connection between abortion, in vitro fertilisation and gene manipulation was drawn to ask how the question of human rights could be considered in this context. The poser was: ought it not to be the primary question whether neo-eugenics through gene manipulation should be resisted, or was it to be asked in terms of the mother's choice to have a 'blue-eyed baby girl'? Depo Provera, a contraceptive drug, was introduced into the Indian market without conducting Phase IV trials, which meant that the Indian state conducted no research specific to Indian users before deciding to introduce the drug in the market.

The issue in Phase IV trials of Net-oen was of informed consent. In the pre-liberalisation phase, we were informed, all research was to be undertaken by the ICMR. But post-liberalisation, there has been a dramatic change, and the trend has been for pharmaceutical companies, or the NGOs funded for the purpose, to conduct research; their agenda is not beyond suspicion. Pharmaceutical companies have been attempting to dilute the guidelines for scientific research on human subjects. The Nuremberg Code was very strict. The later Helsinki declaration, we were told, relaxed these rules. And efforts are underway to further relax the notion of informed consent for the greater common good. These efforts have been stalled at the international level. But ICMR's 'Ethical Guidelines for Biomedical Research on Human Subjects' has been amended in 2000 to allow proxy consent in some cases, such as in epidemiological situations or in the larger public good. In 1997, the Indian government signed an agreement with the USA that would allow Indian citizens to be used as research subjects in an international research project on human genome for furthering 'international good'. Since this became known, there have been protests—that the bodies of Indian citizens do not belong to the state that it can sign them away.

Court battles around banned drugs being sold in the Indian market have sometimes resulted in prospective banning. But the plea of the pharmaceutical company that the stocks be not destroyed, but that they be allowed to transport it to another jurisdiction outside India has been allowed.50 Sharing information with other potential markets becomes of importance, and ways of doing this may have to be established.

POPULATION POLICIES

There has been a deliberate re-introduction of 'incentives' and 'disincentives', and of punitive measures into state policy:

- The birth of a third child beyond a period of gestation from the commencement of state laws on the subject (including Himachal Pradesh, Rajasthan and Haryana) will disqualify a person from standing for elections to the panchayat, or to continue in office.
- Medical termination of pregnancy and tubectomy has been included in the Maternity Benefit Act 1961 (in 1995) for 'benefit' under the law. The threatened denial of 'maternity benefit' for the birth of the third child and thereafter was, however, shelved after concerted protest, The new provision puts an onus on the woman to keep the size of her family low.
- There are private proposals pending in various state legislatures including Delhi and Andhra Pradesh to

disentitle the third child to ration under the Public Distribution System, and for the parent to be penalised in their jobs if they hold a government job. The Delhi proposal even included provisions that the family could not be allowed to procure a house if there was a third child! These have not yet become law, but they have not disappeared from the public debate altogether.

- 'Social marketing' of contraceptive drugs, supported in Uttar Pradesh by large grants from funders, has been the subject of protest from, particularly, women activists. Social marketing, which includes across-the-counter sales, would inevitably lead to ill-informed use of the contraceptives, without an understanding of the sideeffects, or of the meaning of symptoms that may manifest upon use. The prioritising of reducing population at the cost of women's health is being stoutly resisted.

ORGAN TRANSPLANT

A racket in the sale of kidneys was exposed in Karnataka in the late 1980s and early '90s. There were allegations that the 'donor' was duped and his kidneys were removed and 'donated'; or that the donor had sold his kidneys as a commodity may be sold to raise resources—poverty was the characteristic that distinguished the donor. A series of exposés confirmed that there was a pattern to the sale and purchase of kidneys, which implicated, among others, doctors and hospitals.

The dust refused to settle, and in 1994, Parliament enacted the Transplantation of Human Organs Act 1994, which allowed organ donation either only after death, or where the receiver was a near relative of the donor, or it is actuated by 'affection, or attachment towards the recipient.' In the last-mentioned case, an Authorisation Committee has to approve the donation. The Act, in its prefatory text, says it is 'to provide for the regulation of removal, storage and transplantation of human organs for therapeutic purposes and for the prevention of commercial dealings in human organs.' The issue seems to have acquired a subterranean residence since. This may be an area which must be regularly revisited to prevent exploitation, and worse. In a different context, the issue of surrogacy has entered Indian parlance; but the human rights, and legal, implications have not been pursued with much rigour.

TRAFFICKING

While trafficking in women is rampant in many parts of the country, and also across borders, it is Kerala that the sexual exploitation of women and trafficking has been exposed, and the accused brought to trial and conviction. The *Surinelli* case, the *Ice Cream Parlour* case and the *Vidhura* case are undiluted narratives of sexual exploitation. In the *Surinelli* case, forty persons, including prominent political figures and persons from the establishment among them, were convicted after a prolonged trial in 2000.

They are now on bail while their appeal is pending. Some women's activists have been studying the issue of migration and trafficking—whether for prostitution, labour in sweat shops, domestic work which is often ill-paid and oppressive, or as mail order brides – while recognising that while migration makes women vulnerable to exploitation—and violence, migration is often not wholly involuntary. Women, for instance, migrate to escape violent domestic situations too. Shorn of its moral content, activists say, the law regarding trafficking could actually help women trafficked into situations for which they did not bargain.

BONDED LABOUR

Though the Bonded Labour Act is of 1976 vintage, it was not till the Supreme Court's judgment in December 1983 that the recognition of bonded labour acquired a national reach. As the champion of the bonded labour said it, it is that needs to be dealt with to get people an experience of human rights.

- Minimum wages
- Minimum guarantees of employment
- Child labour
- Land rights and
- Alcohol

Identification, release and rehabilitation of bonded labour have happened essentially by court supervision. In Tamil Nadu, there is a separate ministry that has been set up to deal with bonded labour; this was following a report given to the Supreme Court of the extent of bonded labour prevalent in the state.The issue of bonded labour has been handed over by the court to the NHRC, which has set up a committee including activists, advocates and bureaucrats with experience, to find a means of dealing with the issue.

We watched while a political activist working among bonded labour discoursed with a body of bonded labourers from Rajasthan. They were seeking his help in getting free, and getting land which could help them retain their liberty. The advice was that they get together a mass of similarly positioned people before launching a campaign in their district. The confidence they exuded that bringing together 25,000 people in the district would not be an unmanageable task was an indication of the dimensions of the problem of bonded labour.

ANTI-LIQUOR MOVEMENTS

There is a connection that seems to exist between liquor and violence, particularly domestic violence. Many parts of the country have witnessed anti-liquor movements in assertion of the women's right to be free of violence. This includes Andhra Pradesh, Himachal Pradesh and Orissa. Apart from the factor of state interest—particularly in terms of revenue—in the proliferation of liquor, the liquor mafia also has a long reach. There have been reports of women leading anti-liquor movements being killed, in an apparent attempt to stifle protest and resistance. Illicit liquor and the deaths of those who drink the brew – the 'hooch tragedy', as it is termed – is oft-experienced, and it is common to find people wielding state power, including ministers, being implicated. Last year, for instance, Kerala reverberated with reports of deaths in just such a hooch tragedy. In Uttarakhand, the demand for prohibition was closely linked to the struggle for statehood and is a challenge before the new government.

HIV AND AIDS

The right have been issues that have been raised in the context of AIDS, particularly since the AIDS Bill which was in circulation in the mid-1980s.

- To privacy
- To confidentiality between doctor and patient
- To informed consent
- Against discrimination

The identification as 'high risk groups' or as 'high risk activity' has been considered both in pragmatic and rights-related terms. While categorising people as 'high risk' on the basis of the class to which they belong has been rejected by rights activists, it has in fact been adopted in practice. The question of confidentiality has been adjudicated in the 'right to marry' case in which the Supreme Court held that the right to marry is not an absolute right. Referring to the provisions in the Penal Code,the court held that, apart from making a person punishable under the law if he marries and transmits AIDS to a woman, there was duty upon him not to marry. And the doctor, aware of the HIV status of the patient had not disclosed it to persons he knew were likely to be affected by it, he would be a participant in the crime,' the court said. Till a disease/condition is cured,the right to marry will be 'suspended', the court has held.

There are two points of view in this position of the court on the 'right to marry'. A rights group advocating the cause of people with HIV/AIDS, and of persons with a positive status, contend that the right to marry is part of the right to life. A woman activist lawyer has taken the stand that the disclosure mandated by the court is necessary to protect the interests of women. The former group contests this expectation, and holds that this will result in denial of rights to positive people without empowering women. A respondent further located it in the context of 'personhood'—that even while conceding that there may be no right to marry, there would be a violation of the rights of the HIV+ person where there is disclosure without any of the protections that an HIV+ person may need, and to which they would be entitled—particularly given the rejection and discrimination that is known to ensue. The right to treatment, and discrimination—in the workplace, in custodial institutions and in places like hospitals—of positive people are centrally in the human rights arena.

DENOTIFIED TRIBES

British India notified specified tribes as 'criminal tribes', with all members of the tribe tarred by the same brush, and all of them classed as criminals or potential criminals. The Indian Parliament passed a law in the early years after independence repealing this categorisation of tribes. The 'ex-criminal tribes' are now referred to as 'denotified tribes'. While the status of these tribes has changed in law, the prejudices attaching to treatment of these tribes seems relatively unchanged.

The attribution of criminal characteristics to a tribe has not abated. That they continue to be called `denotified tribes' freezes their status. Rampant discrimination, and criminalisation (different from criminality) was reported. The neglect of land reforms, and of improving their conditions of life, was reportedly allowing for the perpetuation of stereotypes about these communities. The very construction of identity was said to be responsible for the human rights violations that they faced, and was acknowledged as a violation on its own.

TOURISM

Tourism's contribution to the violation of human rights has become an area of increasing concern.

- The growth of the sex industry, including the use of children for sexual pleasure, is associated by activists with tourism.
- The displacement and exclusion of people from forest areas, and the introduction of elite tourism is said to be passed off as 'eco-tourism'; activists find this contradictory
- The taking over of agricultural land to create hotel resorts, as is happening in the Diamond Harbour area

in West Bengal, is opposed as being inherently unjust and environmentally unfriendly.

- The images of the reservoir in the Tehri and at the Sardar Sarovar being converted into lake resorts, militates particularly against equity.

These instances merely illustrate a point. Destruction of culture, sometimes through showcasing culture, is another issue. An instance is the Todas in Tamil Nadu. The non-involvement of local communities in making choices about whether, and what kind of, tourism would be brought into their midst was also reported.

RIGHT TO INFORMATION

A concerted, and effective, campaign for the right to information has been underway in Rajasthan, spearheaded by the Mazdoor Kisan Sangharsh Samiti (MKSS). It has caught the imagination of activists and groups across the country, particularly as a tool for preventing and challenging violations as well as asserting the right to development. A norm of transparency has been given prominence, including transparency of the government as well as the group working in the area. The irresistible force it has generated has moved the government, albeit reluctantly, to table a Freedom of Information Bill 2000. Meanwhile, the right to information has been introduced into the law following the Bhopal Gas disaster. Among the persons now entitled to receive information about potential hazards in a factory are also the Inspector appointed under the Factories Act 1948.

The information is to include the means of disposal of hazardous substances, and the arrangements for their storage or transportation. Information on what should be done to limit damage in the event of a disaster is also to be disseminated; the onus is on those running the factory. We did not, however, hear of anyone having used these provisions. The rights inherent in these provisions demand to be asserted.

- The workers
- The local authority
- People living in the vicinity of the factory

BHOPAL

Sixteen years after the Bhopal Gas disaster occurred, and Methyl Isocyanate (MIC) leaked from the Union Carbide plant in Bhopal on 2/3rd December 1984, the victims still wait for justice.

- The payments of pitifully small amounts as compensation
- The shrinking of their remedies, including the way the appeals system has been worked to reduce the entitlement of the victims;
- The difficulties in access to medical care
- The disbelief, even all these years later, that they were indeed victims of the disaster52
- The absence of a legal aid system
- The immobility of the state in the matter of the extradition of Warren Anderson of the UCC; the reduced gravity of the charges against the Indian accused; and the snail's pace progress of the trial
- The vanishing corporation, where mergers result in the original corporation pretending to a civil death, and the vanishing liability. The recent takeover of UCC by Dow Chemicals is an instance.
- The absolving of liability which has been introduced into the law and which is reportedly being used by MNCs coming into the country in the liberalised era54

The difficulties in bringing an MNC before Indian courts have not yet found answers. Neither has the problem posed by the state often being a tort-feasor itself. There are also reports of continuing harm to the people in the vicinity, and to water sources, emanating from the plant site, where chemicals continue to be stored in vats.

- Continued care of the victims of Bhopal
- Access to the information gathered by ICMR, and
- Monitoring and research connected with the Bhopal Gas disaster, at least over a period of fifty years have been set out as priorities owed to the victims of the disaster

A Draft Code of Conduct for Corporations was discussed by a group of persons brought together in Geneva by the Office of the High Commissioner for Human Rights on March 30-31, 2001. The First Draft Code envisages

- Social responsibility of corporations, and
- Corporations as human rights watchdogs.

These could be difficult roles to reconcile with the experience of Union Carbide in Bhopal, Enron in Maharashtra and with the shadow of corruption and the unviability of the Power Purchase Agreement, Cogentrix in Karnataka and the allegations of corruption and the anxieties about environmental degradation, in Kashipur in Orissa and the dominance given to mining interests, to name a few instances.

The introduction of genetically modified cotton where corporations experiment on Indian soil, and take no responsibility for the consequences of use of genetically modified (GM) technology, is another instance. The resistance to the 'terminator' seeds reflects the concern of farmers and others about the destructive power of corporate profit-seeking on their autonomy and self-sustenance. The various, even if failed, attempts to use the international patenting regime to appropriate the use of *haldi, neem* and *basmati,* for instance, to serve multinational corporate interest has raised questions of rights of people over resources in contest with the profit motive. Issues of liability are weak in the Draft Code's first version.

The importance of involving persons from jurisdictions of corporate conduct which may have to be accounted for in a code may have to be recognised, and participation in the settling of international standards and making of international law facilitated.

ENVIRONMENT AND POLLUTION

Environmental litigation has been among the visible aspects of contending with pollution. The courts, particularly the Supreme Court, have been accorded primacy in the matters concerning the environment, by environmentalists as well as the state. The court has used

- Closure
- Relocation
- Clean-up technology as remedial tools, and
- The polluter pays principle and
- Pollution fine as reparative and sanctioning measures.

There has also been an induction of the precautionary principle, and a statement of the acceptance of the norm of sustainable development, including within it the concept of inter-generational equity. The preventive principle does not find similar spaces in judicial dicta. The loss of livelihood, and the denudation of the resources of land and water, were witnessed, for instance, in

- Limestone quarrying in Dehradun, where the court ordered closure of the mines, rehabilitation of mine owners, and afforestation and restoration of the land (1980s)
- Tanneries in Kanpur (1980), Vellore and Calcutta (1990s) which were located along rivers, and where the court ordered closure, and the establishment of effluent treatment plants before reopening the units
- A complex of industries in Andhra Pradesh, where the court ordered clean-up technology, and compensation to affected farmers (1990s)
- The Bichhri (Rajasthan) case of hazardous waste negligently disposed on premises of four industries which had been closed down and left after being in operation without requisite environmental clearances; the court set out the polluter pays principle. But the difficulties besetting restoration where toxic damage has occurred was also evident in this matter.

Conservation of forest resources and the right of the tribal to live in, and live off, the forest is set out elsewhere in this report. The relocation of industries from within Delhi, and the consequent closure and loss of employment of large numbers in the workforce has emerged from within an environmental context. It is related later in this report while dealing with conflicts and the prioritising of rights. The locating of a nuclear power plant in the Sunderbans is another instance of the anomalies that 'development' is imposing on a people and on the environment.

POLITICAL VIOLENCE BY NON-STATE ACTORS

Variously termed as 'militancy', 'terrorism', 'non-state violence', the use of violence in pursuing political ends has been in existence for over a couple of decades at least, in a number of states. The state response has been varied including

- The enactment of the TADA, and other extraordinary laws, including the treatment of political violence as 'organised crime' as has happened in Andhra Pradesh, Madhya Pradesh and Maharashtra
- The identification of such political activists as 'enemy' of military forces as in the ITBP Act which defines 'enemy' as including 'all armed mutineers, armed rebels, armed rioters, pirates and any person in arms against whom it is the duty of any person subject to this Act to take action.'
- The unleashing of state violence, as happened in the Punjab particularly in the late '80s, and the beginning of the '90s. Or, again, as being witnessed in the encounter killings in Andhra Pradesh.
- The implicit equation of state violence with non-state violence in placing both in the agenda of the NHRC, while yet leaving violations by the Armed Forces beyond the NHRC's direct reach

The question of political violence has gone through phases in the civil liberties movement. In the 1970s, a political journalist told us, he had walked out of a civil liberties organisation because they had taken a decision to focus on state violence, and not speak to condemn violence by non-state actors. In the 1980s, silence about the violence of the militants in Punjab, which included the deliberate and often indiscriminate killing of civilian targets, was held out as evidence of the partial and one-sided image that the civil liberties movement conjured up; there was an uncertainty that crept in among civil liberties groups too.

In the 1990s, there was an open debate, most specifically

in the context of Andhra Pradesh, where one point of view held that political violence to overpower and alter systemic violence could not be condemned; and another point of view emerged that revolutionary violence was not equal to, or the same as, people's response, and that sustained violence over decades injured the weak and the vulnerable the most. 'Systematic and calculated violence begins with the enemy, ' a civil liberties activist says, 'but soon turns to agents of the enemy within and among one's friends.'

There is also the question of congruence between means and ends, he adds. The abduction and disappearance of Sanjay Ghosh at the hands of the ULFA in 1997 did lead to re-appraisal of the presumptions about revolutionary violence and the latitude that should be permitted it. A civil liberties group, for instance, spoke of its position as opposition to 'systematic, significant and sensitive killing by armed opposition groups.' An activist said: 'unless a revolutionary movement develops a tradition of human rights, there is a problem.'The ranks of 'surrendered' militants (SULFA in Assam, Surrendered PWG in AP) has raised human rights issues—not only in terms of their rehabilitation but also for how they are used by the state. Caught between the cadres that they have walked away from, and the police or security forces who are now their protectors, it has been noticed that an inordinately large number of 'surrendered' militants die violent deaths.

It also appeared evident to civil liberties groups that the surrendered militants are set up as stooges to carry out 'executions, which would then be passed off as a clash between the cadres and the deserters. Their position is plainly vulnerable. In Andhra Pradesh, we heard that cases against surrendered naxalites are never dropped, leaving them open to blackmail and to being manipulated. Recent brutal killings of civil liberties activists, often in broad daylight and open to public gaze, are suspected to have been engineered on order of the state government, using surrendered naxalites. Political violence in North Kerala and West Bengal seems to claim victims with regularity. It is an occurrence about which activists in both states spoke. In West Bengal, activists spoke of 140 CPM workers having died in 1999-2000 (over one and half years). This is concentrated mainly in the Hooghly, they said, but had spread to Calcutta too. It has percolated to the grassroots and, they said, it has ceased to have ideological basis. Peace talks, and mediation, seem to be ways in which intervention has been attempted by human rights activists.

CLAMPING DOWN ON PROTEST

Protest, dissent and resistance are most often treated as 'law and order' problems and the state responds accordingly. This not merely reduces matters of development choices, economic and physical displacement and political difference into a case of law and order, but, in the process, it results in employment of aggression in putting down protestors or those who challenge the decision or the authority of the state. The protests against reservation in educational institutions, and the demand for a separate state in the hill areas of Uttar Pradesh came to a close with the formation of a new state Uttaranchal. The 'Uttaranchal' movement was accompanied by violence when the state attempted to quell the protests and agitations that took place.

The crackdown on the protestors on their way to holding a public rally in Delhi on October 2, 1994 'resulted in a lot of bloodshed including loss of many lives, infliction of injuries on persons belonging to both sides, outraging the modesty of women ranging to ravishments.' Activists in Uttarakhand refer to it as the 'Muzaffarnagar' happenings (*Kaand*). Approached, the Allahabad High Court had the CBI enquire into the allegations of violations. Prosecution was launched, but the accused officers subsequently discharged. In the meantime, the High Court had given directions for payment of damages and compensation. On appeal, the Supreme Court set aside this order in May 1999. While castigating the High Court for stepping beyond its brief, the Supreme Court made no observation on the excesses committed by the police.

The clamping down takes many forms:

- The imposition of prohibitory order under s.144 Cr.P.C.

- The refusal to grant permissions to take out processions
- The arrest of protesters
- Implicating protestors in criminal cases.
- Tear gas, lathi charge, firing on protesters
- The branding of speech and action of protesters as seditious, or as obstructing development and therefore being against the national interest
- The forcible removal of protesters from the site of protest.
- Forcible breaking of hunger strikes

The disappearance of Khalra who, along with Kumar, investigated mass cremations in three districts in Punjab is one of the startling instances of attacks on human rights defenders. Lawyers appearing for naxalites are regularly intimidated and threats held out to them. Anti-liquor activists have been killed, and there is little doubt that the liquor mafia is behind the killings. Organising or supporting people in resisting displacement, and the taking away of land or water resources for mineral exploitation or prawn culture, has led to cases being lodged against activists. The killing of Shankar Guha Niyogi by assassins paid by industry is another attempt at killing the leader to weaken a movement. The contempt jurisdiction of courts, which has been used liberally particularly in recent years, constitutes a potent threat to free speech, expression and to protest.

The conflict between the Supreme Court and the Narmada Bachao Andolan and its members and allies in the matter of contempt has resurfaced after the judgment of the court allowing the raising of the height of the dam. Truth, incidentally, is no defence in a matter of contempt. The device of 'subjudice' is also often used to still discussion, and to refuse to share information with those seeking access to it. In the more extreme manifestations of clamping down, there is custodial violence and encounter killings. It is also evident that civilians often get caught in the crossfire. They may be subjected to harassment including body searches, detention, rough questioning by security forces and routinely treated with suspicion. Search and seizure of private dwellings, even of whole villages are common. Reports of fact-finding teams in Kashmir record this in graphic detail. Caught between militants and the security forces, civilians face the dual threat of either being punished by the former for being 'informers', or punished by the latter for harbouring or aiding militants.

DISABILITY

The 1990s has seen a visibility, and position for the disabled in public spaces. The emergence of disability groups seems definitely to have made a difference. The enactment of Persons with Disabilities (Equal Opportunities, Protection of Rights and Full Participation) Act, 1995, which was received by law persons with a certain scepticism as soft law, has acquired a significance with disability groups activating the law. The 'disability audit' of public buildings and spaces undertaken by the physically disabled in Delhi in April 2001, is an illustration of the potential of the law to help those who can use it.60 The introduction of 'disability' into the census is seen as another step ahead for the disabled.

A disability activist in Hyderabad spoke of the trauma that those disabled by accidents experience. He said it was not uncommon that accident victims would call, seeking help from depression and the push to commit suicide caused by the loss of limb or faculty.

Those physically disabled from birth would use their experience with disability to help the recently disabled to cope, he said. Even when the First Citizen's Report was produced in 1985, the effect of fluorosis on the people in parts of Nalgonda in Andhra Pradesh was described. In the intervening years, it appears some efforts have been made by a non-state agency to provide 'filters' to the people living in the fluoride-affected areas; a cursory visit was sufficient to reveal that most people have, but don't often use, these filters. The visit was to Mada Yedevelly at Narkatpalli Mandal in Nalgonda district. A school teacher who led the way said that it is known to have the highest fluorosis rate in India. There are about 1600 people in the village now, said our respondents. 200 or so have moved out, they said. Till ten years ago, they used to drink the water, they said. Then, when they realised its devastating effects, they started getting water from other areas, where they go to work, for instance.

There is a tank where water from another village, Puthurenipalli, is brought, but that is not free of fluoride either; only less so than their village water. There is a defluoridation plant established by the Dutch government in Yellareddigudam gram panchayat, but that is a little way away. The connection between the plant and the village water supply was not evident. And there are still distended limbs, prematurely aged bodies and a range of milder signs of the persistence of fluorosis.

These illustrations of the causing of disability, as a result of accidents or by inadequate attention to public health issues, is accompanied by the absence of state policy to take preventive or reparative steps. There have been some attempts at making easier the securing of an amount in compensation, but there is very little in evidence to deal with the post-accident trauma, or rehabilitation of these victims.

CORRUPTION AND CRIMINALISATION OF POLITICS

Even when the First Citizen's Report was produced in 1985, the effect of fluorosis on the people in parts of Nalgonda in Andhra Pradesh was described. In the intervening years, it appears some efforts have been made by a non-state agency to provide 'filters' to the people living in the fluoride-affected areas; a cursory visit was sufficient to reveal that most people have, but don't often use, these filters.

The visit was to Mada Yedevelly at Narkatpalli Mandal in Nalgonda district. A school teacher who led the way said that it is known to have the highest fluorosis rate in India. There are about 1600 people in the village now, said our respondents. 200 or so have moved out, they said. Till ten years ago, they used to drink the water, they said. Then, when they realised its devastating effects, they started getting water from other areas, where they go to work, for instance. There is a tank where water from another village, Puthurenipalli, is brought, but that is not free of fluoride either; only less so than their village water. There is a defluoridation plant established by the Dutch government in Yellareddigudam gram panchayat, but that is a little way away. The connection between the plant and the village water supply was not evident. And there are still distended limbs, prematurely aged bodies and a range of milder signs of the persistence of fluorosis. These illustrations of the causing of disability, as a result of accidents or by inadequate attention to public health issues, is accompanied by the absence of state policy to take preventive or reparative steps. There have been some attempts at making easier the securing of an amount in compensation, but there is very little in evidence to deal with the post-accident trauma, or rehabilitation of these victims.

CORRUPTION AND CRIMINALISATION OF POLITICS

Earthquakes, floods and droughts have recurred with rigorous frequency. While some of these happenings have indeed been 'acts of God' or 'force majeure', a relationship between land and water use and droughts, for instance, has been drawn by activists and researchers. The post-disaster treatment of the affected population has given rise to rights issues. The relative neglect of those devastated by the Orissa cyclone in October 1999 is contrasted by development workers with the relatively improved treatment of those afflicted by the Gujarat earthquake in January 2001. The victims of the Uttarkashi earthquake in 1991, in the meantime, have said that they were yet to see anything beyond aid in the immediate aftermath of the earthquake reach them. The development of a rights perspective in the context of such disasters may shift the emphasis from welfare to rights.

CONFLICT AMONG RIGHTS

The expanded assertion and recognition of rights, and the dimensions to rights that are emerging, have given rise to situations of conflicts among rights, and consequently, among rights activists. Choices are being made, and a prioritisation of rights occurring in a range of areas. The neglect of women's rights in the human rights arena for decades after the Universal Declaration on Human Rights (UDHR), and the Constitution of India, has had the women's movement demanding, and acquiring even if partially, recognition of women's rights as human rights.

There were some among our respondents who held that human rights are those which are asserted against state action and inaction. A human rights lawyer, on the other hand, saw human rights as a strategy which ought not to be confined within an inflexible definition. For people in the women's movement, however, human rights are about patriarchy and systemic oppression and violence; domestic violence and death in the matrimonial home could not, clearly, be excluded from the universe of human rights issues.

As a civil liberties' activist told us, in a pamphlet they prepared in 1990 (when the debate about whether violence and death in the home should be on their agenda), she compared statistics in dowry deaths with encounter killings: it was 2000:300. Though it stoked a lot of controversy, the women members of the organisation were very happy that the issue had been raised, she said. The emergence of women's rights in the human rights universe has also brought with it some contradictions which demand to be addressed.

A MORE JUST DEAL FOR WOMEN AND FAIR TRIAL STANDARDS

In cases of violence against women: registering a case; getting effective investigation underway; the ordeal of trial for the victim, particularly in situations of rape; the difficulty in obtaining evidence in offences within the home, as also in cases of rape; and the low rate of convictions had women's groups, and on occasion, the National Commission for Women, demanding changes in the law to deal with these issues.

Over the years the demand has been for:

- The recognition of certain actions/practices as actionable offences—domestic violence, cruelty in the matrimonial home and 'dowry death'. While the first is under consideration of Parliament, the latter two now find a place in the law. S. 498-A IPC, which makes punishable a 'husband or relative of husband of a woman subjecting her to cruelty' has become contentious. On the one hand the extent of violence in the matrimonial home is undeniable, and restraining the perpetrators and protecting the victim-woman is imperative. On the other hand, the experience .of abuses of this provision which defines an offence that is cognisable62 and nonbailable, which may land families in prison pending bail, is said to have caused resentment against, and distrust of, this provision. Those who would not drop the provision because of the occasional misuse, point out that there are hardly any other protective measures to help a woman battered in her marital home, nor any other deterrent provision to add caution to offending members of the matrimonial family.

- Enhanced punishment for certain offences against women. The introduction into the law of 'minimum sentences',63 and higher sentences has also happened. Implicit in the demand for prescription of higher penalties is the need to secure deterrence—if the low rate of conviction takes away the possibility of deterrence, it is sought to be reintroduced through a higher penalty where conviction does result. It has also been a measure of the state's, and popular, perception of the seriousness of the offence. The conflict lies in this, that it comes at a time when the virtues of imprisonment are in serious question. It is not evident that the conditions in prisons, and the violations of the rights of prisoners which is now common knowledge, has been reckoned with while asking for enhanced sentences. But the conflict became most apparent when death penalty for the offence of rape was mooted. When it was first suggested in the mid-1990s, there was very little by way of audible objections from women's groups; some women's groups extended it support. It was when the issue was raised again in 1998, that there was an avalanche of protest from women's groups. The NCW too released a report of a study it had done which showed that most of their respondents opposed the prescription of death penalty for rape. For some in the women's movement, the opposition to death penalty for rape appears to have been a pragmatic position—since it would only make the women more vulnerable if the penalty were so severe. For others, the pragmatic argument was a means of opposing the spread of death penalty into areas where it is not, already. What is disturbing is the persistence of the Home Minister in holding out the death penalty as a promise to women, as a statement of seriousness about the problem.

In this context the failure to challcnge the prescription of the death penalty for offences in the Commission of Sati (Prevention) Act 1987 also becomes an area that needs to be re-visited.

- Shifting the onus of proof. This has already been introduced into the Evidence Act 1872 in 1983 and 1986. S. 113 A raises a presumption as to abetment of suicide by a married woman where she commits suicide within seven years of her marriage, and it is shown that her husband or in-laws or a relative of her husband had subjected her to cruelty. S.113 B raises a presumption of dowry death where it is shown that soon before her death she had been subjected to cruelty or harassment by the accused for, or in connection with, any demand for dowry. S.114 A presumes absence of consent in certain prosecutions for rape. A respondent reasoned that she had opposed this shifting of onus of proof because it would open the gates for the state to extend the shifting of onus to other areas; see what has happened in TADA and such laws, she said. Also, while the violations are certainly heinous, the criminal justice system is structured to require the prosecution to prove guilt; it is often not possible for an accused to rebut an accusation, she said, even where the accused may be innocent. Further it is a dilution of fair trial standards. The contrary position is that there are offences where such a presumption is not necessary if justice is to be done to the woman.

- A separate criminal code for women. This was a proposal that emanated from the NCW and was widely discussed in 1995-96. This was intended to make the trial less traumatic for women, speed up the criminal judicial process, and it was expected to raise the conviction rate. There were discussions of making some inroads into the rights given to an accused under the law. This proposal, however, appears to have been shelved.

It was suggested to us that child sexual abuse being of an extraordinary nature, there should be a relaxation of fair trial standards in dealing with it.

HIV, AIDS AND DISCLOSURE

The two conflicting positions on disclosure by a hospital/doctor about the HIV+ status of a person has been set out supra while mapping human rights issues. To that discussion of the issue may be added that the view on disclosure seems to have been influenced by the context of the proposed marriage of the petitioner in that case. It may be appropriate to consider the reach of the principle of disclosure while weighing the rights content of the court's decision.

AIDS AND HIGH RISK GROUPS

The AIDS campaign has given visibility to women in prostitution who had so far been unable to requisition public spaces. There are few who deny that women in prostitution need to be empowered to prevent their becoming ready victims of HIV transmission, as also of passing the virus on. However, the programme of intervention to protect from AIDS has re-introduced the idea of high risk groups, and women in prostitution as constituting such a group—a notion that was contested in the 1980s as discriminatory, and with the potential of leading to victimisation of targetted groups.

ABORTION IN THE CONTEXT OF WOMEN'S HEALTH AND SEX SELECTIVE ABORTION

When Parliament passed the 1971 law legalising abortion under certain conditions, the statement of objects and reasons listed three reasons for passing the law:

1. *As a health measure*: When there is danger to the life or risk to the physical or mental health of the woman;
2. *On humanitarian grounds*: Such as when pregnancy arises from a sex crime like rape or intercourse with a lunatic woman, etc.; and
3. *Eugenic grounds*: Where there is substantial risk that the child, if born, would suffer from deformities and diseases.'

By 1995, when the Maternity Benefit Act 1961 was amended, the insertion of population control provisions into the law was being acknowledged, and resisted. The 1995 amendment, however, did give a renewed emphasis to placing the onus for family size on the woman when it incorporated 'leave with wages for tubectomy operation' as a 'maternity benefit', even as it gave medical termination of pregnancy the same position in law as miscarriage.

This is a statement of the adoption of abortion as state supported policy. The question of abortion as a right, and abortion as a population control measure may need to be re-visited. There was also a proposal to limit the provision of maternity benefit under the Act to women workers up to the second child; this however seems to have been dropped, perhaps because of the protest that met the proposal at almost every turn. The Pre-natal Diagnostic Techniques (Regulation and Prevention of Misuse) Act 1994, which was modelled on an earlier Maharashtra law, was enacted expressly 'to prohibit pre-natal diagnostic techniques for determination of sex of the foetus leading to female foeticide. Such abuse of techniques is discriminatory against the female sex and affects the dignity and status of women.' The punishment for transgressing the prohibition of the law is intended to be deterrent. Yet, in the seven years since the law was enacted, there have been no prosecutions of which any of our respondents made mention. The conflict inherent in asking for abortion as a matter of right, and believing that sex selective abortion needs to be curbed requires to be squarely addressed.

SEXUAL HARASSMENT IN THE WORKPLACE

After the Supreme Court's Vishaka guidelines, demands for translating them into policy and practice are being made. The allegations of sexual harassment by persons in positions of leadership within the human rights community, and the lack of procedures prescribed in Vishaka even within the human rights community, has been raised as an area of conflict in the context of human rights.

FREEDOM OF EXPRESSION, PRIVACY AND CENSORSHIP

The depiction of women, as also of violence against women, has raised difficult questions of censorship and of free speech and expression. The control that capital has over the media has been recognised, and it is not the free speech rights of corporations that is in issue here. Feminists worry that the power to determine what is 'obscene' or 'indecent' could curtail the use of media to interrogate, for instance, rape: for the depiction of rape could be viewed as 'obscene' and explicitly addressing the issue proscribed. Even as feminists, and women, find public spaces for their speech and expression, the space could get restricted and reconstructed by censorship. The Miss World contest organised in Bangalore in 1996 gave rise to similar, uneasily quietened questions.

The responsibility of the researcher, and the impact of publishing research findings, has been in issue in the Almora case, where research published in September 1999 became a subject of singular controversy in April 2000. The research, on AIDS and the local community, used the responses from a sample of respondents who spoke about the sexual practices in the area, from where male migration for work is very high.

Promiscuity and adultery were spoken of. The protesters were angry at the depiction of the community in the report. That the research was funded by a foreign donor agency added a dimension to the protest. The NGO later apologised, and withdrew the report. By then, three activists had spent 45 days in jail. In the meantime the state had moved in to impose the NSA on them. This last deed was roundly condemned, and much of the human rights community spoke as one to attack the state action. The questions raised by the research and the report, however, continue to hang in the air.

PROSTITUTION

There has been considerable movement in public perception. Most significant though has been the openness with which the practice, proliferation and problems of prostitution are now discussed. Inevitably, perhaps, there have been conflicts that have surfaced in this area of women's rights. On the one hand is the demand that sex work be recognised as real work. In the mid-'90s this was articulated as sex work being seen as labour. There was also a demand that labour laws be applied to sex work. That appears to have been gradually amended to the demand that sex work be accepted as labour in terms of the dignity that labour commands. A collective of women in prostitution identified three R's—Respect, Recognition and Reliance.

The women in the collective also spoke about the right to say 'No' in the course practice of their profession, and said they had to be given the right of 'self-determination'. While there was no demurring about the need to protect women from exploitation—from the police, the pimp, the madam and the client—there were dissenting voices on recognising prostitution as sexual labour. As one respondent said it: 'Feminists are being included in a much larger agenda. They are giving patriarchy and sexual exploitation a sugar coating by calling it work. Earlier patriarchy oppressed women by calling them 'mother goddess' and curbing her freedom. Today patriarchy oppresses her by calling her the 'bread winner'. She continued: 'I accept that today the state is doing little to stop trafficking. But the day sex work is seen as work under law, that will be the end of all efforts to stop trafficking.' A woman from the collective, however, said: 'Trafficking can only be stopped by us. Only we know what is happening in our areas. We are telling the government they should give us the right to act.' She however conceded that not all areas where prostitution is practised and trafficking occurs were yet capable of being so monitored. We see ourselves as workers, she said, and we want a union that will give us a base. A 'mela' which was organised by the collective in Calcutta in March 2001 reportedly met with stiff resistance from some women activists, while others stood up for the rights of the women to organise themselves. It is sometimes depicted as an issue of 'agency' of the woman as against those who see women in prostitution as victims, and subjects of exploitation.

Six aspects which a woman in the collective adverted to if they were to be considered to be 'labour', and their association recognised, were:

1. Police raids would not happen.
2. Mental torture in the rescue homes would cease. Also, when the girls are released by pimps, they say they have paid huge amounts when they actually pay far less in bond. Bonded labour is therefore rampant in the present dispensation, she said.
3. A self-regulatory examination board, with a multi-sectoral member composition would be able to prevent the entry of minors into prostitution. The two criteria of age and willingness would be applied by them. Now, we don't have even the right to stay where we are, she said.
4. The right to say 'No' would get established.
5. Teasing to demean women in prostitution would reduce.
6. When they retire, they are not even able to go back home; once they are declared to be labour, that will change. That would be real rehabilitation, she said.

There was some conceptual confusion about 'decriminalising' and 'legalising' prostitution. While most of our respondents saw a need to decriminalise to prevent them from being a vulnerable group, the mix up with legalising prostitution which many among our respondents were unable to accept—dogged our discussion. A proposal that the travel of single women across political borders be controlled, which was under discussion with the NCW, was dismissed by some respondents as being a prescription for obstructing freedom of movement of women and as likely to serve no other end. The children of women in prostitution are seen by the law as being potentially in 'moral danger'. The Juvenile Justice Act 1986 and its successor legislation the Children in Need of Care and Protection Act 2000—allow for their children to be taken over by the state. A judge of the Supreme Court had even said that the women should be 'coaxed, cajoled or coerced' to give up their children.65 This clash of a complex of rights and of perceptions needs to be more fully understood.

ENVIRONMENT

In the past fifteen years, environmental concerns have acquired a dominance which, it seems, have re-prioritised, and sometimes dislodged, rights.

Reduced Pollution and Hazards v. Workers' Livelihood

The issue was most starkly represented in the Delhi Relocation case. When 168 industries in the first instance, and thereafter all 'hazardous' industry in Delhi, were ordered to be closed or relocated, the conflict between the right to reduced pollution and hazards, and workers' jobs exploded into prominence. The matter arose out of a PIL filed by an environmental lawyer. The condition in which such an order would leave the workers—whether the industries closed down or relocated—was not considered till after the decision was made. The order, coming from the Supreme Court, has had an effect of finality and narrow negotiability which has pushed workers' rights very low in the hierarchy of rights into a residuary position. In Kerala, the Grasim industries pollution case has engaged the environmentalists since the 1970s, and the workers from even earlier. Between 1985 and 1988, the industry closed down for reasons unconnected with the pollution. Environmentalists and workers then fought on the same side to have the industry re-started; the loss of jobs was then the primary concern.

Since it re-started in 1988, the environmentalists have been gradually moving away from an appreciation of labour's concerns, since they do not see that environmental concerns and workers' jobs can be accommodated in a single solution. The environmentalists have voted for battling the pollution at all costs, even as they are chagrined at having to leave labour out of the reckoning. In Trivandrum, we heard of people whose livelihoods had been dislocated by the pollution of the coastal waters demanding that either the industry close down, or they be absorbed into the industry in replacement of livelihood lost due to the pollution. In Tuticorin in Tamil Nadu, among the salt pans is located a chemical industry.

A drying pond stands mute testimony to the potent pollution being caused by the industry. The salt workers' cooperative is maintaining a stoical silence about the pollution, since any protest from them may result in loss of jobs for about 1800 workers employed in the industry. In Vellore in Tamil Nadu, when the Supreme Court ordered that tanneries be closed, around 8000 workers were reportedly laid off. On the one hand, a labour activist said that it is time that workers developed a position which takes public health, pollution and environmental issues into account. On the other, the practice of using the court system, in PIL, to project a uni-dimensional view of the issue by environmentalists was attacked. The present priority accorded to environmental issues was seen as allowing the environmentalists to get away without having to reconcile conflicting concerns.

Shelter v. Conservation

The displacement, by court order, of residents of slums bordering, and encroaching in some measure, into the Borivili National Park in Mumbai has raised similar concerns. The clash between environmentalists and those espousing the cause of the slum dwellers has been violent, and the positions apparently irreconcilable.

Shelter v. Beautification

A petition asking for garbage disposal in Delhi has allowed the Supreme Court to order demolition of slum dwellings. While doing so, the court has likened giving land for rehabilitation to 'an encroacher' to 'rewarding a pickpocket'. In this vein, there has been a mass-scale illegalising of structures which house the poor. In the same order, the court has directed that garbage disposal being a public purpose, land should be released to the municipal corporation, free of cost. The court has been re-working priorities, and groups approaching the court increasingly recognise that environment, as expansively defined, is likely to take precedence over other rights such as shelter and workers' livelihood. There has been greater scope for negotiation, however, when the survival of an industry is concerned—clean-up technology (particularly ETPs and CETPs) which, at best, is recognised to be a partial answer, have been accepted as an answer to the charge of pollution.

Tribals v. Forests

The presenting of the conflict in these terms, i.e., tribals vs. forests, has tended to marginalise the tribal communities. There has been denudation of the rights of tribals who habitually reside in forests and live off forest produce. The creation of national parks and sanctuaries has led to installing the concept in law of exclusion of the tribal from the forest. Where they are being allowed access, their rights are severely circumscribed—by identity cards, timings, numerous checkpoints and a very limited range of permitted activity—leaving them often at the mercy of the forest officer. A distinct school of thought has emerged which advocates against the exclusion of tribals, and which sees a role for tribal and forest dependent communities in the conservation of forests. The reconstructing of the rights of tribal communities is, largely, except for the rare exception, being done without the participation of the affected communities.

Anti-Smoking Law v. Workers

The workers in the tobacco industry have found their jobs

threatened by the anti-smoking legislation that has been introduced in some states. Trade unions find themselves impelled to oppose the ban because it will cause reduced sale of beedis and, consequently, reduced employment. They also argued that it was a ploy by large tobacco companies to snuff out the beedi industry since it is the class which smokes beedis which will have difficulty in finding spaces which are not public and where they may smoke legally. Yet, this would present workers as selfcentred and anti-health. The conflict defies easy solution.

TRIBAL LAND ALIENATION

The law, generally prohibits the transfer of land from a tribal to a non-tribal in agency areas, or scheduled areas, except for reasons recognised by law, and by procedure prescribed therein. While this is usually respected as fair and legitimate protection extended to scheduled tribes, and to prevent exploitation of the tribal by the non-tribal, the situation in Kerala has been somewhat complicated. In 1975, the state legislature enacted the Kerala Scheduled Tribes (Restriction on Transfer of Lands and Restoration of Alienated Lands) Act 1975. The law has had a chequered career, with the government attempting to dilute the effect of the law, by amendment, and the courts demanding its implementation in its 1975 guise.

The question of alternative land rather than restoration has also been mooted—but it is not clear that such alternative land exists. While tribal activists have been campaigning for enforcing the 1975 law, others have been muted in their reactions. The reason, our respondents say, is because the land appears to have been transferred for a price to settlers who are themselves only marginalised populations. It would be unjust and iniquitous to dislodge them from lands for which they have paid as much as they can afford, it was said.

This was represented as a case of conflicting interests, but of two equally, if differently, affected communities. Rehabilitation of the already displaced adivasi community appears to be one way of resolving the issue—a view with which tribal activists do not concur, considering it as an erosion, even a denial of the right against alienation of land.

DALIT MOVEMENT AND THE CASTE AS RACE REPRESENTATION

The effort by NGOs to get caste on the race agenda at the Conference for the Elimination of Racial Discrimination has been an attempt to internationalise the issue of caste. Some activists and leaders in the dalit movement have also been involved. While some of them have got on board as in Gujarat, the dalit activists/leaders in Andhra Pradesh and Tamil Nadu have been consulted but have chosen not to enter the arena themselves. This is how a dalit activist leader explained it: 'We need international pressure. So far we have treated it as an internal matter.

This will help the issue get focus.... This has been raised by NGOs, not by the movement. I don't know about donor politics. We only tried to get some control by putting some of our academicians in it. But we are not sure what it means.' A Dalit leader who had not heard of this move objected to the caste-as- race representation. Race is not our politics, he said. Our fight is against brahmanism and casteism, he said. Even if it were to be considered that NGOs may not be able to consult with all affected or concerned persons, groups, organizations or movements before espousing causes, the conflict that could exist where the NGO position and that of movement politics do not converge has to be addressed.

SPEEDY DISPOSAL OF CASES V. OPEN CRIMINAL JUSTICE PROCESS

Overcrowding in prisons has been partly attributed to the problem of transporting undertrials to the courts, and of finding police escort to perform this task. In response there is an emerging practice of magistrates holding court within prison premises. This reportedly happens in Delhi and in Bangalore, for instance. The prison is patently a closed premise, as also beyond the beat of the persons who make the judicial process an open system, including lawyers, reporters and observers. In a different context, the virtues of in camera trials in cases of rape to protect the interests of the victim of rape has also been debated, inconclusively.

HUMAN RIGHTS LAWYERING

In approaching the court, or when an activist is drawn into the judicial process, a question of representation of a political or an ideological position often rises. Illustratively, a feminist litigating for getting custody of her child may be faced with two choices: either to assert the stereotype—the mother as the primary carer of the child, and the child needing the care and attention that only the mother can give—and increase the probability of getting custody, or staying within the politics of feminism and reject such stereotyping which, in turn, may drastically reduce the chances of getting a favourable order from the court.

An instance, again, is in matters of contempt of court, where activists may be advised to tone down their honest opposition to a court order which is patently unjust, even unconstitutional, or perhaps to tender an apology which would serve the requirement of the court, but which may compromise the politics of the contemnor. Difficulties abound where activists are picked up by the police, and there are apprehensions that they may be subjected to torture, or even be killed in a fake encounter—does politics stop at the doorstep of the courtroom? Is it necessary to get the consent of the activist before taking a position in court, in a habeas corpus petition, for instance? And what is to be done where the activist is unreachable?

STRATEGIES AND RESPONSES

AN OVERVIEW

In this stage, a listing of strategies and responses of state and non-state actors is attempted. Those attempted by non-state actors is inevitably more exhaustive, since a large proportion of our respondents belong to this description of person.

Organising People

This may be for effective and informed protest, as has been done by the NBA, for instance. Or in getting people to re-capturing control over their resources, as in the Aruvari Sansad in Alwar District in Rajasthan. Or to form collectives, as with the Durbar Mahila Sammanvaya Committee.

Working on the Right to Information

Led by the MKSS in Rajasthan, it has caught the imagination of activists across states, and fields of activity. It has also resulted in bureaucratic and political acknowledgment of the right/freedom. One aspect of this right is explored by activists who gain access to 'top secret' documents and share them with grassroot level workers as also with the rest of the interested community. This happened with the Land Acquisition (Amendment) Bill, for instance, exploding thereby the unsustainable position that proposed legislation of this kind may need to be kept secret from the people it is likely to affect. The use of information technology to gather facts about offending enterprises, for instance, and disseminating them is another facet of the interpretation of this right.

Iconisation

The changing of a victim into a symbol, as in Mathura (custodial rape), Bhanwari Devi (in defiance of rape and oppression), Dominic D'Souza (AIDS), Budhan (denotified tribes) are some instances. Some places where the violations occurred also lend their names to a construction beyond immediate incident: Muzaffarnagar—the scene of killing and molestation of the Uttarakhand agitators; to activists it appears to epitomise the struggle against odds, but also of an isolation of the struggle from the human rights communities in other parts of the country. Or the 'Stchundur' treatment in Andhra Pradesh, where landlord retaliation against dalit assertion, inadvertent in this case, took place amidst police protection; this is now referred to as a phenomenon. 'Broken People' researched and written by Smita Narula for Human Rights Watch is said to have catalysed dalits into forming a national organisation. There were references to Masanabu Fukuoka's One Star Revolution having helped shape perspective.

Bringing in the Media

While press briefings are frequent, taking the press along

to witness an event is not unknown, e.g., the Disability Rights Group being accompanied by press persons while doing a disability audit of public buildings in Delhi in April 2001. The presence of empathetic persons within the press establishment was also said to make a difference, as when dalits were professional journalists.

Fact-finding, People's Tribunals and People's Commissions

This is a process by which a state tactic has been co-opted by non-state actors. Previously human rights activists would demand judicial enquiry into incidents of violations of human rights. The use of judicial inquiry sometimes in the form of Commissions of Inquiry, to diffuse situations, or the inconclusive, or, sometimes, unfairly exculpatory, nature of the findings where judicial enquiry culminated in a report, discredited this state response. There is also the capacity of the state to scuttle such inquiry once the immediate need to set them up is past. The Srikrishna Commission is a rare instance of a report which commanded credibility, and it too had to go through the vicissitudes of winding up and re-starting. Peoples' Tribunals and Peoples' Commissions of Inquiry have made the shift from legality to legitimacy. With the state privileging retired judges in appointment to commissions of inquiry, People's Tribunals and People's Commissions too have on their panel retired judges, who, in addition, carry the aura of integrity and competence.

The panels may also have other public figures including among them journalists, lawyers, academics and activists. There were two instances of attempts to thwart the functioning of People's Tribunals/Commissions which we encountered. The first was when a panel was constituted to hold public hearings on disappearances in Punjab. In keeping with the demands of 'natural justice', notices were issued to policemen, among others. The state contested the right of the people's tribunal to hold hearings, contending that that is a judicial function which the Tribunal cannot usurp. The activists' position was that this was a process in which participation was voluntary, and this was not an alternative to the judicial process. The High Court, and later, the Supreme Court, upheld the state view, and the tribunal was not allowed to function.

The enquiry into the Srikrishna Commission was similarly threatened by the judge who issued notices for contempt to the People's Tribunal. Extra-mural intervention led him to set aside the notices. The People's Tribunal also explained that their inquiry was intended to facilitate the official inquiry, and was not an act of defiance. Fact-finding missions, which generally follow soon after an episode of violation, are also increasingly used where human rights defenders are subjected to harassment. The issuing of a statement by persons with credibility in the activist universe and generally after a visit to the site, and after meeting with as many of the actors as is possible, is meant to provide an alternative to self-serving versions that may emerge from the state or its agencies.

It is also intended to highlight an event to prevent further violations. It is important to ensure that the accusation of prejudgment which discredits state reports do not taint such non-governmental fact-finding missions. The report of a lawyer who visited Coimbatore to investigate the anti-Sikh riots in 1984 was the basis of a significant petition in the Madras High Court. This constitutes a turning point when 'culpable inaction' by the state was recognised, where injury to person or property could have been anticipated, but the state did not act to prevent such injury.

Visiting Zones of Conflict and Violence

The cutting off of a free flow of people between areas of conflict and violence and the rest of the country also cuts off the possibility of understanding what the people experience, of information being shared, of extending solidarity and support. The report of the Women's Initiative in 1994, 'Women's Testimonies from Kashmir: The Green of the Valley is Khaki' is testimony and photographic depiction of the women in Kashmir. Uma Chakravarthi and Nandita Haksar's 'Delhi Riots' is a testimony collected even while curfew made it difficult to reach the victims and witnesses of the anti-Sikh riots in Delhi.

People to People Dialogue

This has been held, for instance, in the North East to break the barriers of distance and incomprehension. This also helps in exploring, in areas where the issue is of self-determination or autonomy, after the conflict, what is to follow. The meeting of Naga women and Kashmiri women, both caught in situations of conflict, organised in Delhi in April 2001 is another instance.

Negotiating Conflict

The efforts of the Committee of Concerned Citizens in Andhra Pradesh to reduce the violence practised by the state and the naxalites is documented in 'Report of the Committee of Concerned Citizens (1997-2000)'. Comprising persons with whom both the state and the PWG would not be unwilling to speak, the CCC started its correspondence with asking the state for a cessation of 'encounter' killings, and asking the PWG to desist from killing its adversaries. While the state response has been more formal than substantive,66 the PWG has had the CCC recognise the fundamental nature of land reforms and land re-distribution before violence ceases. The openness of this process of talks and dialogue, and the establishing of credible persons as dialogists, is a significant aspect of this process.

Truth Commission

This was organised in the context of deaths of young women in their matrimonial home in Karnataka. A panel heard the parents and relatives of the murdered woman, giving the victim's version a space that it is not able to find in the systems of the state.

Dissemination

A group of disabled persons working among the disabled in Andhra Pradesh, and producing a newspaper and running a press, said they had printed and disseminated 3000 copies of the 1995 Disabilities Act. The response, they said, was excellent. They also spoke of sending out 10,000 letters to motivate handicapped people. The CEDAW too has been widely discussed, disseminated and translated and training modules developed for understanding, and using, the CEDAW. The widespread use of posters setting out the rights of the accused as ordered in D.K. Basu's case and in Joginder Kumar has been taken into police stations too. This has also been translated into the local language in many states. Use of information technology, films, reports, magazines and newsletters, both to gather and to share information. Video films and documentaries which assert facts with a perspective—*e.g.*, An Unfinished War on population policies and women's perception of their bodies, Kaise Jeebo Re on the Narmada struggle, Hamara Shehar on demolitions in Bombay.

Peace Committees

This was particularly spoken of where political violence is widespread and routine, especially in West Bengal and Kerala and was also found in Tamil Nadu in the context of caste violence. Human rights groups send out peace committees to bring warring groups to negotiate peace.

Census

The use of 'census' on the practice of untouchability is seen as a way of squarely placing the issue on the table. Disability having been brought on board as a factor to record in the 2001 census, disability groups have been motivating persons with disability to enter their data in the Census as a step towards recognition of their rights in state policy.

Setting the Non-Negotiable

This establishes the base lines in an issue. For instance, regarding child labour, a non-governmental organisation has set them out like this: All children must attend full-time formal day schools; Any child out of school is child labour; All work/ labour is hazardous, and harms the overall growth and development of the child; Any justification perpetuating the existence of child labour must be condemned.

Legislation

Monitoring changes proposed in law, and in policy, which

may affect people's rights. This may also involve the critiquing of proposed drafts and preparing alternative drafts which would be people friendly. The forest laws and the laws relating to land acquisition, as well as the rehabilitation policy went through this process. The Bill on domestic violence was prepared by non-governmental effort and has found its way into parliament. The Women's Reservation Bili has survived disinterest and active antagonism in Parliament because of the activists who have battled to keep it on the agenda. In the 1980s, the changes to criminal law which dealt with crimes against women were the result of demand from the women's movement. Participating in state processes, as in presenting memoranda to the Committee to review the working of the Constitution, or intervening with the Law Commission is also practised.

Campaigns

The Campaign against Death Penalty is one instance. Campaigns often accompany other modes of intervention, legislation or recognition of rights (or wrongs), for instance. Campaigns may also take on issues such as opposition to the WTO, or to the manner of opening up of the Indian economy to multinational power companies, for instance.

Resistance and Protest

This may take the form of rallies, padayatras, cycle rallies, processions, dharna, bandh, hartal and roadblocks. Apart from the 23 conditions that the Madras High Court has imposed on processions,67 the Kerala High Court has declared that bandhs are unconstitutional since they deny freedom of movement and the right to carry on one's avocation.68 This stands affirmed by the Supreme Court.69 Bandh seems to have got devalued as a means of protest because of the indiscriminate use of protest because of the indiscriminate use to which it has been subjected by political parties. This is particularly true in Kerala, where activists broadly supported the court's decision. This appropriation of non-governmental methods by governments—in power or in the opposition—appears to have robbed it of its legitimacy and meaning.

- Land invasion.
- Seminars, workshops, lectures, preparing of manuals, holding state and national level consultations and conventions, training of activists and grassroot workers and getting a dialogue going among them, pamphlets and posters are usually used.
- The formation of networks has become frequent, as has the induction of issues and the broadening of agenda to accommodate such issues. This has also helped to move towards an understanding of the indivisibility of rights.
- Signature campaigns.
- Alternative election manifesto.
- Participatory methods of decision-making and policy making. The 'Van Gujjars proposal for the Rajaji area' published in 1997 where, through an overtly consultative process among forest-dwelling Van Gujjars, a scheme for community forest management in Protected Areas was drawn up.
- Budget analysis from a range of perspectives, including analysis of what it does for women, children and health.
- Social Development Report.
- Use of PIL in the Supreme Court and the High Court, using the NHRC and the State HRCs and human rights courts. In some states, either the SHRC has not been established,70 or the SHRC is not a credible institution, and the NHRC is more regularly approached. The National Commission for Women (NCW) has also been used and, in a certain period of its functioning, it was seen as an institution which provided solidarity, by the unqualified acknowledgment of the justness of women's claims.
- Training of judges and police personnel. This has been most commonly on gender sensitisation and or human rights.
- Advocacy on rights of people with the state and agencies of the state.

Help Lines

This has been established for street children, lesbians and gays, and for women in distress. While the first and the last mentioned have endorsement in state policy and practice, help lines for lesbians and gays is denied legalised spaces for operation. Help lines have also existed for some years now for those with suicide on their minds.

Trial Observers

This appears to be an underused method of demanding accountability in judicial and quasi-judicial processes. Yet we did hear of its use in two situations: at the Justice Mohan Commission of Inquiry into the Manjolai tea estate incident where 17 people drowned in the Tamaraparani river—6-7 persons attended the hearings each day of its sitting. And, the Kerala State Commission for women had two lawyers attending as trial observers in the Vidhura case.

The state has adopted strategies, and measures, dealing with human rights violations, and for pre-empting the occurrence of such violations. While some of these strategies and measures are perceived by activists as having supportive potential, others are seen as providing spaces for human rights violations with impunity; this is particularly so in the case of extraordinary laws. The establishing of 'Commissions' including: the NHRC (by Act of 1993), the NCW (by Act of 1990), the National Commission for Backward Classes (by Act of 1992), the National Commission for Safai Karamcharis (by Act of 1993). It is a widely held opinion that the NHRC was established in response to international pressure. Though the Protection of Human Rights Act says that there shall be 'two members having knowledge, or practical experience in, matters relating to human rights' there has been no person from the human rights community in the NHRC; nor does there seem to be enthusiasm among the members of the human rights community to be appointed to the NHRC.

The NHRC has standardised compensation as a response to human rights violations. It does recommend disciplinary action and prosecution of errant officers, but this is not invariable. There has been an acknowledgment of custody deaths, and there is a direction that all cases of custody deaths be reported to the NHRC within 24 hours of its occurrence. The numbers have been seen to be increasing each year; the NHRC puts it down to increased reporting.

There is a direction that post-mortem of persons who have died in custody be videotaped; it is not apparent that this has made a difference. The NHRC was at one with the human rights community in demanding that TADA be not re-enacted. It also recommended ratification of the Torture Convention, but the government does not have to heed the NHRC, since its opinion is only recommendatory; and the Torture Convention remains not ratified.

The exclusion of the armed forces from the purview of the NHRC is identified by activists as a grave lacuna in the Act that establishes the institution. This is especially so since human rights violations by the armed forces is a matter of concern and contention in the conflict-torn regions of the country. It is also that this exclusion is viewed in the context of the NHRC's reach over 'terrorism', and, therefore, found anomalous. In defending its human rights record before the Human Rights Committee, the state has used the NHRC, along with PIL, as reason to believe that all human rights violations have avenues for redressal within the state. The Supreme Court, too, has passed on the burden of PIL cases which deal with human rights issues, included bonded labour, mentally ill in institutions and women in 'protective' homes, to the NHRC.

This shift from a binding fundamental rights jurisdiction to an institution with recommendatory powers has been viewed with growing concern by activist lawyers. The judge-heavy composition of the NHRC has influenced the procedure of 'hearing', setting out of a 'case', and even 'affidavits' and 'arguments'. The Annual Report of the NHRC is to be placed before Parliament, making it a public document. The government is to give an Action Taken Report along with it. In the Annual Report of 1998-99, the NHRC refers to the nontabling of the report of the previous year; the more significant recommendations from the previous year have been reiterated in 1998-99. There has been no challenge to this governmental neglect. The soft approach, sometimes amounting to a clear negation of rights, as in the Punjab Disappearances case, has been castigated by activists. The impact of directives issuing from the NHRC, on custody deaths for instance, is unclear. Documentation of cases, and the reports of investigations, is not easy of access, and no system has been devised for ensuring such transparency.

State Human Rights Commissions (SHRCs) have been set up only in some states. Andhra Pradesh, with its escalating record of encounter killings, has not established a SHRC. In West Bengal, activists do approach the SHRC, but they explained that they were confronted with popular prejudices—such as judging a victim of custodial torture as not worthy of the energies of human rights activists; and their concern being 'misplaced'. An orientation to human rights was found missing when such poses were struck, they contended. Activists in other states, such Tamil Nadu, seemed to prefer approaching the NHRC rather than the SHRC; a question of competence and demonstrated seriousness of purpose at the state level, they explained.

COURTS

The setting up of human rights courts at the district level has begun, and activists have engaged with the process of establishing rules and guidelines in terms of the procedure to be adopted by these courts. These don't seem to have become functional yet, and they remain sidelined and hazily constructed within the dominant judicial system. Also, activists in Tamil Nadu said that human rights courts were restricting themselves to civil and political rights; it will lead to a defining of what constitutes human rights in this lexicon, they said. Mahila Courts, or courts for women, have been set up in some states, including Karnataka.

The appointment of women as judges to person Mahila Courts, and the setting up of all women police stations, are measures that are expected to make the system more accessible, and sympathetic, to women. Some respondents said that conscientisation of judges on women's issues was of importance; appointing women as judges was no guarantee that the necessary sensibilities would enter the system, they said.

COMPENSATION

Like the NHRC, the state too uses compensation as a remedial tool. Ex gratia payments made to victims is a response that has got standardised especially in areas of conflict. The state generally provides compensation for victims of 'terrorist violence'. Victims of violence practised by the security forces, or state violence, is not accorded this recognition.

EXTRAORDINARY LAWS

While using the language of 'law and order', 'public order' and of 'terrorism', the state, at the centre and the states, has enacted extraordinary laws. These represent an assumption of extraordinary powers premised on security and safety of the state and of the population at large. The Indian state is also in the vanguard in negotiating an international law on terrorism. Cross-border terrorism is identified by the state as a major threat to human rights, and more prominently, to the security of the state.

OTHER LAWS

The state has enacted, re-enacted, or amended, laws which deal with rights of populations considered vulnerable. The Persons with Disabilities (Equal Opportunities, Protection of Rights and Full Participation) Act 1995 is one instance. More recently, the Juvenile Justice Act 1986 was replaced by the Juvenile Justice (Care and Protection of Children) Act 2000. Both these laws have been through the process of consultation. In the case of the Persons with Disabilities Act, in 1998, the government set up a committee to review the legislation. The Committee held regional consultations where interested persons could state their position before the committee. No changes have, however, been brought into the legislation since then. Consultations were sponsored by the government and other agencies when changes to the JJ Act were being considered. A division of opinion on children in conflict with the law was discernible at a stage in the consultation. This was not investigated further, nor resolved. The government instead consulted with a closer group of professionals and the Juvenile Justice (Care and Protection of Children) Act 2000 was enacted as a result.

COUNSELLING

The setting up of Crimes Against Women cells in Delhi, for instance, is intended to provide a place for registering complaints seeking help, providing counselling and, where relevant, reconciliation. Violence in the home has been the primary target. We also heard of the counselling of the families of naxalites by the police, though we did not get insights into the intent, and techniques employed in counselling.

CENSUS

The inclusion of the category of 'disability' in the 2001 census has been a statement of recognition of persons with disability being persons requiring specific state attention. Apart from providing a basis for asserting their rights, it has also placed persons with disability within the agenda of the Planning Commission. Women in prostitution have, however, been agitated by their profession being classed with beggars and the unemployed, particularly since it is being done at a time when they are asserting that prostitution be recognised as work.

SAMATHUVAPURAM (A PLACE OF EQUALITY)

This is a state-sponsored scheme in Tamil Nadu, expressly intended as an intervention to reduce caste clashes in the state. Envisioned in 1997-98, the scheme is to create a settlement of 100 houses as part of, but some distance from, a village, where contiguous houses will house persons belonging to different castes/religions, even as a large proportion of the houses are allotted to scheduled caste families. The beneficiaries are selected at the gram sabha, and they are only to be people from the villages immediately in the vicinity of the new settlement. 150 samathuvapurams are planned. The second and the 77th samathuvapuram were visited. There was a case of a caste clash that broke out in the 2nd samathuvapuram where a dispute over filling water from a common tap resulted in a dalit woman being assaulted by a family belonging to a higher caste. Local political activists explained that the issue had been resolved with the withdrawal of allotment of the house to the higher caste woman and her family, and their being sent back to their abode in the original village. This is an experiment that calls for long term follow up.

NATIONAL COMMISSION FOR WOMEN

Established by statute in 1990, this was one of the consequences of the demand of women's groups that women be given a space in intervening on their own behalf. The NCW has, over the years

- Intervened where women's rights have been violated, as in the case of custodial rape, or where young women have been kept confined by their families to prevent them from going away with a man they choose to marry and live with;
- Constructed laws, with regard to domestic violence for instance, to be lobbied for acceptance by parliament;
- Held public hearings into the treatment of oustee-women affected by the Maheshwar dam, for instance
- Conducted surveys, of women's views on the imposition of death penalty for rape, for instance.
- Held consultations on a separate criminal code for women, for instance, or on the issue of cross-border trafficking;
- Organised meetings to mount pressure on issues such as the reservation of seats for women in parliament and the legislatures;
- Intervened in court cases, as where a woman was awarded the death penalty by the Allahabad High Court, and an appeal was made to the Supreme Court.71

The Supreme Court has on occasion, asked the NCW to prepare a scheme for the care of victims of rape.72 Some states, such as Kerala, have also set up a State Commission for Women.

PUBLIC INTEREST LITIGATION (PIL)

This is a jurisdiction that was sponsored by the court, but which developed with the participation and enterprise of activists and the press. The 1990s have, however, seen an appropriation of this jurisdiction by judges and by lawyers, often acting at cross-purposes with activist concerns. At its inception, the PIL jurisdiction of the High Courts and the Supreme Court, with a relaxed rule of standing and simplified procedure, where even a postcard sent to the court highlighting human rights violations could be converted into a petition was a means of asserting the court's relevance in the human rights arena.

The court has used:

- Commissioners to do fact finding
- Expert agencies to assist in deciding upon a course of action
- The issuance of directions, and the monitoring of their implementation by the court through report-back methods
- The involvement of all governments, at the state and the centre, since many of the issues have been systemic, and widespread, e.g., the condition of undertrial populations, or the cleaning up of cities

PIL was conceived as a 'non-adversarial' process, though located within an adversarial judicial system. In 1988,73 the Supreme Court asserted its hold over a case, and the cause, even where a public interest petitioner may seek to withdraw the case from the court. The power of the court to reach issues has expanded with PIL, as has the Supreme Court's exercise of its constitutional power to do what it considers necessary in the 'interests of complete justice'.74 The rights orientation of the court has therefore acquired significance.

Conflicts among rights have manifested over time. The use of the courts, and the PIL jurisdiction, by activists, and other public interest petitioners, has come into contention particularly since the Delhi Industries Relocation case, Almitra Patel and the proceedings in the Bombay High Court in the Borivili National Park case. The cradle scheme in Tamil Nadu was initiated by the state government to prevent female infanticide. The midday meal scheme has been a means of reducing malnourishment among children, while bringing them into the schoolroom. Among schemes to improve the status of the girl child, we heard of a government scheme where if a girl child studies up to standard X, the government will pay Rs.10,000 on marriage. In the nature of 'help lines', which are sometimes located within the offices of high-ranking police personnel, we heard of a 'Crime Stopper Control Bureau' in Tamil Nadu. The coopting of NGOs in monitoring and implementing laws, policies and schemes has been routinised in the last decade.

It may take the form of:

- Membership of a commission, such as the Rehabilitation Council of India
- Membership of committees set up by the government to make policies, e.g., in the making of a population policy
- Appointing NGOs as monitoring agencies, e.g. under the Equal Remuneration Act 1976.
- Empowering NGOs to take action under the law, e.g., s. 13 of the JJ Act 198675
- Funding NGOs carrying out programmes devised by state agencies, e.g., providing child care facilities for children of women in prostitution
- Participating in training of judicial officers and policemen, for instance, in gender issues, matters of human rights, and child rights.

In the Janmabhoomi programme of the Andhra Pradesh government, one example of the process of involvement of the people in reviving, or creating, resources—in desilting tanks lying long in disuse, for instance—is achieved through giving work contracts to collectives such as Mahila Mandals. This, however, is not accompanied by a transfer of rights to the local people. The impact this has on the panchayat system may need to be studied. The changes in the role, and autonomy, of the NGOs in relation to the state was adverted to by many respondents, and may need a more systematic appraisal.

COMMISSIONS OF INQUIRY

The appointment of judges to constitute commissions of inquiry under the Commissions of Inquiry Act 1952 is a commonly used device to quell immediate protest and agitation, and to provide a veneer of impartiality to the investigation. This process has lost quite significantly in terms of credibility, since most commission reports come long after the event, and all too often gives a clean chit to the government. The Srikrishna Commission of Inquiry into the Bombay riots of 1992-93 following the demolition of the Babri Masjid is held out by activists as an exception. There is an appropriation by human rights activists of the device of 'Commissions of Inquiry', and this device has been resorted to regularly in the past decade. The legal aid system, now established under the Legal Services Authorities Act 1987, is one potential intervention in the arena of human rights. It however remains litigation-dominated, and is unavailable at the points in the system where human rights violations may occur. The dearth, near-absence, of legal aid available for the victims of the Union Carbide disaster in Bhopal has been represented as one instance of the incapacity, or neglect, of the legal aid system in responding to counselling, litigative and consultative needs of a victim-population.

Bibliography

Alan, R.: *The Interrelationships of Economics with the Social Sciences*, Paris: Institute of Economics,1999.

Albertoni, E.A.: *Mosca and the Theory of Elitism*, UK: Oxford University, 2000.

Bayly, C.A.: *Rulers, Townsmen, and Bazaars: North Indian Society in the Age of British Expansion*, Cambridge: Cambridge University Press, 2000.

Bhambhri, C.P.: *Constitutional, Educational, and Inherited Social Imbalances*, New Delhi: National Institute of Educational Planning and Administration, 2004.

Bartoli, H.: *Economie Unidimensionnelle*, Paris: Institute of Economica, 1991.

Buchanan, J.: *Economics and its Scientifc Neighbours*, London: Westview Press, 2003.

Bhikhu, P.: *Crisis and Change in Contemporary India*, New Delhi: The Book Review Literary Trust, 1998.

Cahman, W.: *Sociology and History and Research*, New York: Free Press, 2005.

Carrithers, M.: *The Assembly of Listeners: Jains in Society*, Cambridge: Cambridge University Press, 2005.

Dogan, M.: *Fragmentation of the Social Sciences and Recombination of Specialties*, New Haven: Yall University Press, 2001.

Eugene, F.: *Politics and Social Conflict in South India: The Non-Brahman Movement and Tamil Separatism*, Berkeley: University of California Press, 1997.

Galbraith, J.K.: *Conditions for Economic Change in Underdeveloped Countries*, Paris: Institute of Economics, 2000.

Hasnain, N.: *Shias and Shia Islam in India: A Study in Society and Culture*, New Delhi: Harnam, 1999.

Intriligator, M.: *Independence Among the Behavioral Sciences*, New York: University of Chicago Press, 2000.

Karashima, N.: *Towards a New Formation: South Indian Society under Vijayanagar Rule*, New Delhi: Oxford University Press, 1996.

Kumar, R.: *The Social History of Modern India*, New Delhi: Oxford University Press, 2001.

Lewis, W.A.: *The Theory of Economic Growth*, US: University of Chicago Press, 2002.

Mahalingam, T.V.: *Administration and Social Life under Vijayanagar*, Madras: University of Madras, 2004.

Marion, J.: *Scientific Analysis is a Subset of Comparative Analysis*, New Haven: Yall University Press, 2001.

Raye, R.: India: *A Compendium*, New York: American Geographical Society, 2002.

Rigney, D.: *Patterns of Interdisciplinary Citation in the Social Sciences*, US: Princeton University Press, 1999.

Smelser, N.: *Handbook of Sociology*, London: Sage Publications,1988.

Stein, B.: *Peasant, State, and Society in Medieval South India*, New Delhi: Oxford University Press, 2000.

Tilly, C.: *Big Structures, Large Processes, Huge Comparisons*, New York: Russel Sage Foundation, 1999.

Index